# Durkheim and National Identity in Ireland

# Durkheim and National Identity in Ireland

## Applying the Sociology of Knowledge and Religion

James Dingley

ISBN: 978-1-137-44258-1

Library of Congress Cataloging-in-Publication Data

Dingley, James.
    Durkheim and national identity in Ireland : applying the sociology of knowledge and religion / James Dingley.
        pages cm
    Includes bibliographical references and index.
    ISBN 978-1-137-44258-1 (hardback)
    1. Knowledge, Sociology of. 2. Religion and sociology. 3. National characteristics—Ireland. 4. National characteristics—Northern Ireland. 5. Durkheim, Émile, 1858–1917—Political and social views. I. Title.
    BD175.D56 2015
    941.5—dc23
                                                                    2014035458

A catalogue record of the book is available from the British Library.

Design by Amnet.

First edition: March 2015

10 9 8 7 6 5 4 3 2 1

# Contents

Acknowledgments     vii

Introduction     1

1   Durkheim as a French Nationalist     11

2   Durkheim's Sociology of Knowledge     33

3   Nations and Nationalism     63

4   Ireland, the Revisionist Debate     101

5   Science and the Arts in Ireland     127

6   Ireland and Nationalism     151

Conclusion: Knowledge, Truth, and the Problem
of Useless Knowledge     185

Bibliography     193

Index     205

# Acknowledgments

To my former supervisor Prof. Sami Zubaida (Birkbeck College, University of London) and Dr. Brian Fitzpatrick and Mr. Mick Shannon (both formerly of the University of Ulster) who all assisted me greatly in the original PhD thesis on which this book is based. Since then I should also thank Dr. Peter Catterall (University of Westminster) for his help and support in developing and refining the work over recent years.

# Introduction

There are few attempts at theoretical analysis, either political or social, in the study of Ireland (Whyte, 1991, chapter 11) and fewer reviews of Northern Ireland's "Troubles" (such as Tonge, 1998; McGarry and O'Leary, 1995) offer any theoretical explanations or perspectives of them. Meanwhile, apart from the Marxists, social theory is almost totally lacking in Irish studies and helps explain Whyte's (1991, p. 246) plaintive question: "Why has research on the Northern Ireland problem not been more effective?"

Few studies have had much impact, although the influence of postmodernism is identifiable in contemporary policies of multi-culturalism, pluralism, the celebration of diversity (Crozier and Froggatt, 1998), and consociationalism (Taylor, 2011), the foundations for the Belfast Agreement (1998), which essentially just constructed a complex set of technocratic constitutional arrangements to (hopefully) manage divisions, not resolve them. This also reflects how most "Irish" problems are viewed from a political science perspective and from nationalist all-Ireland imperatives and assumptions.

Even in politics there are few studies of Ireland primarily from the theoretical perspectives of ethnicity and nationalism, although books on nationalism have utilized Ireland as an example (such as Kellas, 1991; Dingley, 2008; or Hastings, 1997). Few of the standard texts on Ireland or Northern Ireland even mention ethnicity or nationalism, as a brief look at their indexes attests, although exceptions exist (such as Boyce, 1991; Lyons, 1982; or Coulter, 1999). Even books whose avowed rationale is to "explain" Northern Ireland (such as Whyte, 1991; McGarry and O'Leary, 1995; and Tonge, 1998), provide virtually no explanation in terms of theory, tending toward summaries of the actors' own perspectives.

Thus analysis of the troubles has tended to the superficial or technocratic, concentrating on the overt divisions but not on why they exist or are so divisive; why Protestants and Unionists identify as British, while Catholics and Nationalists identify as Irish. This leads to confused ideas of "religion falsely dividing Irishmen" or "British imperialist plots" to divide and conquer that serious analysis finds wanting (Howe, 2000; Whyte, 1991; O'Halloran, 1987).

Genuine analysis and explanation appears profoundly lacking, while ill-informed debate abounds and the Province remains deeply divided with conflict simmering below the surface. Problems of deep division, sectarianism, and discrimination still dominate (Nolan, 2012; Bell et al., 2010), but few ask why someone would discriminate against another who is living in the next street and different only in religion. Equally unasked is why neighbors with no other apparent differences assert different national identities (assuming, along with Howe, 2000, and Whyte, 1991, that ideas of perfidious British manipulation are untenable). Lack of such questions may well help to explain why the Belfast Agreement (1998) has broken down on several occasions, constantly verges on crisis, and leaves Unionists deeply disillusioned.

Lack of theoretical analysis is a major weakness in understanding Northern Ireland, normally cast as a political (national) and not a social problem, constantly seeking political constitutional settlements and ignoring social relations for political ones. But this rests on a false dichotomy between ideas of society and nation, for, as Giddens (1987, 1995) observes, the political context of sociology is too frequently ignored as is the fact that the emerging nation-state of the nineteenth century was sociology's essential frame of reference:

> Society is the object of study of sociology—more specifically, that form of society associated with the modern era. Understood as a bounded unity, "society" here refers to the nation-state. But very little attention has been given in social theory to examining the nature of such a phenomenon. (Giddens, 1987, p. 22)

More specifically:

> If any aspect of the general world view of Durkheim and Weber has been consistently under emphasised in most modern accounts, it is their nationalism. While it could be an exaggeration to say that it has been ignored, it has typically been seen as something in some way marginal or extraneous to their work. (Hickox, 1976, p. 196)

Consequently, nation gets cast as something other than society, a polity exclusive of social factors, such as values, customs, culture, or social structural. Yet in classical social theory society was an implicit reference to the emerging nation-state, to construct the social cohesion for an integrated polity, making nation a social reality, defining its boundaries, consciousness, and internal cohesion; a truly national community and shared identity. And for Durkheim this was his specific mission in France.

Where social theory is used in studying nationalism it is mostly as an aid to inform thought on it. James (1996) provides a good example, when he refers to the overt debt that Gellner owed to Durkheim (p. 96), but even here the idea that society for Durkheim or Weber equated with nation is scarcely entertained. Yet, as Llobera (1996, p. 146) observes, Durkheim was much criticized for his French chauvinism and (p. 145) that "what gives the nation its moral value is that it most closely approximates to the society of mankind."

Thus classical sociology inferred society as nation and its social construction. Politics was about the technical mechanisms for ordering and developing a national society, not separate from it. That there may not be a perfect fit between nation and society, as in Northern Ireland, or that nation-states contained several societies was a problem for sociology to analyze and politics to implement sociological conclusions as part of the same. Both society and nation are broad, imprecise concepts that emerged together in the nineteenth century, as Europe underwent massive socio-economic and consequent political change. These created new problems of social and political order (Nisbet, 1996, in sociology; or Gellner, 1983, and Breuilly, 1993, in nationalism) that required much rethinking (beyond the hardened bureaucratic boundaries of modern academe).

In Europe, society and nation had a much more immediate being and significance than in the UK (Anderson, 1992, chapter 2; or Hickox, 1976, chapter 8), sociologists had to address the formation of national societies in a more directly political manner, because they had not previously existed, such as German or Italian unification. As Greenfeld (1993) observes, England, the core of British-ness, was the first modern nation; it developed accidentally before the age and theories of nationalism; other states then had to consciously catch up with her and her growing success.

However, even British sociology reflects political and national realities: Spencer's (late nineteenth century) sociology virtually rejects the idea of society as an entity by stressing a utilitarian, individual contract theory in which society is regarded as an epiphenomenon (which Durkheim's work, 1984 [1893], critically rejected). This reflects the lack of a conscious British/English nationalism for an identity that stressed the autonomous individual, a non-social polity, Imperial identity, and pre-age-of-nationalism ideology (Greenfeld, 1993, pp. 86–87). Contemporaneously an Anglo-centric Britain was more concerned with external Imperial problems than with nation/society, regarded as non-problematic because Empire and individualism were so obviously successful and internal socio-political problems (fractious dissidents, the unemployed and unemployable) could be exported out to colonies (Anderson, 1992, pp. 92–93). European states did not have such colonial safety valves and had to solve the problem at home.

European sociology therefore had to address problems of internal social integration and cohesion for political stability in a concrete way. Thus Durkheim stressed the importance of a single, non-religious, mono-lingual educational system to ensure socialization into a single unifying (national) culture and identity to overcome ethnic and religious divisions rampant in France. National identity was therefore socially constructed, making sociology a central part of state (national) cohesion policy making, something often not grasped in the UK, especially Northern Ireland, where social division (multi-culturalism) is social and political policy.

Multi-culturalism also informs the consociational theory on which the Belfast Agreement (Taylor, 2011) is based, which makes multi-culturalism official state policy, built on arguments (such as Ruane and Todd, 1996) for the equality and tolerance of ethnic and religious differences, granting them equality and parity of esteem, cemented together into a harmonious society via Education for Mutual Understanding.

This ignores the fact that the differences now to be tolerated and granted parity of esteem are the same ones that have caused division for four hundred years and that these differently (socially) constructed identities may be based on imperatives that are antagonistic and even conflicting. Equally, they ignore questions of whether one culture and social structure is more or less well equipped to provide individuals with the right skills and knowledge pertinent to successfully function in the relevant economic, political, and administrative world of Northern Ireland as part of the UK. In other words, culture, social structure, and identity are assumed to be politically "neutral" (something the European sociological and nationalist traditions would have found naive), reducing conflict and division down to just attitudes of mind.

Consociationalism and multi-culturalism are also heavily influenced by post-modernism, itself more informed by literary theory (Howe, 2000, p. 234) than social theory, ideas that Durkheim would have found naive, dilettantish, and irrational, lacking a grasp of social/national reality (Jones, 2001, pp. 220–21). As Durkheim wrote in *Division of Labour* (1984 [1893]), the toleration of difference in modern society is based on a deeper shared culture of exchange, understanding, and reciprocity, where compatible and reciprocal differences make social cohesion and toleration possible by making us interdependent, and so they have an integrative function. But this necessitates a shared culture of toleration based on the individual, understanding, exchange, and shared values. This is totally different from exclusive cultures that cannot reciprocate or exchange and have opposed interests, values, and identities restricted to their immediate cultural group, which leads to inter-group indifference or antagonism, the situation pertaining in many multi-ethnic European states.

Classical social theorists, such as Durkheim, Tonnies, and Weber, would have had severe reservations about current Northern Ireland policy and its failure to grasp the relationship between identity, nation, and society. They needed molding into a complementary, integrated whole, not sectioned in two. Thus sociology can tell us much when looking at contemporary Irish national problems, whose origins lie in a nineteenth-century nationalist ideology that built upon social and religious divisions dating back to the seventeenth century (Kennedy, 1996, p. xiii). Such divisions similarly confronted most nationalist movements and sociology throughout Europe; and Durkheim's sociology overtly addressed French ones. Unsurprisingly, although overlooked, he has exercised an influence over some of the most influential writers on nationalism over the years (Gellner, 1983; Eriksen, 1993; Greenfeld, 2006; Smith, 1998).

Where theory has been used in Irish studies, it usually comes from *the revisionists* (Brady, 1994; Boyce and O'Day, 1996) who have become associated with British or Unionist perspectives. Revisionists emphasize a scientific approach to history, which is deemed biased by Irish nationalists. Thus, attempts to develop theoretical arguments often get bogged down in accusations of being anti-Irish, since the critical, scientific analysis associated with rigorous theory (empirical evidence, quantified data, rational analysis) has generally been critical of nationalist claims. Nationalists emphasizing emotional themes of suffering and trauma (Fennell, 1993; or Rolston in Miller, 1998) have thereby failed to withstand much rational analysis (Howe, 2000; or Kennedy, 1996)—a key theme in this study, since Durkheim's sociology of knowledge explicitly emphasizes the importance of the objective (science) over the subjective (emotional) in social analysis, which has important implications for different concepts of truth and reality.

This goes to the core of opposed identities in Northern Ireland, where different ideas of truth are fed, codified, and transmitted through separate Catholic (scholastic philosophy and subjective identification) and Protestant (scientific philosophy and objective identification) socialization via different educational, social systems, religious organizations, and structures (primary creators and transmitters of knowledge). Cultural ideas of truth, being, and identity are importantly bound up with religion, taking one back to a conflation of the social with the political and now also the religious. Indeed, it is this centrality of religion that helps to make Durkheim's sociology so pertinent.

Nationalism is regarded as a nineteenth-century product reflecting the demands of industrialization and modernity (Gellner, 1983; Hobsbawm, 1992; Breuilly, 1993; or Smith, 2000). This then makes Ireland a good example, since modern Irish nationalism is a product of the same period (Bew, 2009; Kennedy, 1996; Boyce, 1991; Foster, 1989a; or Lyons, 1973). And modernization and industrialization, Enlightenment developments, are precisely what impelled sociology. Meanwhile, the nineteenth century witnessed the rise of an Irish Unionism that was predominantly Protestant and a Nationalism almost wholly Roman Catholic. This places religion at the heart of national identity in Ireland, as with most nationalisms (Llobera, 1996; Smith, 2003; Dingley, 2011a and b). And religion dominated much classical sociology, especially Durkheim's:

> What gives distinctiveness to sociology's incorporation of the religio-sacred is not the analytic and descriptive attention men such as Durkheim and Weber gave to religious phenomena. It is rather the utilization of the religio-sacred as a perspective for the understanding of ostensibly non-religious phenomena such as authority, status, community and personality. (Nisbet, 1996, p. 221)

This alone makes Durkheim pertinent in studying Ireland. Another pertinent sociological observation, usually ignored in Irish studies, is that (Protestant) Ulster developed an industrial economy while (Catholic) Ireland developed a peasant-proprietor one: "Ireland was also economically divided. The industrial development of the North-East marked it off from the rest of the country and helped to heighten the Ulster Protestant's sense of solidarity" (Buckland, 1981, p. 5).

Once again, given the attention afforded in the literature to problems of modernization and economic development (Gellner, 1983; Hobsbawm, 1992; Breuilly, 1993; Smith, 2000; Greenfeld, 2003), this should be significant in understanding Ireland and for sociology since economic development and religion were core concerns in classical sociology because they posed serious problems for modern social order, integration, cohesion, and culture. Durkheim's entire *The Division of Labour in Society* (1984 [1893]) is devoted to it, where he identified the intimate relationship between religion and society, how both radically changed with industrial development, generating new, different forms of social identity and cohesion (class rather than religion). Further, Durkheim emphasized religion's role as a symbolic representation of society, thus equating society with religion (social with cosmic order).

The importance of religion in Ireland is a commonplace, but why it's so important is rarely studied. Sociologists of religion (Bruce, 1994, 1989; Dingley, 2013) note the importance of religion to ethnic identity in Ireland

and Bruce (2000) especially warns against ignoring peoples religious beliefs. However, attempts to utilize social theory to explain the relationship between religion and socio-political behavior are few, apart from limited efforts to apply Weber and Tawney, but, as Kennedy observes (1996, pp. 113–15), they have been found wanting in explanatory value.

Durkheim offers a more complex religious analysis than Weber, Tawney, or Marx. For him society and religion mirror and causally affect each other. Also, religion functions to provide regulatory social and moral frameworks relevant to specific socio-economic structures of relations; it provides the basis for a specific set of cognitive and moral knowledge; and it also functions to provide a network of relationships through which socio-economic relations are pursued within a shared cultural and moral context. Clashing socio-economic needs and interests would then be reflected in religious conflict; knowledge of what is technically right would be reflected in knowledge of what is morally and socially right. This might help yield a better understanding of the intractability of religious conflict in Ireland (or anywhere) and the inability to form a single Irish, or Ulster, community or conscience collective (nation).

Durkheim helps bridge a gap between political and economic explanations. For, while economics has been used by Marxists (according to Whyte, 1991, some of the best) to explain Northern Ireland's divisions, they lack explanatory depth:

> Richard Rose's *Governing Without Consensus* (1971) can in its theoretical sections be taken as a sustained attack on Marxist and other economic interpretations of the Northern Ireland problem. Rose's key claim is that the conflict is so intractable because it is *not* economic. Economic conflicts about the share out of material benefits, are bargainable: conflicts about religion and nationality are non-bargainable and therefore much harder to resolve. (Whyte, 1991, p. 192)

Durkheim specifically provides explanation here, in *Division of Labour* especially, by linking together religion, economic development, and social and moral development with social organization (structure) as intimately bound up with economic organization (division of labor).

Thus in different socio-economic structures Durkheim finds the basis for different religions and moral codes, which also act as symbolic representations for each other. Different forms of economic behavior and organization imply different moral imperatives. Communities pursuing different material interests and related skills require different moral codes and often conflicting forms of cognitive and moral knowledge, implying opposed concepts of truth and reality. Thus religious and national conflicts become moral ones, even cosmological, which helps explain the role of religion and takes conflicts beyond material bargaining onto a cosmological plane. Inter-community struggles become ones of truth and falsehood, good and evil, order and chaos, godly and ungodly, defying rational material explanation, they permit the rejection of normal earthly constraints. Material interests become transmogrified into ultimate questions of being and moral absolutes that become intractable.

Religion links to the role of (religious) symbols, which is another important area of Durkheimian analysis that assists in understanding Northern Ireland, where symbols so often ignite conflict (Bryson and McCartney, 1994; or Loftus, 1994). It is what parades or banners symbolize rather than the parades, flags, emblems, or banners themselves that cause rioting and violence (Jarman, 1997; or Ryder and Kearney, 2001), representations of what denies "us" by "them" (Belfast's 2012–13 flags protest, Dingley, 2014), or representations of "our" order, truth and reality, over "theirs" (Smith, 1991; Eriksen, 1993; Hobsbawm and Ranger, 1992). This should then be understood in terms of the religious identification of much nationalism, where religious symbols have become national symbols, such as patron saints and crosses or crescents on flags (Smith, 1991, 2003; Greenfeld, 1992; Dingley, 2011a and b; Hastings, 1997). From a Durkheimian perspective the very existence of different religions may symbolize different national identities.

Thus Durkheim's sociology can be a valid way of understanding nations and nationalism, especially in Ireland. Equally, one can test his sociology by reference to a concrete example in Ireland, while such a test also examines sociology's usefulness in understanding the real world.

Finally, for readers unfamiliar with religious studies, two important concepts that are vital to understanding the religious divisions in Ireland and throughout Western Europe need to be explained to make the following text explicable. The first is the doctrine of ultramontanism: This literally means beyond the high mountain and was developed within the Roman Catholic Church after the Napoleonic Wars. Ultramontanism stressed a new discipline to the central authority of Rome and the Papacy, a new sense of rigid conformity to the Church and its teachings, a single church, united in its theology and dogma and increasingly hostile to challenges to its authority and any compromises with other authorities.

Partly this was a reaction to the Napoleonic Wars, regarded as the culmination of Enlightenment toleration and liberal progress, which had severely undermined the Catholic Church's spiritual and temporal authority and that of the entire ancien régime of which it was part. As such it was quite reactionary and intransigent in all its antipathies to modern ideas of liberalism, democracy, toleration, free inquiry, and most of the things it associated with modern industrial society, which it regarded as the root cause of all of Europe's problems. Consequently it created a "closed confessional milieu with its own view of the world" (Kung, 2001, p. 171) in splendid isolation from everything else surrounding it. And it was these attitudes that Cardinal Cullen brought back to Ireland from Rome in 1848 and imbued into the modern Irish Catholic Church (Remond, 1999; O'Leary, 2006; Kung, 2001; Lee, 1989b).

Second is scholastic philosophy, which intellectually accompanies ultramontanism. This has been the "official" philosophy on which Catholic theology and dogma has been based since the Middle Ages. First introduced by Thomas Aquinas (consequently sometimes known as Thomism) it was based on his interpretation into Latin of Arabic interpretations of Aristotelian philosophy derived from original Greek texts discovered by the Muslim Arab conquerors of Baghdad (then a major center of Christian learning and philosophy) in the eighth-century AD.

Catholic scholasticism worked down from a preconceived given order of the world, natural and God given and revealed via the Catholic Church, making Catholicism the revelation of God's divine order. This led to a philosophical outlook where all had to be interpreted within the Catholic scholastic system, knowledge only existed within it and therefore had to be interpreted within it, which in turn led to tortuous reasoning and hair-splitting debates (casuistry) to fit everything into it. All knowledge and therefore truth existed only within the Catholic Church thus making it the sole legitimate authority on all matters spiritual and temporal and hence its judgments final and salvation only through it.

Scholasticism had been under attack since the fall of Constantinople (1453) and the exodus of Greek scholars to the West, bringing not only original manuscripts of Aristotle but also Plato and Platonic counter-arguments. This was fundamental to the Renaissance, Reformation, and Enlightenment, especially the birth of modern science, which almost immediately became locked in an ongoing battle with scholasticism and Catholicism. This is because science and scientific philosophy works in the opposite direction, from empirical data and evidence upward, identifying causal relations that may not fit into existing schema and supposed orders and which invariably contradict perceived scholastic wisdom. Science unravels its own natural orders and one has to follow its causal relations in an open-ended manner based on verifiable evidence, not religious belief; hence Papal bans on Copernicus and Galileo, whose observations and precise mathematical calculations flatly contradicted traditional Catholic teaching concerning the earth as the center of the universe.

Modern scientific philosophy suggested other, new causal relations, truth, and knowledge, which simply made Catholic teachings and any other scholastic systems of knowledge redundant. Science also severely undermined most of the assumptions on which the ancien régime was founded, in particular the traditional (scholastic) ideas of social and political order on which both the Catholic Church's and traditional monarchies' authority rested. Hence the protective appeal of a closed ultramontane world and the antipathy to science and modernity, also the concern to retain control over social relations, the basis of social order, and political power, making the church the sole arbiter of truth and legitimacy.

Finally, science and Protestantism, because of their emphasis on reading and knowing for oneself and the need for discussion, debate, and critical appraisal of other peoples' work, findings, and interpretations, imply a liberal and tolerant culture. Openness and freedom of thought to criticize and develop new ways and understandings are crucial to both, and in turn imply democratic ideals, making them a serious threat to all traditional authority but a direct threat to scholastically based and hierarchical systems (Russell, 1996; Shapin, 1998; Kenny, 2007; Grayling, 2007; Gaukroger, 2008).

Almost certainly Durkheim would have had these things in mind in France and throughout Europe when he was working. As a champion of liberalism, science, and the scientific mind and as a tireless campaigner against the dark forces of mysticism in social analysis and politics, he would have clearly recognized that Catholic scholasticism and ultramontanism were major opponents he and the modern world faced. And in France they were resurgent in the late nineteenth century (as the Dreyfus Affair signified; Tombs, 1996) and French right-wing Catholic thought was very influential on Irish Catholicism of the time (McCormack, 2012) making Durkheim even more pertinent to an understanding of national identities in Ireland.

# CHAPTER 1

# Durkheim as a French Nationalist

D urkheim's (French) nationalism is vital to understanding his sociology, especially his commitment to the Third Republic, desperately
trying to rebuild France after her shattering defeat in the Franco-
Prussian War (1870), the Paris Commune (1871), and the resultant turmoil
and humiliation of defeat: "His experience of the French defeat may have
contributed to a strong (though in no way militant) patriotism, a defensive
sense of national decadence and a consequent desire to contribute to the
regeneration of France" (Lukes, 1975, p. 41).

However, for Durkheim it was even more complicated: He came from
Alsace-Lorraine, lost to Germany in 1870, making him a refugee. He was also
a Jew, attacked by the right, particularly the Catholic Church, because "Jews
were blamed for defeats" (Lukes, 1975, p. 41). France had been taken to war
by Napoleon III whose regime had extended full citizenship to Jews. Not
surprisingly, reactionary forces of the ancien régime, such as traditional Monarchists and Roman Catholicism, were quick to blame France's defeat on her
revolutionary tradition, equality and liberalism, and the abandonment of traditional ancien values (traditional religion, established order and hierarchy).

Thus Durkheim perceived a need to rebuild France while also protecting
the progressive trends that emancipated someone from his religious and social
background, an outsider to the old elites. This implied supporting modern liberal ideas of individualism, civic inclusiveness, objectivity, and tolerance that
integrated everyone equally as individual citizens and broke down the old hierarchical orders, ethnic divisions, and religious exclusiveness that he regarded as
causing France's defeat. Thus his sympathies "lay strongly with republicanism
and progressive social reform, in the face of the reactionary sentiments of the
monarchists and the catholic right" (Giddens, 1978, pp. 12–13).

Hence Durkheim advocated the revolutionary ideals of liberal republicanism against the mystic ideas of social elitism, Catholicism, monarchy, and

ethnicity, with a corresponding concern for social and national solidarity. This impelled him to the importance of scientific values and objectivity in both sociology and politics, seeking civic (national) values to replace the old elite ones; rationality not mysticism. France needed rebuilding on scientific, rational, and objective criteria that alone were capable of including all of its citizens equally, as individuals, to avoid past divisions and defeats. And the strongest, bitterest, and best-organized opposition to such ideas came from the Roman Catholic Church, a bulwark of reaction, which saw science, equality, civic identity, individualism, and toleration as bitter enemies to their traditional socio-political domination as a pillar of the ancien régime (Burleigh, 2005; Chadwick, 1998; Remond, 1999):

> In fact it would be no distortion to view Durkheim's entire sociological career as an intransigent and relentless battle fought on two major fronts: against the dark, unfathomable forces of mysticism and despair on the one hand and against the unsubstantial ethereal forces of the dilettantic cult of superficiality on the other. (Alpert, 1961, p. 18)

Modernizers also wished to emulate Germany, whose educational, industrial, material, and scientific development, shared linguistic culture, and recent successful wars (1860s) and unification (1870–71) made her an object lesson.

Durkheim wanted a new France where all non-Catholics could participate as equals, and also one based on intellectual (scientific) rigor and objectivity: concerns with real implications for Ireland, with its intellectual and religious divisions, symbolized in the revisionism debate (objective, scientific analysis versus mystic, emotional romanticism).

Durkheim was therefore deeply committed to the Third Republic (1870–1940) attempting to rebuild France according to modern scientific principles and help to establish its authority, legitimacy, and a socio-political order that rejected Catholicism and monarchy, who bitterly opposed it. Only the previously excluded, such as Jews, Protestants, scientists, the newly educated middle classes, and the property-less, would benefit from its progress. Consequently the Third Republic sponsored such people through higher education, and they in turn actively supported it:

> Many of these became teachers in state institutions, and constituted for many observers the core of active support for the Third Republic. The national education system thus selected a meritocracy which in many respects became a new "establishment," based not on titles, land or industry, but on examinations. (Clark, 1973, p. 172)

Durkheim fell into this category of educated, committed individuals with their interest in education, especially scientific—the bedrock for their advancement. This in turn implied new, non-religious social and civic ideals, with scientific moral values to replace the traditional mystic and highly divisive religious ones that had excluded all non-Catholics. Consequently, civic values became official French policy specifically to aid social integration and cohesion and overcome religious divisions.

Nineteenth-century France had been bitterly divided religiously and ethnically, with 50 percent of its population not even speaking French (German, Basque, Breton, Flemish, Italian, and Occident formed clear ethno-linguistic communities within France) nor did they identify with France, to the extent that policies of internal colonization were espoused to ensure everyone became French (Weber, 1976, chapter 29; Tombs, 1996, chapter 16). This helped initiate the search for a new moral code (a civic, national religion) to help integrate and bind everyone as French speaking citizens and develop a new sense of shared, national community:

> The net result was that Republican France was eagerly concerned with philosophy, with morality, and with moral education—not from intellectual disinterestedness but from practical considerations of finding a substitute for traditional Christian teachings, so as to legitimate itself and win the broader support of new generations of schoolchildren, wrestling them away from the moral authority of the Catholic church. (Tiryakin, in Bottomore and Nisbet, 1979, p. 195)

And Durkheim was at the forefront of this, reflected in his interests in education, morality, and civil ethics, especially ones grounded in objective and rational principles. This accorded with modern Enlightenment values in an age of science and industry, with proven ability (in scientific and industrial terms and the German example) that would provide a concrete platform for a lasting, real unity—hence, Durkheim's dislike of mysticism and dilettantism.

The entire country needed recasting along modern scientific lines; to accord with the objective needs of modern industrial society became Durkheim's focus. This was both ethically correct (for equality) and functionally necessary (for industry) in the modern world: A scientific age required scientific, not religious or mystical, morals, whose inculcation should be part of the state's socializing (secular education) role, developed by sociology to provide the relevant knowledge. And in 1904 France officially cut its educational ties to religion and made state education secular, which contrasts strongly with Ireland where denominational education still reigns supreme.

In effect Durkheim argued that there are objective, determining criteria behind socio-political cohesion and integration which lie in an objective moral system that treats all citizens objectively as individuals, which in turn provides an objective reality to the nation/society. This in turn implies objective criteria for state policies to ensure national cohesion and integration, which responds to the objective reality of their milieu. This is made explicit in Durkheim's social realism, whereby he insisted on the reality of society in itself:

> The nation can be seen to have acted as the main reference for the social reality which Durkheim used to critique doctrines which reduced explanations of social phenomena to the level of individual psychology or which inflated society to the level of all humanity. Durkheim's sociological model seemed more realistic because it dealt with the confluence of social forces within a bounded society. (Thompson, 1982, p. 38)

Social realism implied society as a fact, composed of other subsidiary facts, and opposed to the facts of other societies, making a factual reality of nations, which could not simply be willed against the facts, only constructed around and upon them with objectively scientific policies.

French nationalism and its milieu were the dominant facts of Durkheim's life and sociology, from which he now sought the facts pertinent to France's humiliation in 1870 and what would most aid her recovery. To this end he was sponsored by the Third Republic to study in Germany and learn from its success (Lukes, 1975, pp. 86–95). In this way he could help establish the, "necessary political reforms following the shattering effects of the . . . Franco-Prussian War of 1870–1." (Giddens, 1996, p. 11).

Simultaneously Durkheim wanted to protect the liberal individualism and freedoms the Republican and Enlightenment traditions had bequeathed, grounded in scientific ideas of objectivity and individualism, which he also saw threatened by revolutionary socialism and its own brand of social (class) divisions. Additionally he rejected revolutionary socialism's vague ideas of universalism and English utilitarianism and classical economic universalism, which he regarded as ignoring social realities (Giddens, 1995, pp. 116–35; Jones, 2001, p. 111–31). What he sought to promote was a genuinely inclusive and objective nationalism that could then lead to international cooperation.

This gave Durkheim's sociology a specific trajectory, to create a liberal, inclusive, and cohesive France able to resist German domination and emulate its economic and cultural success, and that of other modern industrial societies, which he implicitly equated with nation: "For all practical purposes Durkheim used the terms "people," "nation," "state," "la patrie," and "society," synonymously, to denote a collective being with a personality distinct from and superior to that of its individual members" (Hamilton, 1990, p. 118).

He insisted on the reality of different societies, of which men were products, thus accounting for national differences, also; that man owed even his individuality to society. Much of the purpose of Durkheim's *Suicide* (1970 [1897]) was to establish the reality of society and social forces leading to individual decisions to commit suicide. Rates varied from society to society according to the nature of social relationships (deduced from an analysis of international suicide statistics). Suicide was therefore a social phenomenon, resulting from social relations, and rates varied according to social circumstances—social facts.

The implication is clear, different societies, with different social structures and cultures, result in different patterns of (national) behavior, making social integration and cohesion across them difficult. Man is a social being and society has an autonomous force and being over him, hence a factual status, which in modernity is realized in the nation. Nation is the modern reality, or "social milieu," that shapes man and takes him beyond his individual being to implant characteristics and identity in him, which binds him to the group that shares this identity and characteristics and separates him from others:

> 'Society is not a mere sum of individuals; rather the system formed by their association represents a specific reality which has its own characteristics' and it was 'in the nature of this individuality, not in that of its component units, that one must seek the immediate and determining causes of the facts appearing there.' (Durkheim, in Lukes, 1975, p. 19)

This immediately differentiates Durkheim from Spencer and Anglo-American social theory where society is regarded as merely a sum of individuals and their contracts.

The specific reality of the social and its characteristics were defined via the systems or networks of relations—structure. These alone provided the means, boundaries, and conduits for the creation of social facts: relations made knowledge and vice versa. Relationships that tie and bind us and how they operate are part of a shared social being from which we derive our characteristics and knowledge of self and others. Different structures of relationships, usually derived from a collective's operating environment, form the external basis for social differentiation between societies while also creating an inner content of different understanding, meaning, and knowledge:

> He insisted that the structural method should relate not simply to external forms of association, but also to the material and intellectual content of collectives. Furthermore, although the search for structure presumed a certain degree of stability in social phenomena, it had to be born in mind that structures were dynamic and emerging. (Thompson, 1982, p. 18)

This dynamism of society helped explain its lack of hard definition, and nineteenth-century societies were changing radically due to industrialization. However, structures existed and enabled one to identify societies as entities, and boundaries could be identified by looking at relations and their limits; also, finding the most relevant and dynamic relationships influencing a structure as a whole. Thus nations could be identified by seeking out their most pertinent relationships, which gave meaning and purpose to their original structural existence and imposed constraining social forces on individuals. In this way nation, national characteristics, and interests can be identified in behavior functional to the maintenance requirements of a social (national) structure.

And because individual and society are intimately linked, the nation is of fundamental importance as the social fact and milieu for socialization. This links Durkheim to another important aspect of nationalism, the German philosophical tradition (especially Kant), which strongly influenced contemporary France, partly due to unified Germany's obvious success. Influenced by Renouvier, Durkheim took Kant's categories of thought, which Kant believed existed autonomously in the mind, and reinterpreted them as the structures of society, so that categories of thought (ways of thinking and relevant knowledge) reflected social structure and relationships:

> Renouvier's view of knowledge and reason (his epistemology) implied that categories of thought such as space, time, substance, cause, etc., could be other than they were. Durkheim developed this into a sociological epistemology which implied that categories ordering thought and experience varied from society to society and were socially determined. (Thompson, 1982, p. 31)

This implies that social reality, at least, is a product of relationships—social structure, which gives man his sense of reality, truth, what is, and ought to be: This became the basis for Durkheim's sociology of knowledge. Societies (nations) now had an objective basis—structures of relationships. And because structures are dynamic, not fixed, one can identify the variables to be influenced in affecting the development of nations, primarily the nature and quality of relationships—hence, much of Durkheim's concern with education, religion, and civic morals, since these directly affected the form and quality of relationships; also, Durkheim's concern in *Division of Labour* to identify different types of structure and the functional role they played and the prerequisites they required in communal and individual life. This in turn helps explain the relevance of Durkheim's sociology of knowledge to an understanding of nationalism.

Nation and national identity can now be interpreted as a product of social structures, which form the social and individual basis for national identity. It also helps explain ideas of "national will" and "national self-determination" via reference to the social forces within and functional requirements of those structures to maintain the continued existence of a bounded set of relationships; also, the importance to the individual of the national since their sense of being and identity is dependent upon them.

This does not imply wholly fixed and determinate structures and dependencies. As Schmauss (1994, pp. 12–14) has observed, there has been a tendency to interpret Durkheim's structural functionalism in a very static manner via the tradition of American sociology. This is a false perception (Jones, 2001, pp. 5–10) since he always emphasized society as dynamic, thus the entire *Division of Labour* is about the evolution of society from mechanical to organic structures as part of an ongoing process. *Division of Labour* was a theory of historical development and change as the material milieu of a society alters and its internal structural differentiation changes.

Such a theory of social change corresponds with the emergence of nationalism, whereby the division of labor, the key structural change related to economic development and industrialization, acts as the dynamic for social, impelling corresponding political, change. Therefore as socio-economic external and internal relationships change so must their political relationships extending over them, redefining political boundaries to control vital relations. This Durkheimian theme is central to much of the theory on nationalism (Gellner, 1983; Breuilly, 1993; Eriksen, 1993; Smith, 1998) and especially the Marxists (Kellas, 1991, p. 61). Most of the literature stresses that nationalism is very much a response to economic change, particularly industrialization, which required substantial changes in social and economic organization and relations, implying new knowledge.

However, national disputes are intractable precisely because they are not wholly material, which is where Durkheim helps bridge the divide between material and non-material explanations by emphasizing a sui generis reality of society. That is, relationships are grounded in the material but also have an independent reality able to react back on the material and develop their own autonomous life. Relationships then form a social and moral claim over the individual that extends beyond calculated material interest because their being, both moral and material, depends upon it. Nation thus acquires an existence in its own right as a social fact with all the social force that Durkheim gave to society. Thus there is a moral imperative to nationalism, taking it beyond simple economic self-interest.

## Core Elements of Durkheim's Society

Central to Durkheim's sociology is his concept of the "conscience collective":

> In the Division of Labour, Durkheim defines 'the conscience collective or commune' as the 'set of beliefs and sentiments' common to the average members of

a single society (which) forms a determinate system that has its own life. The French word 'conscience' is ambiguous, embracing the meanings of two English words 'conscience' and 'consciousness.' Thus the 'beliefs and sentiments' comprising the conscience collective are, on the one hand, moral and religious, and, on the other hand, cognitive. (Lukes, 1975, p. 4)

Thus:

The totality of beliefs and sentiments common to average members of a society forms a determinate system with a life of its own. It can be termed the collective or common consciousness . . . By definition it is diffused over society as a whole . . . In fact it is independent of the particular conditions in which individuals find themselves . . . links successive generations to one another. Thus it is totally different from the consciousness of individuals, although it is only realised in individuals. (Durkheim, 1984, pp. 38–39)

This is both a moral and a psychic idea, built around shared concepts, beliefs, values, skills, behavior, intellectual and cultural knowledge; a way of life, of seeing and believing, which creates a sense of solidarity, identity, and purpose among those sharing it:

A social cohesion exists whose cause can be traced to a certain conformity of each individual consciousness to a common type . . . Indeed under these conditions all members of the group are not only individually attracted to one another because they resemble one another, but they are also linked to what is the condition for the existence of this collective type. (Durkheim, 1984, p. 60)

This cohesion is a product of artifice and natural causes (reflecting theories of national formation), the functional necessities for existence in a particular milieu and a conscious construction in response to it; the cohesion is therefore life-sustaining and built on cooperative relations. It creates a society that is, in itself, real and an important source of psychic and physical life that exists apart from the individual, acting upon and through them in a determinate manner:

The individual is dominated by a moral reality greater than himself: namely, collective reality. When each people is seen to have its own suicide rate . . . when it appears that that the variations through which it passes at different times . . . merely reflect the rhythm of social life; and that marriage, divorce, the family, religious society, the army, etc affect it in accordance with definite laws . . . these states and institutions . . . will be felt to be real, living, acting forces which, because of the way they determine the individual, prove their independence of him; which, if the individual enters as an element in the combination whence these forces ensue, at least control him once they are formed. (Durkheim, 1970, pp. 38–39)

Society is a reality, a social fact, which imposes a moral obligation over the individual that takes primacy over self-interest and constrains individuals to act according to collective needs. These needs are those values, acts, and skills (knowledge) necessary to maintain the collective, which has its own life—sui generic—which is related to the environment in which the collective has to survive, the individual's survival being in turn dependent on the collective. Thus individual and collective are intimately related, mentally and physically, making the individual a collectively dependent being, while the collective is dependent on individual conformity. This would offer an explanation for the importance of nation in a social world dominated by nationalism.

The collective was symbolically represented via religion, which Durkheim interpreted as the origin of social consciousness, ways of telling men how to act socially (morally): "Originally, it pervades everything, everything social is religious; the two words are synonymous" (Durkheim, 1984, p. 119).

Society is moral and is religion; God is its ideal symbolic representation and the worship of God is the worship of society, additionally religion involves the moral instruction relevant to its maintenance, which would explain the close relationship between religion and nationalism, religion representing the moral imperative acting over the individual to put one's nation before self-interest. Thus religion/morals inform individuals of collective norms and values, guiding behavior and thoughts toward the needs for collective existence.

Consequently, "alien" morals, religion, and other types of outside knowledge, pose threats to any collective's existence, disrupting its relationships and undermining its solidarity, threatening both individual and social existence. New knowledge would also threaten elite positions, since theirs is directly related to mastery, if not monopoly, of collective knowledge, while even non-elites might suffer from emotional loss, existential insecurities, or ontological insecurity at the demise or redundancy of old knowledge (Kinnvall, 2004; Krolikowski, 2008). In this one can find imperatives to national autonomy and resistance to change, especially separatist nationalism.

Collectives thus provide the solidarity on which individual well-being and existence depends. One consequence of this is that different collectives may not be able to tolerate each other:

> Every strong state of consciousness is a source of life; it is an essential factor of our general vitality. Consequently, everything that tends to weaken it diminishes and depresses us, the result is an impression of being disturbed and upset . . . It is therefore inevitable that we should react vigorously against the

cause of what threatens such a lowering of consciousness . . . It is as if a foreign force had penetrated us . . . it provokes a veritable disorder . . . an emotional reaction of a more or less violent nature. (Durkheim, 1984, pp. 53–54)

Thus different societies (social structures) cannot mix without doing violence to each other, and therefore need separating out, with clear boundaries and their own space or careful integration. Herein lies an explanation for nationalist and religious conflict within state borders and the need for a single national identity and institutions, otherwise religions and societies will continually be competing to impose their knowledge (cognitive and moral) on the polity, and which social order and moral values and legitimacy should prevail (as in Northern Ireland). For the moral regulation functional to one society will inevitably contradict that necessary for another leading to conflicting relations and no solidarity.

This provides a rational basis for separate nations and intra-nation-state conflicts, via Durkheim's concept of the conscience collective. The alternative to separation would be integration, which would require the construction of new integrative structures, knowledge, and consciousness (reality), hence Durkheim's interest in education and the development of civic morals in an ethnically and religiously divided France. His ideas were closely followed by the French government (Lukes, 1975, chapter 6) and helped prompt policies of internal colonization (Weber, 1976 pp. 485–96), which highlights the nationalism of Durkheim's and his great student Mauss's sociology:

"A materially and morally integrated society" characterised by the "relative moral, mental, and cultural unity of its inhabitants, who consciously support the state and its laws." It is clear that France around 1870 did not conform to Mauss's model of a nation. It was neither morally or materially integrated; what unity it had was less cultural than administrative. Many of its inhabitants, moreover, were indifferent to the state and its laws, and many others rejected them altogether. "A country" says Karl Deutsch, "is as large as the interdependence it perceives." (Weber, 1977, p. 485)

National integration, with a shared common consciousness founded upon a single reality, even if partially constructed, was the purpose behind Durkheim's sociology—lessons for Northern Ireland? Traditional religion in France did not offer a common consciousness or morality relevant to the modern, industrial world, consequently the state had to generate a new (civic) religion (society) able to embrace all (Catholic, Huguenot, Jew, and non-religious) to reflect France's new reality.

And because, for Durkheim, the individual soul was their sense of collective being, their conscience and consciousness any social/national consciousness and conscience had to be genuinely inclusive and non-problematic for all individuals. It was the enervating and psychic force guiding men's actions in practical morality (ethics), the basis for solidarity. This was the force over and above the individual, acting on and through them to the collective good, sacrificing to it and constraining individual behavior to social ends and ideals, recalled to men via symbolic representations: "Collective ideals, he argued, 'can only become manifest and conscious by being concretely realised in objects that can be seen by all, understood by all and represented to all minds: figurative designs, emblems of all kinds, written or spoken formulas animate or inanimate objects'" (Lukes, 1975, p. 423).

Ceremonies and rituals, particularly, provide such recalls and reanimation of collective consciousness, although with greater intensity since they are social and utilize involvement, such as national days, parades, and memorial services. The role of symbols in nationalism provides some evidence for Durkheim's sociology, since his "proof" lay not in abstract theoretical debate, which consumes much modern sociology (Jones, 2001, pp. 218–24), but rather its applicability to interpreting and understanding the real world beyond the university, rather than internally perfect academic concepts: "That is, he did not pretend to have proved his theories of the origins of religion and of the basic categories of thought. Rather, he argued that these theories provide the best explanation of the facts" (Schmauss, 1994, p. 232).

Society (nation) was a fact that existed, often imperfectly in conceptual terms, and its existence, dynamics, and function needed explanation; and the test of Durkheim's sociology lay in its ability to do this. He believed that, once understood, a science of society could help achieve social integration by identifying functional realities, analyzing functional needs, and suggesting positive and progressive policies, especially for Republican France. However, under the influence of post-modernism, his concepts of progress and modernity are ones that much sociology avoids today (Dodd, 1999, pp. 1–8).

Post-modern sociology stresses subjective and interpretative dimensions, narrative, and discourse as reality, while Durkheim emphasized an objective and external reality:

> through the dialectic of reality, conscience, representation and thing (*chose*); second, through a logic of social truth, and third, through a relational view of reality, then we can repudiate not only accusations of a false scientism, but also that he neglects the processes by which social reality is an emergent property of meaningful interaction, that is, "sighs, gestures and language (Walsh, 1972: 37)." (Jones, 2001, p. 134)

Durkheim's society was a real collective consciousness in which education was vital for its development and transmission, a concern dominating his work and reflected in *Moral Education* and *Civic Morals*. For, while the collective grew out of a material and social environment it also needed some conscious construction, structure, and historical guidance to codify, share, and pass on its knowledge (cognitive and moral), originally a religious task. This provided permanence, solidity, and concrete reality to the collective consciousness, while also integrating, maintaining, and nurturing it. Here Durkheim saw the teacher as the direct descendent of the priest and modern education as the equivalent of religious instruction. Indeed his pedagogy has been criticized for overemphasizing this dimension: "Durkheim's pedagogy relies upon an unduly narrow conception of education as socialisation through the authority of the teacher, seen as the agent of 'society,' the 'interpreter of the great moral ideas of his time and country'" (Lukes, 1975, p. 135).

Again, most of the literature on nationalism stresses education's role in making the national. But Durkheim also stressed social reality in education over mere indoctrination and manipulation; for, while it helped develop a collective consciousness in individual minds it was only successful if it corresponded to their external realities. The consciousness developed can then be used to identify legitimate borders to societies, since they will restrict relations, knowledge, and consciousness in a way that would define the nation. Where men are not bonded into the relevant relations, knowledge, and consciousness, they become excluded from the collective and thus are not part of the nation and are aliens even in their own land.

This collective consciousness, symbolized through religion, in turn sanctifies the social and all related and vital to it. Durkheim used this to explain the sacredness of land (O'Brien's *God and Godland*, 1988; Smith, 2003, chapter 6), whereby individual rights to land ownership are derivative of the collective (sacred), only through it do individuals have rights to portions of the land (national territory) or other material resources. From this base Durkheim interprets taxes and tithes as forms of religious sacrifice to God (collective) that reconfirm the individuals' sacred rights:

> It is to this society that these annual tributes will be offered, by which the believer originally bought the right from his deities to till and cultivate the land. These sacrifices, these first fruits of all kinds, are the earliest forms of taxes. First, they are debts that are paid to the Gods; then they become tithes paid to the priests, and this tithe is already a regular tax that later on is to pass into the hands of the lay authorities. (Durkheim 1992, p. 163)

Thus an important link is forged between membership in the collective, religion, sacrifice, land, and nation that helps explain the sacredness of the nation. Nation is sacred because it is collective and land is sacred because it belongs to the collective, but only that land over which collective relations and consciousness exist. This helps provide a reality to nation, national rights, will, and self-determination based not just on material interests but also on moral (sacred) imperatives.

This introduces a fundamental aspect of Durkheim's sociology, the concept of reality, particularly social reality and truth, the core of his sociology of knowledge. For him the ultimate reality of society lay in its structure of relations and their functional requirements, and, as Jones (2001) or Schmauss (1994) have indicated, not in some mechanistic and determinate manner. Durkheim's structural-functionalism, as explored in *Division of Labour*, was one of change and progress, of societies responding to changes as their milieu changed: "There is a dialectical exchange between internal and external relations—that is between persons and things" (Jones, 2001, p. 69).

This was the core of Durkheim's theory of progress; relations changed and impelled new concepts and truths that challenged older ones. This corresponds with his idea that societies evolve from primitive to advanced, indexed via increasingly complex and sophisticated social relations, which progressively free the individual from collective domination (mechanical solidarity) to enable greater individual autonomy (organic solidarity). This was closely associated with the growth of moral density (population growth and closer living relations) enforcing greater reflection, then specialization and the progressive development of the division of labor, particularly with industrialization and increased exchange relations. Here the nature of social relations changed gradually from solidarity through closeness, conformity, and similarity (segmental peasant society) to solidarity based on extended relations, individualism, and reciprocity between differences (modern industrial society).

The entire knowledge basis of society (consciousness) changed as relations changed and extended, new relations generating new knowledge required more new knowledge and encouraged greater reflection. Relations were the social reality and their truth. Truth was knowledge of relations and the permanence of relations reflected in a stable order, which had important ontological implications (Giddens, 1991a and b) for concepts of being since changes in social order affected ideas about permanence, reality, and being. Social order thus has an important ontological function that nations help maintain.

This tied into the rise of science as the basis for truth, replacing religion but growing out of it. Mechanical solidarity was dominated by religious truth, where mysticism, folklore, and other traditional and parochial forms of knowledge predominated. Organic solidarity was associated with the rise of science, new material truths that displaced mysticism, folklore, and tradition, but, most important, replacing religion as the arbiter of truth (Pagden, 2013).

Scientific truth was universal, enunciating and operating according to universal laws that denied parochial custom and mysticism. Truth became universal, material, and realizable in this world, thus undermining the established authority and legitimacy of traditional knowledge and truth (religion) or at least removing religion to a distant realm. However, science and scientific truth are not wholly opposed to religion since they grow out of religion (Porter, 2000; Merton, 1973; Burke, 2000; Shapin, 1995; Pagden, 2013).

Indeed many early scientists were often deeply religious men (as were many nationalists) concerned to show how science revealed God's laws (of nature), thus offering rational explanation for the existence of God by discovering His laws (Porter, 2000, chapter 5; Uglow, 2003). However, and significantly for Ireland, ideas of rational religion and science were almost exclusively Protestant and replicated in networks of Protestant relations (churches, congregations, dissenting academies) and industrial (Uglow, 2003). Science followed the progressive development of relations in socio-economic development and emerged with the same industrialization that induces organic solidarity. Science is the knowledge base of organic solidarity and posed a contradictory knowledge (truth) base to the mechanical solidarity associated with peasant society.

Durkheim associated the rise of science with industry and the division of labor, leading to more extensive relations of greater depth and complexity. This helped stimulate increased reflection, deeper thought, and criticism, which impelled greater rationalism, the basis for science. Science was a function of extended relations, which undermined old parochial, religious relations, mysticism, and traditional religion as truth (Shapin, 1995; Gaukroger, 2008): Empirically founded rationality replaced custom and emotion, and industry and scientific economics replaced self-sufficient peasant society and the old moral economy (Porter, 2000, pp. 386–87).

Throughout the British Isles industry and science were predominantly Protestant interests, especially in Ulster with its close links to staunchly Protestant Scotland (Herman, 2003, pp. 63–64). This helped link all sectors of the industrial and Protestant British Isles as British (Colley, 1996). And Britain in the eighteenth and nineteenth centuries was regarded as the center of progress, development, and the Enlightenment, closely watched by the rest of Europe (Porter, 2000, chapter 1).

However, Catholic Ireland did not enter these relations or values, its core relations were peasant, segmental socio-economic ones, where traditional religion (truth) dominated. Enlightened and Protestant progress implied loss to Catholic Ireland, non-truth, not part of the British reality, reconfirming traditional Catholic truth. But to an elite southern Protestant Ascendancy (landlords over Catholic peasants) and an industrial Protestant Ulster Enlightenment, progress and being British did equate with truth, reality, and universalizing forces.

Durkheim indexed progress via the development of division of labor and movement away from segmental social structures (a few close and undifferentiated relationships) to societies built on extended, complex, and differentiated relationships. Segmental social consciousness and solidarity was maintained via similitude and conformity, of which there could be many since they responded relatively passively to their local physical environment. Segmental knowledge was simple, unchanging, and closely adapted to relatively unchanging environments, reflected in strong local traditions, customs, myths, and folklore, which provided a rich source of practical knowledge adapted to local needs. In such a milieu the individual was dominated by collective conscience, sentiments, and conformity to local norms: "As long as mythological truth reigns, conformism is the rule. But intellectual individualism appears with the reign of scientific truth; and it is even that individualism which has made it necessary . . . thus social unanimity cannot henceforth establish itself around mythological beliefs" (Durkheim, in Jones, 2001, p. 16). Thus the mythological beliefs of nationalist (Catholic) Ireland run counter to the requisites for moral integration with the scientific values of Unionist (Protestant) Ireland/Ulster.

Additionally, segmental society was also indexed via laws that repressed differences and individualism for strict conformity to religious codes that dominated men's consciousness. Relations were comparatively few, simple, close, and conformist, tradition and custom prevailed and cognition and knowledge were bounded by religion. Such a situation is precisely that described by historians of Catholic Ireland (Brown, 1981; Lyons, 1982; or Foster, 1989a).

The opposite applied in modern society. Differences increased concomitantly to increased specialization, due to industrial division of labor, and relations increased in terms of number, scope, extent, and depth, and reciprocity between interdependent differences became the basis of solidarity and collec tive consciousness. Interdependence, not similitude and conformity, bound men. Industrial society often combined previously separate ones into larger units of exchange and interdependence, which required scientifically standardized criteria for universal exchange. Consequently, the law changed from repression of differences to regulating exchange between differences, thus progressively freeing individuals from collective restraint and religious sanction: "There was a general identification of repressive law and religious law in primitive societies ('offences against the gods are offences against society') and of primitive religion and mechanical solidarity ('religious consciences are identical there')" (Lukes, 1975, pp. 238–39). Thus:

> Penal law, and generally that penal repression, had progressively declined with the regression of mechanical solidarity and the advance of organic solidarity; and that this decline was a function of the growth in social complexity, organisation, administration, specialisation and individual autonomy, and an increasing respect for justice, equality of opportunity and individual dignity. (Lukes, 1975, p. 258)

Thus religion progressively faded from public life with increased individuality and reciprocity, while knowledge became increasingly secularized—science, whose universal principles and standardized laws enabled reciprocity via shared knowledge and forged universal links. Religion didn't cease to exist, since man was still of the collective, but became a distant force, expressing more individual and abstract values as man was less acted upon by his collective.

A universalizing conformity and consciousness was now required for functional reciprocity and toleration of difference, which implied science and scientific values, laws, standards, and truth applied to all. The new, distant God became one of tolerance to harmonize differences that were functional to the reciprocity required of division of labor and increasingly eschewed mysticism, custom, folklore, and traditions. A God of science who exalted the individual and knowledge that was more rational, deeper, and sophisticated was required that directly threatened the old God.

## Science, Enlightenment, Progress, and Modernity

Modern society was, for Durkheim, not simply organic solidarity, science, and division of labor but inherently progressive, the legacy of the Enlightenment, of which the French Revolution was an offspring. Its defense and its Republican tradition were central to Durkheim's sociology and his own Jewish emancipation: "The Republic, then, was not only acceptable. On occasion it even seemed worth defending with some vehemence. And this was particularly true of the Jews, to whom the word 'equality' in the national motto meant more than an empty symbol" (Hughes, 1961, p. 58).

For Durkheim, therefore the Revolution represented the birth of a new God and religion: "In the general enthusiasm of that time, things that by nature were purely secular were transformed by public opinion into sacred things: Fatherland, Liberty, Reason. A religion tended to establish itself spontaneously, with its own dogma, symbols, altars and feast days" (Durkheim, 1995, pp. 215–16).

Revolution, Enlightenment, science, democracy, freedom, and progress, had real meanings for Durkheim, strongly influenced by Renouvier's work on Kant that asserted both a rational and real basis for man and society and who identified progress with reason and science (Thompson, 1982, pp. 30–31; Lukes, 1975, pp. 54–58). They saw reason and rationality as progressively freeing man from collective domination, which formed the basis for Durkheim's attack on mysticism and Romanticism and created his border between mechanical (mystic and religious) and organic (rational and scientific) societies. Rational societies were also more cosmopolitan, with increased economic specialization and extended relations reaching toward more scientific thought:

> Civilization has a tendency to become more rational and logical . . . That alone is rational that is universal. What defies the understanding is the particular and concrete. We can only ponder effectively upon the general. Consequently, the closer the common conscience is to particular things, the more exactly it bears their imprint, and thus the more unintelligible it is . . . Not being able to reduce them to logical principles we are inclined to view them only as bizarre.
>
> But the more general the common conscience becomes, the more scope it leaves for individual variations. When God is remote from things and men, His action does not extend to every moment of time and to everything. Only abstract rules are fixed, and these can be freely applied in very different ways. (Durkheim, 1984, pp. 231–32)

In nationalism, the relationship between enlightened (science, industry, and modernizing) nationalism has been a common theme, just as mysticism, peasant lifestyles, and religion has been associated with Romantic (ethnic-separatist) nationalism that created barriers to modernity. Here Durkheim predates the literature: "As we advance in evolution, we see the ideals men pursue breaking free of the local or ethnic conditions obtaining in a certain region of the world or a certain group, and rising above all that is particular and so approaching the universal" (Durkheim, in Giddens, 1996, p. 202).

But, importantly, it is the individual breaking free from the (ethnic) group and mechanical solidarity for universal values that reflects progress, not segmental groups breaking away from universalizing societies to protect group (parochial and mystic) differences that reflect progress. This may be a point of confusion for postmodernist proponents of multi-culturalism who confuse individual and group differences. Individual differences imply a universal, liberal, and progressive culture breaking down barriers and freeing the individual from collective domination, while group differences imply cultural barriers, mysticism, lack of individuality, and repressive social relations. A multi-cultural society would be something of an oxymoron since it would imply opposed social forces as the basis of society and be genuinely restrictive of the toleration and individual relations on which differentiated individual social relations depend.

An important aspect of early enlightened unification nationalism, specifically the French Revolution, was that it aimed to break down ethno-linguistic and religious differences within states and between them, aiming for a universal humanity that was bound up with ideas of extended trade relations. Industrial Ulster was bound into extended, international trade relations, Catholic Ireland's peasant economy was not. This is important because "Durkheim claimed . . . that the fundamental categories of thought were located in the organisation of society, social forms produced the forms of thought" (Turner, in Durkheim, 1992, p. xxvi).

The social organization (organic, industrial division of labor) that informed Ulster's consciousness was fundamentally enlightened, emphasizing individualism, cosmopolitanism, and rationality, keys to liberal democracy:

> The more deliberation and reflection and a critical spirit play a considerable part in the course of public affairs, the more democratic the nation. It is the less democratic when lack of consciousness, uncharted customs, the obscure sentiments and prejudices that evade investigation predominate . . . With feudalism, there is diffusion of social life, and obscurity and lack of consciousness are at their worst. (Durkheim, 1992, p. 89)

Irish nationalism openly espoused a peasant-proprietor economy, self-sufficiency, emotive Romantic notions and custom along with traditional (Catholic) religion.

Another cultural area of difference between social structures lay in different values and morals related to suffering, passion, and violence, for, since the individual is more acted upon, in all senses, under mechanical solidarity they are likely to tend toward a more violent and passionate attachment to society, not a reflective one:

> The gods we worship live only in the privations and sacrifices to which mortals subject themselves. Sometimes, human victims even are exacted and it is this toll that expresses in mystic form what society exacts from its members. We can imagine that such training over generations is likely to leave in the consciousness a disposition to cause suffering. Moreover, all these sentiments are, too, very vivid passions, since they will tolerate no opposition and tolerate no question. Characters formed in this way are therefore in essence a product of the passions: they are driven by impulse. Passion leads to violence and tends to break all that hampers it or stands in the way. (Durkheim, 1992, pp. 116–17)

Most of the literature on ethnic nationalism has noted its predisposition to passion and violence (Kedourie, 1993; Greenfeld, 1993; Nairn, in Hall, 1998; Dingley, 2013), while enlightened nationalism has been noted for its rationalism, tolerance, non-violent individualism, and utilitarian ideas of happiness. Thus, again Durkheim predates the literature on nationalism when discussing law and the modern state: "A duty to be directed towards the law, (ensuring) that the law is aggressive and expansive should become peaceful, moral and scientific" (Durkheim, 1996, p. 50).

These are indices of progress for Durkheim. The state acquires a more prominent and reflective role as society develops, with a growing concern for internal regulation of society that progressively replaces religion as the organizing force. Rational development of society and the individual in an increasingly complex environment becomes necessary, an organ to think on behalf of the collective as a whole:

> The planning of the social milieu so that the individual may realise himself more fully, and the management of the collective apparatus in a way that will bear less hard on the individual; an assured and amicable exchange of goods and services and the cooperation of all men of good will towards an ideal they share without any conflict . . . This is so, because, as social life becomes more complex, so does the workings of its functions become more delicate. Further, since the more highly developed systems are precariously balanced and need greater care if they are to be kept going, societies will have a greater need to concentrate their energies on themselves. (Durkheim, 1992, p. 71)

States need to address their internal collective organization more effectively, hence a growth in state functions and activity, with inevitably greater centralization and rationalization, which often conflict with regional interests and collective consciousness. Here we have the basis for breakaway nationalisms, a region not integrated into the dominant relations and consciousness that identifies a separate state as in its interests.

Indeed the dominant interests of a metropolitan state may well be perceived as oppressive by a nonintegrated region because the state's activity and moral regulation may be dysfunctional and disruptive to regional interests and consciousness. A new state to fend off "progress," or at least implement it more commensurately with regional needs, may be identified by dominant regional interests: knowledge of collective good via networks of regional relations.

The new regional state now identifies progress parochially as anti-progress, acquiring certain aspects of modernity (nationalism) to fend off progress. This gives many ethnic nationalisms an image of progressiveness that belies their substance (as with Catholic nationalist Ireland: "Liberty came to Ireland in a Protestant guise," p. 161, and "The Enlightenment was its enemy," p. 165, de Paor, in Kennedy, 1985) Here a segmental mechanical structure united to ward off the disruptive incursions of an organic (British, including Ulster) solidarity.

Ulster Unionists wanted to retain the status quo, only reluctantly accepting an Ulster Home Rule Parliament within the UK; they wished to retain their progressive (industrial and scientific) culture and links. Meanwhile, nationalist Ireland revolted against progress and Enlightenment, wrapped up in the language of alternative (Romantic) values. But, because of Home Rule, Ulster developed into a small, semi-autonomous and isolated region, which bred an inward and regressive attitude at variance with its progressive origins.

It is not only state functions but also the type and nature of state laws that serve to index progress from mechanical to organic solidarity. Laws that progressively free the individual from mechanical solidarity are less religious and reflect secular, rational values associated with modern organic solidarity:

> Penal repression, had progressively declined with the repression of mechanical and the advance of organic solidarity; and that this decline was a function of the growth in social complexity, organization, administration, specialization and individual autonomy, and an increasing respect for justice, equality of opportunity and individual dignity. (Lukes, 1975, p. 258)

Once again, it is not a preference for progressive or repressive law but what is functional to the state of society. Different rates of progressive laws will provide a real dividing line between conscience collectives and social structures where the needs of one would be harmful if imposed on the others. Such was the case in nationalist Ireland where the laws pertinent to an industrial society were quickly discarded in an independent Ireland and an adherence to Catholic social teaching became the norm (Whyte, 1971).

Science also indexes peace and toleration, primary moral imperatives for Durkheim. Being reasonable and rational would contrast with passion, sentiment, emotion, and violence as moral imperatives in societies dominated by communal and authoritarian discipline (explaining the IRA; Dingley, 2012), which is not a matter of choice but functional to the nature of social relations.

Different moral imperatives cannot co-exist because they deny each other (another critique of multi-culturalism); different concepts of reality, truth, and purpose inevitably conflict, which helps to understand the violence of much nationalist sentiment and the need for defined borders. Conflicting moral imperatives also explain sectarian sentiments and discrimination between different national identities, providing sectarianism and discrimination with a real causal basis (not all prejudice is mindless), which is not to legitimize them but to explain them, thereby identifying real causes to respond to, rather than moral exhortation alone. And this brings one back to ideas of truth and reality and the importance, therefore, of Durkheim's sociology of knowledge and social action.

# CHAPTER 2

# Durkheim's Sociology of Knowledge

For Durkheim, religion and sociology were ways that society became conscious of and represented itself. Religion was a symbolic representation of society; to be social was to be religious, which was to be moral and know how to behave socially. Morality and being social were the same; society, morality, and religion therefore formed a trinity, integral parts of his system. Moral rules made man social and religion symbolically represented society from which man knew how to be social (moral) and the means by which man knew himself.

Religion was a source of knowing, the original source of all knowledge, man's first attempt to know and interpret his reality, seek causes, and develop reflexive thought, which directly develops into modern science. Implicit, also, was that sociology, as the science of society, had a religious role, with the sociologist as a modern-day priest, the holder of social knowledge. For Durkheim history was the progress of human thought from primitive religion to Enlightenment values (science) and as man's knowledge changed as society did so too his morality, with sociology as its ultimate revelation.

Durkheim was actually trying to reach down to some of the most fundamental aspects of man's being:

> It has long been known that the first systems of representations that man made of the world and himself were of religious origin. There is no religion that is not both a cosmology and a speculation about the divine. If philosophy and the sciences were born in religion, it is because religion itself began by serving as science and philosophy. Further, and less often noted, religion has not merely enriched a human intellect already formed but in fact has helped to form it. Men owe to religion not only the content of their knowledge, in significant part, but also the form in which that knowledge is elaborated. (Durkheim, 1995, p. 8)

For Durkheim, therefore, knowledge is social because it is a product of society, the core of his sociology of religion: knowledge of things external to the individual and of himself, because for Durkheim, man, apart from his biological make up, is a social product. Consequently, man's sense of being, of who and what he is (identity), is a product of the society of which he is a member. Consequently, nations and society are more profound than mere passive objects for study. If society is real then man's sense of reality must come from society, and what is real is society (nation). And if society forms the basis for nationalism then nations have a real basis that links to the reality of man's existence. Man's being as a cognitive individual is intimately tied to his sense of being social, a collective product. Durkheim is addressing a major ontological problem.

Nationalism both reflects a social reality and helps create it, since reality is socially constructed and reaffirms itself in everyday real life. Society, for Durkheim, is the only being over and above the individual, the sole transcendent force able to affect the way we think, and therefore act, on a cognitive level. Society implants in our minds ideas and sentiments of what is and is real: This is a reality in itself and also a reflection of external reality. Also, since Durkheim regards every society as a product of its milieu (environment) and how it relates to it, any society reflects a deeper reality than merely its existence since it also reflects factors vital to its existence.

Durkheim's society responds to its environment, which helps construct the internal relationships (structures) that define it. Those relations then structure man's knowledge of the world, which becomes reality. Each society has its own structure and reality corresponding to its needs and functional to its milieu. (Durkheim later modified this relativist concept of knowledge and truth into a universal one whereby progress and science lead to an ultimate truth.) But consistently Durkheim asserts that each religion (truth) is real for its society and milieu: "Easily the most striking feature of . . . 'Les Formes elementaires de la vie religieuse,' is his insistence that religions are founded on and express 'the real'" (Fields, in Durkheim, 1995, p. xvii). "Fundamentally then, there are no religions that are false. All are true after their own fashion: All fulfill given conditions of human existence, though in different ways" (Durkheim, 1995, p. 2).

No religion is false because it symbolically represents what is real—society. But some societies are at higher levels of development and therefore represent higher truths. (Truth is ultimately an abstract, universal concept for Durkheim, revealed through increasingly abstract science and levels of being.) But for itself, each society is a truth because it is the transcendent and ultimate force in its members' lives.

Meanwhile, individual mentality is shaped by the mental constructs that constitute Durkheim's "representation collectives," that is, social constructs (ideas of truth and reality) that are implanted in and become real in the individual mind and become real for members of a collective, constituting their own reality. The defense of that reality in the face of progress, new knowledge, and truths may well help provide important explanations for many aspects of nationalism.

Durkheim's knowledge is therefore a collective representation in the individual's mind, a product of periods of cooperation within the same milieu that led to the development of common ideas and sentiments:

> What constitutes the strength of the collective states of consciousness is not only that they are common to the present generation, but particularly that they are for the most part, a legacy of generations that have gone before . . . The common consciousness is in fact formed only very slowly and modified in the same way. Time is needed for a form of behaviour or a belief to attain that degree of generality and crystallisation, and time also for it to lose it. (Durkheim, 1984, p. 233)

Coping with one's milieu caused a structure of relations to build up over time producing a reality over the individual that placed him in defined roles and relations with others that appeared autonomous. It stimulated the development of reason by enabling men to overcome their individual and empirical limitations through cooperative behavior and establishing causal relations that assisted men to go beyond their individual limitations. It then developed to help men go beyond what was known at a merely sensate level. Both literally and metaphorically man can transcend his individual situation via a structure of relations that stimulate thinking and reasoning, thus socially man can move onto a higher reality and transform his life.

A shared knowledge was also a functional necessity for the social life that enabled man to transcend his empirical reality, for men can only commune and cooperate if they have shared concepts and categories:

> If, at every moment, men did not agree on these fundamental ideas, if they did not have an homogenous conception of time, space, cause, number and so on. All consensus among minds, and thus all common life, would become impossible.
>
> Hence society cannot leave the categories up to the free choice of individuals without abandoning itself. To live, it requires not only a minimum moral consensus but also a minimum of logical consensus that it cannot do without either. Thus in order to prevent dissidence, society weighs on its members with all its authority. (Durkheim, 1995, p. 16)

If individuals lose shared knowledge, collective acts become impossible and they also lose important aspects of themselves as social products. Equally any new knowledge, or challenges to old, within a collective can cause acute disruption and anguish since reality and truth are now disputed, causing ontological insecurity (Giddens, 1991a and b).

## The Social Origins of Knowledge

In an early study with Mauss of primitive forms of classification, he maintained that the genesis of the categories of thought is to be found in the group structure and relations and that the categories vary with changes in the social organization. In seeking to account for the social origins of the categories, Durkheim postulates that individuals are more directly and inclusively orientated toward the groups in which they live than they are toward nature. The primarily significant experiences are mediated through social relationships, which leave their impress on the character of thought and knowledge. (Merton, 1973, p. 17)

Society is a reality that develops its own self-consciousness via its internal structure of relations, the result of regular interaction between collective members and the performance of rituals and ceremonies that dramatically recall social existence. The structure is regularly re-created by new members entering into it and so it extends over time and the individual, and so assumes an image of immutability and natural permanence, the timelessness that nationalists claim to the nation.

Resulting from this, a collective develops a consciousness of itself, both cognitive and moral, that constitutes a collective mental life elevated over the individual, a higher sense of being, knowledge, and reality. And this reality develops its own categories of time, space, and place beyond the individual, within which are all the beliefs, ideas, and sentiments that make up a particular society and define it:

The totality of beliefs and sentiments common to the average members of society forms a determinate system with a life of its own. It can be termed the collective or common conscience . . . it is diffused over society as a whole . . . it is independent of the particular conditions in which individuals find themselves . . . links successive generations to one another. It is, something totally different from the consciousness of individuals, although it is only realised in individuals. (Durkheim, 1984, pp. 38–39)

This is implanted via collective members and comes to dominate individual thoughts and behavior; it also corresponds to the social milieu and its consequent structure of interactions. From this both a moral and a cognitive social life is structured from which men study their environment and attempt to interpret, rationalize, and explain it and their relationships within and with it.

Thus, for Durkheim, unlike Kant, the social structure and categories of society form the basic categories of thought (rejecting innate capacity to categorize) to classify and systematize. Rather, man borrows from the structure of social relations and imposes upon his external world the categories of thought existent in society:

> Durkheim and Mauss . . . believe that the human mind lacks the innate capacity to construct complex systems of classification such as every society possesses, and which are cultural products not to be found in nature . . . the model is society itself. The first logical categories were social categories, they maintain, the first classes of things were classes of men; not only the external form of classes, but also the relations uniting them to each other, are of social origin; and if the totality of things is conceived as a single system, this is because society itself is seen in the same way. (Needham, in Durkheim, 1970, pp. xi–xii)

Society as real and natural has its own characteristics as, too, does its knowledge, morality, and religion, with an assumption, lacking alternative knowledge, that the entire universe is similarly ordered. Both cognitive and moral knowledge (meaning and how we conceptualize) are specific to society, functional to it and its relationships. Knowledge acquires status precisely because it is seen to have explanation, work, and real benefits. Reality and knowledge are reconfirmed because they are seen to operate effectively in the milieu that created them, providing causal explanation commensurate with expectations, while men reconfirm reality by behaving in an expected way (continued over generations)—national characteristics.

But outside of one's collective, knowledge and understanding may become redundant, having little meaning or relevance, therefore how to behave both morally and practically become highly problematic for individuals. The maintenance of one's collective thus acquires paramount importance for psychological and material well-being. Change, particularly radical progress affecting social relations, poses serious threats for individuals because it alters reality, posing fundamental problems (of order and ontological security) for individual and society.

The ability of ordinary people to cope with making a living or daily life may be disrupted, such as job skills made redundant or how to resolve material problems. For elites, whose position is often founded upon unique collective knowledge (usually due to their strategic position in the system of relations), change becomes a threat to their position. In this can be seen an important impetus for nationalism; the protection of collective knowledge, particularly an elite's, in a changing world. Change that threatens the reality and status of knowledge holders is resisted, thus religion feels peculiarly threatened by modern science. And those who held important relations and skills pertinent to a rural peasant society similarly felt threatened by industrialization.

Religion, for Durkheim, is thus the transmogrification of reality, the idealization of society's ideas and causal relations; of man with god, the individual with society. It attempts to explain the forces and immanent logic that unites things and men, particularly constructing the unseen relations between men. Religious thought is collective self-knowledge, which alone can transcend the individual and act upon him—a higher being within. And because man is part of social reality it is also part of him, it and its ideals exist within and animate him—Durkheim's soul. The individual soul is the sacred, the collective within each person: "The idea of the soul is not without a foundation in reality . . . and we can say that in a sense, there is divinity in us. For society, that unique source of all that is sacred, is not satisfied to move us from outside and to affect us transitorily; it organizes itself lastingly within us" (Durkheim, 1995, p. 266)

The soul is also a product of the past, of ancestors who link past, present, and future; it is part of man's way of knowing himself and his place in the cosmos, through the collective, and it engenders social ideals in man, the things to which he should aspire.

Also, Durkheim's soul is the origin of the individual's personality, that which is progressively individualized. The soul is therefore also separate from the individual and his situation, with a degree of autonomy, and so able to rise above a situation and see the wider (collective) whole. Thus knowledge becomes sacred, of the soul, and as it progresses so too does the sacredness of the individual at the expense of collective conformity. This helps explain the important role of intellectuals like academics, journalists, or literary figures, "wordsmiths"—professional producers and purveyors of national knowledge. It also helps explain the sacred nature of poets, novelists, historians, folklorists, and other definers of national identity as symbolic representations of society.

But the sacred also acts to transform man and society via the progressive development of the individual. By presenting an ideal to be lived up to in contrast to material expediency, the soul opened up an avenue to improvement, to surpass the immediate and think and reflect in the abstract; thus Durkheim's religion developed the ideas and sentiments that would evolve into science, with its own physical and moral forces existing beyond man and directing him, which tend to the universal. Consequently, scientists tend to be less national and more international.

Science stresses the idea of forces acting over us, laws of motion and causality, an order (cosmos) in which man is placed and is now seen to originate in religion. Consequently, religion "is the notion of force in its earliest form" (Durkheim, 1995, p. 205).

The unseen created the earliest speculation on hidden causes of phenomena, and knowledge of it had a binding, moral force because its truth lay beyond the individual, in the collective that existed within them, thus binding them to their collective. But transcendental knowledge also needs revealing and explaining to have a binding influence: the priestly role in religion, now becomes the national role of teachers, state servants, and sociologists.

Because of religion's collective nature and its transcendental ideas it also offers an impression of liberation from physical, profane forces for sacred ones that provide a sense of freedom. Freedom then lies in religion and its truths, which implies the collective as the source of freedom and makes religion worth fighting for. Alternative consciousness, even highly progressive, can be identified as loss of freedom because it denies the knowledge individuals need to transcend the forces they confront. Hence two or more different forces, truths, and realities cannot co-exist within the same sphere, only one explanation can really be true and liberating, the others are untrue and threatening, undermining the moral authority and functional relationships of society.

Consequently, different societies have a natural antipathy unless able to reconfirm each other's knowledge base; with particularly antagonistic relations between mechanical and organic societies, especially where they have to co-exist in the same space (an obvious critique of multi-culturalism). Thus national societies, particularly mechanical, where the individual is dominated by the collective, may engender deep passions when challenged, and passion represented for Durkheim the unreflective dominance of the social and religious, the unenlightened, non-scientific thought that opposed the individual. Hence one may explain the prominence of passion and violence in ethnic nationalism in particular (Nairn in Hall, 1998; Dingley, 2011a).

Knowledge is functional to social needs just as a society creates a functional need for types of knowledge, which functionally relates individuals to society, locating them to precise categories of time, place, and space from which they develop their identity, sense of being, and purpose (ontological security). Originally, knowledge was intimately tied to religion, which provides the moral force and authority to its functional force, which provides the basis for our attachment to nations and national identity; not immutably but functional to social relations.

Religion further led Durkheim to divide the world into two distinct spheres, sacred (relating to society and higher callings) and profane (associated with the individual and self-gratification). Thus the sacred implies some self-abnegation and forgoing of personal interests (the profane) to achieve social consciousness and get closer to the sacred (nation): Closeness to God requires overcoming the profane: "Sacrifices and offerings do not go unaccompanied by privations that exact a price from the worshipper . . . To serve his gods, he must forget himself . . . he must sacrifice his profane interests" (Durkheim, 1995, p. 320).

Sacrifices increase the awareness of the sacred (collective) and help commune more closely with it, which leads logically to the ultimate sacrifice or extreme suffering to fully realize one's soul. The collective, being holy, is only truly known by those who forgo the profane and suffer and sacrifice for the sacred, realizing their passion in a transcendent force not located in the profane world of science and reason, hence the importance of great periods of suffering in national histories.

True knowledge and being is now found in great suffering and passion, especially for the collective. Thus Durkheim provides an explanation for the Romantic nationalists (chapter 3) who reveled in their suffering, religious zeal, and mysticism (Greenfeld, 1993, chapter 4; or Kedourie 1993, chapter 5; Berlin, 2000a; Zamoyski, 1999). Suffering nationalists really commune with their soul, their inner social reality, as they suffer for their nation. Stripped of profane accoutrements, they found a sacred knowledge, inner realization, and liberty commensurate with Durkheim's soul.

The Romantics, therefore, did represent a certain collective reality and truth, even if only successfully achieved when taken up by prosaic interests. They chimed with a reality, with some real resonance among collective members. They had a knowledge of collective being and linked relationships that animated them: the possession of a knowledge, language, or relations that was only functional within a specific social milieu. For Durkheim it was this knowledge that genuinely stirred their souls; the knowledge of Patrick Pearse (MacDonagh, 1983, pp. 85–88) was true and functional to the collective representation (Gaelic, Catholic, peasant society) that existed in him. However, Pearse's reality was unreal and non-functional to the collective representation he rejected (British, Protestant, industrial society).

Knowledge of functional truth in turn implies moral truth; the correct causal relations imply the correct collective behavior. Thus collective consciousness contains not only technical knowledge but moral obligations, which provide direction and purpose in life. Without this, man faced the problem of anomie that Durkheim (1970, pp. 288–90) saw as causing contemporary France's malaise, that is: Lack of moral regulation that instructs us how to behave socially and become socially integrated, which leads to individual suicide and social disintegration.

This knowledge not only needed constructing but recalling via periodic religious rites and ceremonies to impinge and reconfirm the collective message, its truth. The very continuity and regularity of such rites acted as a transcendent force commanding obedience. Meanwhile, the modern scientist similarly repeats experiments to the same end, except more methodically, and so confirms the truth passed on to him, just as priestly rites reconfirmed religious truth and knowledge. To Durkheim this merely illustrated the continuity of logical thought and inquiry from primitive man to modern science, simply transferring moral authority to science as the new religion (Durkheim, 1995, conclusion).

And no knowledge, ideas, or belief system attains a status of truth unless actively shared and confirmed by others: "This is so because society cannot make its influence felt unless it is in action and it is in action only if the individuals who comprise it are assembled and acting in common" (Durkheim, 1995, p. 421).

Only the collective has authority to validate knowledge, and each has its own structure of knowledge. Thus causality is only understandable within its social context (milieu) with reference to its categories of space, time, and place; consequently, each collective understands events in its own real way, which others may find unreal.

Consequently, sympathy between different collectives and their interpretations of reality, what counts as fact, reasonable, and just may be incomprehensible to other collectives. Should one collective dominate another, with different structures and knowledge, its activities would lack moral authority and appear false, arbitrary, and a denial of freedom and liberty, especially on the subjective level of how truth is experienced. In this way one can explain claims of imperialism or oppression by ethnic minorities or secessionist nationalisms where there is little supporting empirical evidence. However, the idea of empirical and objective evidence may be regarded as oppressive by non-empirical cultures where such criteria deny the validity of subjective truths.

Consequently, there exists some real basis for ideas of national interests and self-determination if nations are viewed as collectives of socially structured knowledge. The fact that a collective reconfirms its reality by its own existence, its transcendent forces and their reaffirmation via continually recurring structures of relations and behavior gives it reality. Also by its external relations with other collectives, who always appear to respond to collective behavior in predictable ways.

For Durkheim the origin of all religious and scientific belief is experience:

> This entire study rests on the postulate that the unanimous feelings of believers down the ages cannot be mere illusory. Therefore, like a recent apologist of faith, I accept that religious belief rests on a definite experience, whose demonstrative value is, in a sense, not inferior to that of scientific experiments, though it is different. (Durkheim, 1995, p. 420)

Only society is such a force, experienced most effectively at social gatherings, such as religious ceremonies, scientific congresses, or national festivals, which increase man's social consciousness. The performance of rituals, rites, and the re-consecration of collective symbols help stimulate collective mental life, forming and reforming social ideas and ideals as collective manifestations that are implanted into individuals. They then place their own stamp upon them to become real in the individual's own mind, thus bonding them to society: "It is in assimilating the ideals worked out by society that the individual is able to conceive of the ideal. It is society that, by drawing him into its sphere of action, has given him the need to raise himself above the world of experience, while at the same time furnishing him with the means of imagining another" (Durkheim, 1995, p. 425).

The world of ideas and ideals by which man advances is bound to society and the basis of his own reality, images, and sentiments. Without his society the individual loses the source of his inspiration, mental stimulus, and moral guidance, while society also reconfirms its ideas and ideals, reality, and truth by holding them in common. Alternative ideas and ideals pose threats to material and ontological security.

Science, like religion, for Durkheim, is simply a new attempt to establish an intellectual connection between man, society, nature, and the forces that connect them, but more critical effort and above individual sentiment. Like religion, science is a fact and forms a positive system of ideas immediate both to the individual and the collective, forming a platform for action. This had important implications since Durkheim regarded how to act as the major moral imperative, which often gave religion primacy over science due to its immediacy in instructing the faithful: "Faith is above all a spur to action, whereas science, no matter how advanced, always remains at a distance from action. Science is fragmentary and incomplete; it advances but slowly and is never finished; but life—that cannot wait" (Durkheim, 1995, p. 432).

Thus politics, a desire to act in human affairs, was more prone to religious type movements (collective sentiment) than science, which helps explain the ubiquity of religion in nationalist movements. Consequently, Durkheim's political sociology, suggests that true democratic government be removed from direct contact with the masses (Giddens, 1996, pp. 6–9) via the development of "secondary" state bodies able to reflect and deliberate (science), thus avoiding populist government or blind political faith.

This reflects two spheres of knowledge for Durkheim; mass knowledge, sentiment based on immediate experience that merely reconfirms the collective and where the social dominates the individual, and deliberative knowledge, where society promotes the individual, and carefully reflects upon itself and its categories and relations to go beyond the sensate to find hidden causal connections and meanings. In the first, reality is defined in terms of real, sensate, and concrete objects. In the latter, reality is less sensate and concrete, becoming more abstract and problematic:

> According to Durkheim, there are "two sorts of knowledge." Intelligence does not present the aspect of a unity but that of a duality. It is split into "two opposite poles": the poles of experience and reason, the empirical and the rational. The realm of empirical experience is the realm of the senses. The empirical dimension of intelligence is the dimension of sense perception. (Lehmann, 1993, p. 123)

The empirical represents what is felt and experienced via feeling and sensation, a seemingly simple and concrete reality requiring little thought because, being close and intimate, it can touch and be touched. Knowledge is direct, unmediated in its experience, and therefore requires little thought or understanding, making it particular and parochial, the world of mechanical solidarity, where the collective dominates and acts upon the individual directly, making its force felt and experienced concretely. This recalls the nature of Romanticism, where external forms of immediate impact are emphasized, such as costumes, customs, and close relations.

Durkheim contrasted this with rational knowledge, which required thought and abstract conceptualization beyond empirical experience as an intellectual exercise, impersonal but still of the collective:

> Collective thought is possible only through the coming together of individuals; hence it presupposes the individuals, and in turn presuppose it . . . The realm of impersonal aims and truths cannot be realized except through the collaboration of individual wills and sensibilities; the reasons they participate and the reasons they collaborate are the same. In short, there is something impersonal in us because there is something social in us, and since social life embraces both representations and practices, that impersonality extends quite naturally to ideas as well as to actions. (Durkheim, 1995, p. 447)

And the object of such impersonal collaboration was to think about empirical reality to transcend it and associated with Enlightenment, unification nationalism, such as the United Kingdom or France, which aimed to transcend ethno-religious boundaries. Rather than passively taking cognizance of itself it critically reflects on itself and its internal and external relations to transcend experiential reality. It seeks causes and relations that are not sensationally apparent, which requires thinking conceptually and using abstract logic to produce new knowledge, non-experiential, which develops a new cognitive and moral consciousness.

Such knowledge implies increased specialization, narrower focus, and greater depth, which becomes synonymous with fragmentation of knowledge and so requires new, extended, exchange relations between specialized knowledge holders, which demands increased tolerance of differences. Greater openness in debate, tolerance of alternative views, a recognition of differences as healthy and productive form a new moral code, in contrast to the closed conformity of religious intolerance that rejected alternative knowledge: the very things that Gellner (1983) discusses regarding the new high culture of modern nations, or the difference between an industrial, scientific, and Protestant Ulster and a Catholic, peasant, and scholastic Ireland.

Thus social ideas fall into two categories of knowledge—empirical and sensate or abstract and conceptual—both derived from their collective's particular logic and conceptualizing: social products implanted into the individual from which they learn and interpret their milieu and experiences. Thus individuals derive collective meaning and understanding from which to generalize and interpret their cosmologies in ways consistent with important others with whom they have to interact.

The immediate and empirical knowledge Durkheim associated with collective (mass) domination led him to warn against crude mass democracy, which could overwhelm the abstract, conceptual knowledge associated with science and deliberation necessary for the modern state. Durkheim equated mass domination with mechanical structures whose cognitive and moral knowledge were incompatible with modern, organic society and its functional needs. However, the two models were idealized forms with a slow progression from mechanical to organic.

Conceptual knowledge, although abstract, produces a body of knowledge that is actually more fixed and determinate. Ideas formed in the mind that follow abstract principles of logic have a permanence that empirical knowledge lacked. The senses are in a permanent state of flux and while fixed to parochial objects can be continually felt and experienced in different, subjective ways, reinterpreted and recast according to no fixed principles. What appears fixed is actually the mystical, and what appears abstract is actually fixed in scientific laws; science leads to fixity across individuals, time, and space. The parochial becomes dependent on individual experience, emotions, time, and place: "Sensual representations are in perpetual flux; they come and go like the ripples of a stream, not staying the same even as long as they last" (Durkheim, 1995, p. 434).

Concepts, by their nature of being, are thought out, rational, and logical, debated with other concepts, and open to critical analysis and evaluation by others who scrutinize evidence and logic and refine and test them. Thus concepts are more fixed while at the same time universally transferable and credible:

> And at the same time as being relatively unchangeable, a concept is universal, or at least universalizable. A concept is not my concept; it is common to me and other men or at least can be communicated to them. It is impossible for me to make a sensation pass from my consciousness into someone else's; it is closely dependent on my body and personality and cannot be detached from them . . . By contrast, conversation and intellectual dealings among men consist in exchange of concepts . . . By means of it human intelligences communicate. (Durkheim, 1995, p. 435)

Whereas concepts are scientific and seek universal causes, experiential thought is local and particular, denying universality and rational analysis. Different states of mind are produced along with different forms of knowledge.

Durkheim thus relates parochial and sensate empirical knowledge to magic and mystery, with collective domination and traditional religion, while rational and conceptual thought is the product of cosmopolitan relations, where collectives act through the individual to go beyond the particular, producing a more stable and standardized world, of greater intellectual depth and rigor. But for these very reasons it is a world of less local color, sensate feeling, and passion. Mental inner and intellectual discipline replaces external constraint, custom, and local authority. Thus local elites have an interest in maintaining parochial knowledge in opposition to cosmopolitan, scientific knowledge.

Abstract conceptual knowledge (science) depends on extended structures of relations able to relate beyond the immediate and sensate, which enables extended interaction that then undermines parochial knowledge. In this can be seen an explanation for many separatist nationalism's that sought to create barriers against cosmopolitan forces. Also, it helps explain Romantic ethnic nationalisms that eulogized peasant knowledge, seeing in their folkways and customs a mystery that defied rational Enlightenment explanation for an alternative reality (MacDonagh, 1983, characterizes Anglo-Irish relations precisely in these terms, as different states of mind).

Ideas and the ability to conceptualize also have important functional implications for language, central to any ability to conceptualize: "It is beyond doubt that speech, and hence the system of concepts it translates, is the product of a collective elaboration. What it expresses is the manner in which society as a whole conceives the objects of experience. The notions corresponding to the various elements of language are therefore collective representations" (Durkheim, 1995, p. 436).

Language is thus a representation of shared meanings and understandings, which bind a collective and represent its relationships and functional needs and is not arbitrary. Language contains functional truths and knowledge and therefore also a moral authority over speakers. It is collectively important partly because it contains concepts peculiar to it but also because it mediates group members' ability to exchange with others, while also restricting alternative relations that can be entered into; thus it constantly reconstructs its own reality and inner mysteries. Equally, language barriers restrict the ability of outside, potentially antagonistic, knowledge from entering into collective consciousness, an important factor for Irish nationalism that wished to keep out corrupting, cosmopolitan English influences.

Language is thus a potent means of confirming society's collective authority as a direct and experiential factor in individual life that gives practical empirical being to national reality, reconfirmed in the long history of the linguistic group able to pass knowledge of itself down over the centuries. Knowledge of self, the collective, and its particular milieu can be thought of in ways unique to the collective. Such thoughts make it impossible for people to negotiate their daily lives without that knowledge/language if they are to live within the collective.

But once abstract concepts invade parochial thoughts, the parochial loses its moral and cognitive authority. Hence the importance of language programs in ethno-separatist nationalisms, while unification nationalisms emphasize a single cosmopolitan language. Only where local experience forms a basis for necessary knowledge does functionality preserve the vernacular because it contains concepts pertinent only to the local.

Further, for Durkheim, the more man conceptualizes abstractly and is less acted upon, the more he can illuminate the "real" world and transform it in pursuit of universalizing truth. The development of single languages, extended relations, and abstract concepts are intimate to Durkheim's overall concepts of truth and reality for they lead to an extended collective, increasingly international and universal, where national knowledge is exposed to more diverse and critical minds to ascertain its truth.

Thus knowledge advances toward a higher international truth, less experiential, via cosmopolitan relations built on abstract thought, increasingly impersonal and functional to extended collective forces:

> It is in the form of collective thought that impersonal thought revealed itself to humanity . . . Solely because society exists, there also exists, beyond sensations and images, a whole system of representations that possess marvelous properties. By means of them, men understand one another and minds gain access to one another. They have a kind of force and moral authority by virtue of which they impose themselves upon individual minds. (Durkheim, 1976, p. 438)

Thus truth progresses toward a concept close to the "idea" in Hegel's nation. And, as old truths get discarded, this implies for Durkheim that through the development of reason there is an ultimate truth, totally impersonal, to which man aspires as against the empirical and sensate truths that are personal and context specific. Thus Durkheim confirms his own positivism and links it into his theory of progress:

> The universe exists only as it is thought of, and "it is not completely thought of except by society." Society is a collective, psychic subject. Reality in its entirety is the object of its thought. It thinks, it sees, it regards, it embraces, it represents, it knows reality. When this total subject and its total object are combined, they form the absolute totality, "the totality outside of which nothing exists." (Lehmann, 1993, p. 131)

The ultimate collective provides the ultimate truth, humanity as a whole, and universal knowledge discards parochial truths for a greater impersonal reality. It unites men in a universal cause, displaces local attachments, and promotes universal understanding and the moral ascendancy of science over religion (the rational over the mystical). But at this stage religion and science are reunited as part of the same sacred cause, the revelation of truth via the social. For Durkheim, science has merely worked through the original social reflection that was represented in religion.

Equally as collective thought progressively abstracts and establishes universal principles of humanity so it progressively releases the individual from collective subservience, the individual becomes less acted upon and more assertive. Abstraction frees the individual from sensate and experiential knowledge and authority, including crude empiricism. And rational thought, for Durkheim, equates with the rise of individualism, of autonomous man in the abstract, of human rights applicable to all and consequently a threat to local authority. The individual is still a product of society, but one where reason strips away superficial appearances to reveal inner essences: "Thus very far from there being the antagonism between the individual and society which is often claimed, moral individualism, is in fact the product of society itself" (Durkheim, 1974, p. 59).

For Durkheim it is obvious that only society can supply that knowledge necessary for the individual to be free from collective domination, to reason and think individually; consequently, social progress makes the individual more autonomous. But this autonomy also threatens strong collective sentiments: One system of knowledge within the same space as another would always pose a social threat.

Two systems of knowledge operating in the same time, space, or place are inevitably antagonistic because their consciousnesses imply different imperatives for thought and action, opposed truths and realities and different subjective meanings and understandings:

> If, at every moment, men did not agree upon these fundamental ideas, if they did not have a homogenous conception of time, space, cause number and so on. All consensus among minds, and thus all common life, would become impossible.
>
> Hence society cannot leave the categories up to the free choice of individuals without abandoning itself. To live, it requires not only a minimum moral consensus, but also a minimum of logical consensus that it cannot do without either. Thus, in order to prevent dissidence, society weighs on its members with all its authority. (Durkheim, 1995, p. 16)

Abstract principles of universal humanity applicable to all don't equate with parochial sensate experiences that defy them. Where such universal principles are imposed on collectives built on empiricist knowledge they would be felt, subjectively, as oppressive, no matter how objective they actually are. Thus some ethnic nationalisms may feel oppressed, even when objectively they are not, if abstract principles are applied to them that don't equate with their experiential or functional knowledge.

This principle was also central to Durkheim's (1996, pp. 54–59) rejection of mass rule as democracy. The masses are often apart from, or only loosely touched by, the abstract universal knowledge of educated elites who form a collective of their own. Such knowledge requires careful nurturing and expertise beyond popular cognition, which must be separated off in state bodies protected from mass sentiments and collective dominance. In this way experts can think rationally and deeply, developing specializations that stimulate individualism, beyond the sensate, to find the hidden, deeper, more complex, and abstract truths.

Herein also lay the importance of state education for Durkheim: to inculcate a more scientific and shared knowledge. But as society grew more complex and extensive education required more careful thought and consideration. A more abstract knowledge base had to be implanted to enable men to rise above their parochial experience and comprehend a greater totality, and identifying this became one of the modern state's major tasks, divorced from direct contact with mass sentiment and religion.

Truth, the sacred, and the individual become synonymous in modern (organic) society, products of the collective but going beyond it, the ultimate moral values rather than a sacred truth that lay in submission to parochial collective wills. However, this would be a denial of truth and knowledge for pre-modern (mechanical) societies. Thus collectives place real barriers in men's minds in terms of their ability to communicate and share ideas, meanings, and understandings, giving substance to the existence of social (national) collectives. But this is progressively weakened as knowledge advances via extended relations and larger collectives. However, Durkheim doubted the feasibility of any world state, or universal collective, rather seeing states increasingly cooperating over shared interests requiring international collaboration (Giddens, 1996, pp. 194–204).

Durkheim's knowledge is actually the substance of the representation collective that society implants in the individual mind; consequently showing his emphasis on the importance of education. Education, both in its formal industrial model and its informal pre-industrial model, is the major means to impart knowledge (socialization), such as collective past, economically functional skills, the maintenance of important relationships, and morality. Especially he saw education as functional to the maintenance of society, hence the need for strong collective control over it as the means by which it created and re-created itself. Hegel's "idea" now acquires some substance via socialization.

Passing on the requisite knowledge and collective consciousness was of primary concern:

> If, as we have attempted to establish, education has above all a collective function, if its purpose is to adapt the child to the social environment in which he is destined to live, it is impossible for society to stand aside from such an operation. How could it remain aloof, since it constitutes the reference point from which education should direct its operations? (Durkheim, 1996, p. 177)

Education constituted social renewal for each generation, and a repository of collective knowledge where the collective became most conscious of itself. Not only would modern states need to closely monitor education but educators would need to feel close to the state if they were to convey the requisite sentiments for maintaining the collective being, which helps explain the leading role of so many teachers, educators, and allied trades in nationalist movements. Education replaces and continues the religious function of social renewal, making it central to collective being, which also makes the maintenance of separate religious-based educational systems dysfunctional to social cohesion in religiously divided societies such as Ireland.

But education's ability to construct social unity is also limited; it has to be functional, meaningful, and relevant to its milieu, to its existing collective consciousness, and for its recipients: "Durkheim conceived education as intimately related to each society's structure, which it reflects and maintains and can only partially change" (Lukes, 1975, p. 129).

Outside of its creative milieu, knowledge had little impact if it didn't conform to structural-functional reality. Only knowledge that reconfirms the structure is easily acceptable or believable, largely because it is functional to the believer. Knowledge that is not functional, or a lack of relevant knowledge to cope with one's milieu helped lead to Durkheim's anomie.

Consequently, education was initially confined mostly to the role of reproducing existing knowledge, with only a limited role as creator of knowledge. Education was itself deeply embedded in the structure of society, as were most of the professional (non-science) knowledge producers (originally clergy, then poets, artists, and philologists). This helps explain their predominance in nationalist movements resistant to developments that threatened their collectives, the innately conservative and parochial ethnic nationalisms that tended to dominate twentieth-century politics (Hobsbawm, 1992; or Gellner, 1983)—the very thought processes that Durkheim objected to in contemporary France.

The progressive (Enlightenment) nationalisms, such as those associated with the French Revolution, were universal, cosmopolitan, and enlightened, associated with industrial development and commercial expansion, new (economic) relations, and commensurately new political structures. They sought a new knowledge in an economic development that implied new, extended structures of collective relationships, and therefore a new creative knowledge, the true force of the Enlightenment (Pagden, 2013), but inevitably the overthrow of old parochial and religious knowledge.

## Knowledge: Mechanical and Organic Societies

The distinction between the sacred and the profane is central to Durkheim's idea of man's duality, an individual and a social being, which correlates with his distinction between mechanical and organic societies. In mechanical society the collective acted upon the individual and dominated him; consequently, the individual personality is closely bound to a common social type and everything is religious. In organic society, the collective is less religious and acted through the individual, leaving him greater potential to develop his own character. Knowledge in mechanical society is therefore more of the collective and implies a sacred conformity: simple, commonly held sets of beliefs of truth and reality that conform to a simple, sensate, closed milieu of segmental solidarity. It is non-scientific and experiential, implying passion and suffering as core virtues and collective conformity in a relatively simple and unquestioned manner. The collective is sacred while the individual is profane.

Organic society implies a greater diversity due to a more open and extended range of relations conforming to the functional demands of specialization and division of labor. Individuals are progressively freed from the dominating constraints of the collective and become more rational, scientific, and disciplined in thought and behavior as they enter a deeper, more complex and abstract world of extended relationships and knowledge. The collective, via the state, works through the individual to create a more autonomous being functional to the demands of new relationships. Here the individual becomes sacred, not conformity and submission to dominant cultural norms.

This does not imply that everyone in a society shares equally in its intellectual development, but that the dominant values and beliefs that perhaps only vaguely infuse the masses but consciously enervate the elite's (high culture) become the representation collective to be lived up to:

> The vaguely diffused sentiments that float about the whole expanse of society affect the decisions made by the State, and conversely, those decisions made by the State, the ideas expounded in the Chamber, the speeches made there and the measures agreed upon by the ministries, all have an echo in the whole of society and modify the ideas strewn there. (Durkheim, 1992, p. 79)

Since knowledge is a product of structure any change in it implies new knowledge, which has great implications for Durkheim's theory of social change, particularly the most fundamental one from mechanical to organic structure. Not only would society need new knowledge functional to new relationships, but its very knowledge of itself, its reality, would change, as would that of its individual members as individuals, along with concepts of time, space, place, and all the other categories by which man takes cognizance of himself:

> The fact, today incontestably established, that all moral systems practised by peoples are a function of the organization of those peoples, are bound to their social structures and vary with them . . . History has established that, except in abnormal cases, each society has in the main a morality suited to it, and that any other would not only be impossible but also fatal to the society which attempted to follow it. (Durkheim, 1974, p. 56)

Thus new knowledge, for new social solidarity, is called for when collectives shift to organic solidarity. And it was just this kind of new consciousness that the emergence of modern unification nations associated with the rise of industrialism impelled (Smith, 1998). But if collectives are developing at different paces then ethnic collectives within multi-ethnic states may develop different levels of consciousness (knowledge) at different rates. This could provide an insight into the rise of modern separatist nationalism, such as Irish.

Where ethnic groups within a pre-existing state can integrate into the new structures of (industrial) relations and share the new knowledge, they can combine to form into a unification nationalism, such as France, Germany, or the UK. But where ethnic collectives cannot develop into the new exchange relations and knowledge, they identify themselves as separate and break away from the old state, such as nationalist Ireland from the UK. The new knowledge that dominated the British state was not functional to the milieu found in nationalist Ireland (as will be discussed), which then developed a separate self-knowledge (of interest).

Discussing a society having knowledge of itself need not necessarily mean that all individuals have equal conscious awareness, but that the relations and knowledge that bind them to others in their collective will inform their sentiments, often only vaguely. Those at the center of networks of relations, such as priests, professionals, or civil servants, collecting, collating, and distributing knowledge will probably be far more consciously aware as actively informed and informers.

## Mechanical Solidarity

This type of society is characteristically closed, stable, close-knit and segmental, self-contained and relatively isolated, and associated with pre-industrial peasant society. Life is slow paced and unchanging, with few but frequent close relations within the collective and very limited external relations. It is parochial and rooted and the individual is acted upon by their close and immediate relations and circumstances in a fixed and determinate milieu.

Knowledge is consequently limited, fixed, and related to immediate and concrete objects, to meet and satisfy immediate needs. In this milieu religion, tradition, and folklore often suffice as relevant forms of knowledge, simple and immediate, sensate and experiential, adequate to its milieu and built up over a long period of time and handed down over generations via proverbs, customs, and sayings, which is rapidly superseded in organic societies: "More advanced societies are only slightly fertile in this way during the preliminary phases of their existence. Later, not only are no new proverbs coined, but the old ones fade away, lose their proper meaning and end up by not being understood at all" (Durkheim, 1984, p. 120).

It is in mechanical societies that one finds a preponderance of mysticism, magic, holy shrines, and religious symbols, where reality is most concrete, experiential, and sensate and religion is preponderant, dominating daily life.

Here Durkheim saw man as primarily acted upon by both his collective and physical environment, his individuality suffused into the collective and responding to its shared demands. His knowledge is that of the obvious, which his senses, perceptions, and empirical experience tell him. The immediate force of his neighbors and the structure of intimate relationships that he enters into, the way the physical environment acts upon him, and the authority of the gods and religious symbolism dominate his life. All these reflect a bounded, parochial life with few external contacts:

> In the middle-ages, it was still difficult for a workman to find work in a town other than his own. Internal customs authorities, moreover, formed around each social compartment a protective belt against the infiltration of foreign elements. In these conditions, the individual is fixed to his native heath by bonds that attach him to it, and also because he is rejected elsewhere. (Durkheim, 1984, p. 233)

The fact that man is acted upon by his social and physical environment also helps create an image of diversity and spontaneity in such societies precisely because the individual is not autonomous. The parochial always displays a wide variety of differences since it responds to local sensate variations that act on man who has not yet developed the individuality to free himself from being acted upon. An appearance of freedom via spontaneity thus masks a lack of (individual) liberty and autonomy that only comes through individual discipline and science, which enables man to transcend his parochial environment.

Bounded relations act to confirm the already existing sensate reality, subjectivity, and passion in life. What one feels and senses becomes real knowledge, not disciplined abstract reasoning transcending collectives:

> A sensation or an image always relies upon a determined object, or upon a collection of objects of the same sort, and expresses the momentary condition of a particular consciousness; it is essentially individual and subjective . . . Under these conditions forcing reason back upon experience causes it to disappear, for it is equivalent to reducing the universality and necessity which characterize it

to pure appearance, to an illusion which may be useful practically, but which corresponds to nothing in reality; consequently it is denying all objective reality to the logical life, whose regulation and organization is the function of the categories. Classical empiricism results in irrationalism; perhaps it would even be fitting to designate it by this latter name. (Durkheim, 1976, p. 14)

This creates new barriers to wider relations, where knowledge and language is restricted to the local collective, which helps affirm a parochial sense of reality and the importance of understanding the local, which can only be known (if at all) from within, via the subjective. It is the irrational and mystical crude empiricism that appears to have such a reality and is central to most Romantic nationalism and has its corollary in the type of subjective and arts-oriented academic work, where statements of feeling, sentiment, and experience substitute for critical analysis and rational explanation, which Durkheim critiqued, or Berlin's (2000) third-rate arts.

Such mechanical structures and knowledge would be reflected in the nature and role of government and the state. Where life is governed by vague sentiments and empirical realities it needs little thought or reflection, consequently requiring limited conscious government. The collective mass infuses and imposes its vague sentiments in an informal, semi-conscious manner:

The one because of this diffusion, stays in the half-light of the sub-conscious. We cannot with certainty account for all these collective pre-conceptions we are subject to from childhood, all these currents of public opinion that form here and there and sway us this way and that. There is nothing deliberately thought out in all this activity. There is something spontaneous, automatic, something unconsidered, about this form of life. (Durkheim, 1992, p. 79)

The collective need not go beyond its existing knowledge and structures, while its vernacular forms a barrier to external influences while containing individuals within its enclosed world. This enhances the sense of mystery involved in mechanical groups, in turn reinforcing the religious experience of the group in its enclosed segmental world:

Thus, originality is not only rare; there is, so to speak, no room for it. Everybody then accepts and practices, without argument the same religion; different sects and quarrels are unknown; they would not be tolerated. At this time religion includes everything, extends to everything. It embraces, although in a very confused state, besides religious beliefs proper, ethics, law, the principles of political organisation, and even science, at least what passes for it. It regulates

even the minutiae of private life. Thus to state that religious consciousnesses are
then identical . . . is implicitly to assert that . . . every individual consciousness
is roughly made up of the same elements. (Durkheim, 1984, p. 90)

A sense of idyll, peace, harmony, and ontological integration is maintained
precisely because of a collective's limited consciousness and knowledge.

## Organic Solidarity

This results from the division of labor, which Durkheim explicitly equates
with economic development, industrialization, and its extended networks
of exchange relations that generate greater specialization. This affects the
development of modern concepts of individualism and relatively autonomous beings functional to the new demands of industrial society. It does not
imply that every individual is equally infused with ideas of individualism and
non-parochialism, what Durkheim argued was that the dominant image society has of its collective self (representation collective) that acts on men and
forms the moral basis of society is of this nature, slowly evolving over time as
the requisite relations develop.

At the lower levels of organic society men may only be dimly conscious
of the new order and still display strong collective sentiments. However, its
implications in their lives are dramatic; they become subject to new and more
abstract forces and extended relations that constitute social reality and consciousness, creating new forces and contacts that create new realities and
truths requiring new moral authority and values functional to the new relations: "Then, gradually political, economic, scientific functions broke free
from the religious function, becoming separate entities and taking on more
and more a markedly temporal character" (Durkheim, 1984, p. 119).

Initially these are often resented and keenly felt as new social conditions
and disciplines are imposed upon men; happiness, for Durkheim, was not
a cause of progress. Frequently, only the new elites benefit and fully understand the changes occurring, but that does not make it any less real, or
inevitable.

Simple peasant society proceeded in unreflective traditional ways, but
industrial society imposed new constructed disciplines and regular routines
to meet the needs of abstract economic forces, often originating in distant
lands. Self-sufficiency and submission to the "forces of nature" no longer
suffice, and men have to learn new habits, thought processes, relations, and
exchange, which lead them to develop new ways of thinking about themselves and society, and society has to conceive of man in new ways, functional
to the division of labor's demands for greater specialization, which stimulates

individualization. Thus emerges a new ideal of the autonomous individual progressively freed from collective conformity (the core of religious experience) and symbolized in changing ideas of God and the sacred:

> God, if we may express it in such a way, from being at first present in every human relationship has progressively withdrawn. He leaves the world to men and their quarrels. At least, if he continues to rule it, it is from on high and afar off . . . leaves more place to the free play of human forces. The individual thus feels . . . less acted upon; he becomes more a source of spontaneous activity. (Durkheim, 1984, pp. 119–20)

Now, where religion remains, it is the individual who becomes the center of worship and collective ideal, as individual values replace communal ones in the worship of God, witnessed in the rise of both Protestantism and science as core elements of industrial culture.

For Durkheim, division of labor generated new knowledge; first, by specialization, leading to greater depth of knowledge in narrower areas, which stimulates deeper and more critical analysis of what is, rather than passively accepting it and conforming to its demands. From this, abstract principles of causality are identified, which link phenomenon at an abstract level, from which science emerges as the basis of knowledge, replacing religion in an increasingly demystified world. Or, more precisely, science grows out of religion and acquires many of its social functions, seeking to understand causal-relations and forces via abstract relations. Industrialization becomes both the appliance of science and the stimulus for scientific research in the modern world.

Science is an abstract understanding of forces immanent in nature and implies universal concepts and relations and not unique parochial ones. Concepts and language thus become more cosmopolitan and truth becomes more universal; consequently, abstract scientific truths become more real in a positive sense. The greater number of diverse collectives involved in defining truth, critically analyzing from different locations to verify each truth, helps to refine truths that are more real because consistent over time, place, and space, which also unites more collectives in shared truths. Abstract, but more permanent, truths are established, which defy mysticism and concrete empiricism. But such abstract, all-embracing truth, by its nature can only be grasped by the rational abstract mind as products of unseen forces, not dissimilar to religion.

Mental discipline and intellectual rigor, rationality, and calculation, relying on reason and logic, replace the sensate and experiential knowledge of mechanical society. Rationality replaces feeling, and positivism replaces mysticism as science replaces, or transforms, religion, while knowledge becomes less subjective and more objective. And increasing universality engenders comparisons and refinements of knowledge on a non-passionate level that provides better quality knowledge: "The fact has often been remarked that civilisation has tended to become more rational and logical . . . That alone is rational which is universal. What defies the understanding is the particular and the concrete" (Durkheim, 1984, pp. 231–32).

Improved cognitive knowledge also invokes a different moral climate that frees individuals from unreasoned and sentimental ties built on feeling and repression, allowing for rational autonomy and freedom. Passion may be colorful and invoke ideas of spontaneity, which appears autonomous because it defies rationality, but rationality alone provides autonomy by freeing men from passions that blind, thus laying the foundations for justice and liberty, which Durkheim equated with progress and individuality:

> The task of the most advanced societies may therefore be said to be a mission for justice . . . Just as the ideal of lower societies was to create or maintain a common life as intense as possible, in which the individual was engulfed, ours is to inject an even greater equity into our social relations, in order to ensure the free deployment of all those forces that are socially useful. (Durkheim, 1984, p. 321)

This is concomitant to the increased and more diverse relations men now have to enter into, a function of specialization, increased depth of knowledge, and consequent interdependency produced by division of labor. First, local, segmental economies are replaced by regional, then national, then international ones as the network of industrial economic and social relationships expands. Thus men develop increased contacts and exchange relations with more diverse people, with whom to share, compare, and refine knowledge, and make them more rationally reflective. Concurrently, specialization demands the exchange of individualized skills and knowledge which develops an interdependency and tolerance.

Whereas previously solidarity was maintained by intolerance and repression of differences for a collective conformity, solidarity is now attained by developing complex webs of interdependency that require tolerance of differences and reciprocity to effect solidarity. The whole nature of division of labor is one built on knowledge of reciprocal relations and exchange of differences—but they must be reciprocal and not antagonistic. But such reciprocity and complimentary relations imply a deeper, shared, scientific consciousness (mono-cultural).

This acts on the individual to increase their awareness of legitimate differences and functional new knowledge, in turn stimulating reflection: "Yet once reflective thinking has been stimulated, it is not easy to set bounds to it. When it has gathered strength, it spontaneously develops beyond the limits assigned to it" (Durkheim, 1984, p. 232).

The increasing network of relationships inherent to modern industrial society encourages men to think outward from their locality and cross borders, which aids a growing criticism of existing knowledge and also implies a new shared knowledge and language (culture) for exchange. This becomes the basis for the new morality of individualism and toleration.

New extended relationships also encourage a new mobility as new opportunities are developed and communicated across localities. Scientific knowledge, by its abstract and universal nature can be applied anywhere in the world and its universal concepts and language increasingly make local cultures and vernaculars irrelevant, even a hindrance. Consequently, local moral and cognitive knowledge becomes redundant and liberty and freedom become matters of release from parochial collective authority.

Durkheim's liberty and morality become implicit to a scientific culture and mental discipline not dominated by religion:

> The more general the common consciousness becomes, the more scope it leaves for individual variations. When God is remote from things and men, His action does not extend to every moment of time and to everything. Only abstract rules are fixed and these can be applied in very different ways . . . they have neither the same ascendancy nor the same strength of resistance. (Durkheim, 1984, p. 232)

Mental discipline and science that enabled men to rise above the sensate, not emotion and passion that masked the extent to which they were tied to and dictated to by their collective environment, are the key to Durkheim's concept of freedom, as it was to the Enlightenment as a whole (Pagden, 2013).

Science, also had another unique attribute: It is critical and analytical, whereas religion emphasizes acceptance and submission, making ideas of change and progress implicit to it. This in turn corresponds with the development of man as an autonomous being, able to change his milieu and position in it (fundamental to scholastic fears about science). The new collective enables men to transcend their environment, whereas the previous collective bound man within it. However, this new collective only achieves its goals through the uniformity of scientific knowledge that opens up a cosmopolitan world.

Meanwhile, religion didn't disappear but increasingly confined itself to an abstract god concerned with universal concepts of the individual and its soul, for both are still of society, just in a different way and to different ends. There is still a need for collective reaffirmation of the (religious) social, whose object is now the individual, and society still needs to regularly recall its collective object:

> The common consciousness . . . increasingly comprises modes of thinking and feeling of a very general, indeterminate nature, which leave room for an increasing multitude of individual acts of dissent. There is indeed one area in which the common consciousness has grown stronger, viz, in its view of the individual. As all the other beliefs and practices assume less and less a religious character, the individual becomes the object of a sort of religion. (Durkheim, 1984, p. 122)

This is important in organic society because the extended relationships and abstract knowledge often produce isolated individuals with little collective experience or direct contacts to recall them to their social/religious obligations and dependencies. For Durkheim, the importance of regular ceremonies of social reaffirmation to unify isolated individuals was therefore important, as was the role of education in instilling the right moral/social knowledge into children.

However, Durkheim despite seeing true liberty in science and organic solidarity also recognized that liberty was functional to one's milieu. That is, the experience of liberty was related to one's ability to utilize it and for it to have meaning and relevance within a structure of relations. If organic concepts of freedom and liberty were applied in a mechanical milieu, they may be felt as oppressive or irrelevant because they would be dysfunctional and disruptive to actor and collective. Thus "true" liberty may only be experienced as such within its own organic milieu while experienced as disruptive and oppressive in a mechanical milieu where it is dysfunctional to negotiating established relations.

Following on it can also be observed certain actors, because of their strategic position in a social structure and their consequent ability to manufacture, gather, collate, and distribute knowledge, will have a greater vested interest in maintaining existing relations and knowledge. Science, industry, and increased relations may help generate benefits for humanity as a whole but they also threaten established networks of knowledge forming relationships and invoke resistance. Thus key actors in mechanical societies may actively resist the organic developments as threatening their existence, that is, actors at the core of established relations, especially religious, who see new knowledge as endangering their God.

This latter point may significantly assist in understanding national movements and conflict, particularly where ethnic-separatist (mechanical) nationalism finds itself opposing a modernizing (organic) metropolitan state. The conflict is genuinely social in that the new knowledge (relations) a metropolitan state encourages is disruptive to those of regional ethnic groups. In particular, given the idea of uneven regional development (Breuilly, 1993), the new knowledge and relations may not yet be functional to the conditions pertaining for the ethnic group, both materially and ontologically. In which case one now has an explanation for resistance to modernization and ethnic conflict, as will be argued, was the case in Ireland.

Finally, Durkheim's theory of knowledge bears close resemblance to the origins of ideas of nationalism. Both were grounded in the young Hegelian tradition Durkheim became familiar with during his visit to Germany and later via his reading of Marx (Lukes, 1975, chapter 4). This tradition emphasized the reality of society, the importance of social structure, the social determinants of human consciousness, and materialism in the realm of human behavior. Feuerbach, a major contributor to modern ideas on nationalism, was especially influential here, arguing that religion is a reflection of man's material condition (West, 1996, pp. 43–44).

Further, like many of his contemporaries and nationalists, Durkheim began with a critical evaluation of Kant's philosophy, which posited a distinction between knowledge and morality and claimed an autonomous realm of knowledge existing externally to the individual. Kant's work is particularly relevant, both for his influence on German and French liberal thought and because of his influence on the evolution of nationalism (Kedourie, 1993, chapters 3 and 4).

Durkheim, particularly via Renouvier's work, had been greatly influenced by Kant (Lukes, 1975, pp. 54–57), which again helps tie Durkheim's sociology to nationalism. But while Kant saw an abstract knowledge, akin to Rousseau's abstract individual, Durkheim saw a knowledge grounded in society, like his individual, a position akin to Marx's.

Meanwhile, Durkheim explicitly rejected English utilitarianism (Durkheim, 1984, pp. 221–22), radical individualism and enlightened self-interest being major targets for his attack (much of *Division of Labour* specifically does this). Closely related to this is his rejection of empiricism as a source of objective knowledge (Schmauss, 1994, pp. 62–63 and 188–89) along with his rejection of mysticism, divine rights, and absolutist religious and monarchical authority claims associated with the "ancien régime" (Giddens, 1995, chapter 3).

The importance of social relations was paramount in the nation-creation project, since they produced bonds of affiliation (*religio* = Latin = bonds/relations) and knowledge (cognitive and moral) unique to those relations: the basis for national cultures. But, importantly, some social relations were capable of expansion and wider inclusion, while others were not, which provides us with an important marker between Enlightened and Romantic nationalism. But generically the major factor is that social relations, and different types of them, form the basis for the social construction of nations as unique bodies of social knowledge (culture) that enable individuals to operate effectively within one set of relations while not in another and share a collective consciousness that forms the basis for their individual identity. And at the same time those relations produce a specific type of person who becomes dependent upon those relations and mastery of the knowledge necessary to negotiate them, which helps produce a sense of solidarity with others who share that knowledge.

Nation can now be seen as a form of knowledge built on social cognition that makes no sense outside of the social. This builds clearly on a philosophical tradition established by German philosophy and given a material basis by Marx: Following in these footsteps, Durkheim stands Kant on his feet, seeing the categories of thought as immanent in society and not in the mind, making nations a social construction and national knowledge a reflection of social structure. This makes the proper study of nationalism sociological.

# CHAPTER 3

# Nations and Nationalism

The twentieth century saw the emergence of many nation-states previously non-existent. Lithuania, Estonia, and Slovenia are just examples of what previously would have been regarded as basically loose linguistic groups or provinces ruled over by metropolitan states, such as Russia or Austro-Hungary, which are now nation-states. Meanwhile, Italy and Germany were geographic and cultural expressions covering a number of independent states with no political unity, which illustrates the problem of Ireland's identity and poses questions about nationalism.

Nationalism is an ideology based on an idea (the nation) that argues that the proper political organization of mankind is effected via independent, sovereign nation-states based on cultural distinctiveness, social homogeneity, and popular consent. "The specificity of nationalism, that which distinguishes nationality from other types of identity, derives from the fact that nationalism locates the source of individual identity within a 'people,' which is seen as the bearer of sovereignty, the central object of loyalty and the basis of collective solidarity" (Greenfeld, 1993, p. 3).

Its essence is that each collective (people) should have its own state to protect and nurture its unique qualities on its own territory. And that the state, representing and protecting its people, should have sovereign power to protect natural and inalienable rights the nation is assumed to possess (Gellner, 1983; Hobsbawm, 1992; Breuilly, 1993). As Kedourie has observed: "Not the least triumph of this doctrine is that such propositions have become accepted and are thought to be self-evident, that the very word *nation* has been endowed by nationalism with a meaning and a resonance which until the end of the eighteenth century it was far from having" (Kedourie, 1993, p. 1).

The above assumption nationalists regard as self-evident and unproblematic; yet reality suggests the opposite, as Ireland, Sri Lanka, and the Balkans indicate, because the world is rarely divided into the neat cultural parcels of populations that nationalism assumes. Consequently, nationalism (mostly a nineteenth-century phenomenon) has created a plethora of conflicts and problems that make its assumptions far from self-evident.

## The Idea of Nationalism

The political ideology of nationalism arose during the eighteenth century, first formally expressed in the French Revolution when the old state (monarchy legitimated by religion) was replaced by the "people" as the sole legitimate authority. The people formed the "nation" with the right of self-determination, exercised by its own sovereign state, over its own territory, thus making its people "free" and able to express and determine their own destiny:

> The equation nation = state = people, and especially sovereign people, undoubtedly linked nation to territory, since structure and definition of states were now essentially territorial. It also implies a multiplicity of nation-states so constituted and this was indeed a necessary consequence of popular self determination. As the French Declaration of Rights of 1795 put it . . . Each people is independent and sovereign, whatever the number of individuals who compose it and the extent of the territory it occupies. This sovereignty is inalienable. (Hobsbawm, 1992, p. 19)

This has now become the major legitimating philosophy of government, whereby nationalism legitimates states and state activities. Consequently, "Nationalism is primarily a political sentiment which holds that the political and the national unit should be congruent" (Gellner, 1983, p. 6). It assumes the nation and equates it with the state.

## The State

The idea of the state is primarily political, and precedes that of the nation (people), emerging in medieval times:

> The state had a distinct territorial character as an entity in a system of sovereign states; its authority had a special quality in its sovereignty; it had extraordinary and growing resources of physical power at its disposal; it was distinguished by the peculiar power of the bonds among its members and by its distinctive purpose. (Blackwell Encyclopaedia of Political Institutions, 1987)

Sociologists, meanwhile, emphasized its formal role in organizing society, with a clear distinction between people and rulers:

Between governing and governed, between authority and those subject to it . . . For if this expression has any one meaning, it is above all, organization, at any rate rudimentary; it is established authority (whether stable or intermittent, weak or strong), to whose action individuals are subject, whatever it be. (Durkheim, in Giddens, 1992, p. 42)

Similarly Weber defined the state, but added a specific territorial limit to its authority:

This system of order claims binding authority, not only over members of the state, the citizens, most of whom have obtained membership by birth, but also to a very large extent, over all action taking place in the area of its jurisdiction. It is thus a compulsory association with a territorial basis. (Weber, 1964, p. 156)

As Hobsbawm noted (1992, p. 19), only after 1789 did "state = people," thus binding state to popular authority, acting on behalf of the people (replacing throne and altar; Burleigh, 2005). And it is this changed perception of the state that Breuilly saw as important for nationalism:

The claim to absolute sovereignty established an impassable divide between the one agency that made the claim and everything else that became the object of the claim. This claim led to a vision of the state, or rather of the crown, as a "public" authority standing for some general principle or interest over and above the myriad "private" interests which made up society. The apparent separation of state from society then raised the problem of how they were connected to one another. In trying to answer that problem the idea of the nation acquired a particular importance. (Breuilly, 1993, p. 82)

Rudimentary states had long existed as organizing authorities over territory and populations, but without touching the vast majority of people, illiterate peasants living in isolated and self-sufficient communities, until late medieval times. States were a product of competing elite groups, such as nobles, churches, and merchants, each bringing their particular interests to bear on it to shape its actions. Thus the state, while theoretically unitary, was more a mix of competing interests, but rarely non-elite ones whose lives it barely touched.

Before entering directly into people's lives the state could largely be ignored, but once it directly affected ordinary lives it prompted people to question its acts and authority. This occurred with the development of trade, increased urbanization, and growing military and government activity, which greatly extended the scope of the state in post-medieval society.

Thus by 1789 state authority was questioned by an increasing number of interests traditionally excluded from it, for whom nationalism offered an alternative basis for state authority (from throne and altar). The American and French Revolutions dethroned both God and monarch and the only alternative authority was the people, which transferred the authority of the state to govern the people to a mandate from the people to act on their behalf.

French revolutionaries, inspired by Enlightenment ideals, merely defined the people as all those living within the state's territory. In doing this they asserted the rationalist principles of the Enlightenment (individual equality, reason and brotherhood with no cultural specificity) regarded as universal and thus applicable to all men in all times and places, echoing scientific ideas and principles of universal laws, individualism, cosmopolitanism, objectivity, and rationalism. This provided the basis for ideas of autonomous individuals with rights, and the states' duty was to uphold them, in consequence of which states now claimed reciprocal rights and duties from the citizen: "It might be said that all men are born equal, with the right to life, liberty and the pursuit of happiness, or, alternatively, that men are under two sovereign masters, Pain and Pleasure, and that the best social arrangements are those that maximise pleasure and minimize pain" (Kedourie, 1993, p. 2). Thus states had a duty for the welfare of their people, although defining welfare was problematic.

Meanwhile, defining territorial borders was unnecessary for enlightenment revolutionaries for whom borders would soon become redundant with progress and universal brotherhood. Both Adam Smith (1776) and Thomas Paine (1792), the great luminaries of enlightened politics, foresaw an international order and economy with a greatly reduced state role (ideals that greatly influenced the United Irish of 1798).

Paradoxically, the opposite occurred as the state more directly affected men's lives while also becoming more detached from them: "The state was less and less a distant, almost another, world which had little to do with those it notionally controlled. Indeed, its control came closer and closer. But this looming presence appeared as something far above its subjects. The state seemed to acquire a life of its own" (Breuilly, 1993, p. 82).

The state became a superior force and being in men's lives, a reality particularly influenced by developments in Germany (the home of modern nationalism; Greenfeld, 1993), where a stratum of highly educated officials (mandarins) succeeded the aristocracy as state functionaries. A bureaucracy evolved that posited the state as a body of abstract law and regulations above individuals, a disembodied superior force, that acted over individuals and to which they owed allegiance (Hickox, 1976). Most of these mandarins were arts and humanities educated and claimed to work for a disinterested general welfare above individual interest (Ringer, 1969, introduction).

Here they directly precede Durkheim's concept of the state, which was increasingly influential in Europe but differed from the British tradition, which saw the state more as an arbiter between individual interests and rights. This generated a (British) minimalist concept of the state (Anderson, 1992, pp. 140–44) that was concomitant with classical economics and utilitarianism as divine forces over the individual as against the European's abstract legal body.

Additionally, European states were influenced by the national economics of List or Schmoller (Roll, 1973, pp. 211–31) and ideals of state (mandarin) directed economies with a national purpose (Ringer, 1969, pp. 143–59). There is thus an important difference in the concept of the state between Britain (and America) and Europe, which would have important ramifications for Ireland and state legitimacy.

## The Nation as an Idea

The modern idea of the nation evolved from German Romantic philosophy and ideas of the state. Originally derived from the Enlightenment philosophy of Kant, Fichte, and Hegel, the Romantics, particularly Herder and Lessing, developed a concept of peoples as linguistically and culturally defined groups, with primordial origins, and unique beings ordained by God. This Romantic national idea lay partly in philosophical developments and partly in response to social and political developments in Germany, especially her humiliation by Napoleon and the socio-political role of intellectuals, which made Romantic concepts very attractive (Greenfeld, 1993 Kedourie, 1993; Berlin, 2000a; Dingley, 2008). These Romantic concepts were driven more by artists and poets, such as Schiller, and folklore, such as the Grimm Brothers (greatly influencing Young Ireland and modern Irish nationalism): a cultural primordial idea of the nation, something that Durkheim strongly opposed.

The roots of the idea of nationalism lay in Kant's (1724–1804) philosophy where he reversed the traditional view of freedom, the ability to operate within external constraints, and reinterpreted it as an "inner," individual, sense of being and experience. Freedom became being true to one's self, feelings and senses as part of a moral virtue and universal superior inner law (an idea derived from Lutheran Pietism, of submission to an inner grace and commands from the soul).

This created a (very Protestant) categorical imperative for self-discovery and self-determination, to know for one's self and not blindly submit to others' dictates, because free will and autonomy marked the way to one's salvation as the authentic voice of God and therefore the greatest good and perfect being. Thus Kant's freedom reflected Lutheranism's quest for God and perfection that could only be known via an inner state, which one must be free to realize (justification by faith not by good works). And important for this self-realization was the role of struggle, engagement, and activism, in pursuit of higher goals:

> Kant's ethical teachings, then, expressed and propagated a new attitude to political and social questions . . . Moral strenuousness became the hallmark of virtue; a course of action could not be good unless it were the outcome of deep moral struggle . . . Struggle, then, must accompany all attempts to realize virtue, in society as well as in oneself. Struggle is the guarantee of higher intentions, and compromise a surrender to base instincts. The autonomous man is a stern activist. (Kedourie, 1993, p. 22)

Although originally an enlightened attempt to objectify moral issues and break away from externally imposed traditional orders (ancien régime) it later opened up the potential for subjective feeling states as the basis for moral evaluation: emotional, not empirical tests.

This was developed by Fichte (1762–1814) who argued that knowledge and being could only be known in the mind as sensations in time and space, therefore reality lay only in our consciousness and ability to assert it—we know it exists because it exists in our minds. This was developed by the Romantics who argued that what we struggled for of our free will acquired substance and was realized as knowledge in our minds, thus asserting subjective experience as a basis for truth.

But for Fichte the world was also a product of universal consciousness, revealed via reason:

> So the world as a whole, nature in all its variety and history in its past, present and future, must necessarily be the product of a universal consciousness, an Ego which embraces everything within itself, and of which everything that happens is a manifestation. This Ego transcends all individuals, and constitutes for them the guarantee for the stability of the world, its orderliness and rationality; and by means of their reason, men can discriminate between mere fantasy and the product of the universal consciousness. (Kedourie, 1993, p. 28)

Consciousness now revealed a rational order in what is experienced subjectively as opposed to its analytical examination for causes, underlying meanings, laws or values (part of Durkheim's rejection of empiricism lay in distinguishing between what is experienced, being superficial, and unfelt essence; Schmauss, 1994, pp. 62–63). This in turn has implications for societies (nations) based on experiential as against scientific cultures, as in Ireland.

Building on Fichte came Hegel (1770–1831) and his phenomenology of the spirit, whereby the "whole" is prior to and greater than the sum of its individual parts, which exist only in and through the whole—something of a tautology—where individual consciousness exists only through a universal consciousness. Therefore the individual can only realize himself through identifying with the whole (true consciousness) while individual existence lies in absorption in the whole:

> A particular consequence of this view, highly relevant to politics, is that the whole is prior to, more important and greater than all its parts. A world takes on reality and coherence because it is the product of a single consciousness, and its parts can exist at all and share in reality only by taking their place in this world . . . Only reality can be known; and the only reality is the whole. Knowledge of the parts is illusory; no parts can be known by themselves, since they cannot exist on their own, outside a coherent and ordered world. (Kedourie, 1993, p. 29)

A full circle is turned whereby part (individual) and whole become one and the same and only understandable and realizable through each other (as in Durkheim's social man). And the individual, in order to realize himself, must become part of that whole, which for Hegel was the state (implying both government and society):

> For him the state was an organism, an "ethical totality," and the only vehicle through which the true individuality of any particular human being, that is, one's humanity, could be expressed. It was the "achievement of all, the absolutely accomplished fact, wherein individuals find their essential nature expressed and where their particular existence is simply and solely a consciousness of their own universality." Like the romantics proper, the romantic Hegel advocated total integration of the interests of the individual with those of the collectivity. (Greenfeld, 1992, p. 348)

Freedom and individuality became subsumed into and only realized through the collective, which is sacred because part of a divine plan, making the state an object of worship (Singer, 1983, pp. 42–43). This blended with another aspect of Lutheran Pietism, that one's individuality was God-given, part of one's calling, again making it sacred: "One's individuality in this sense, an irreplaceable brick, however tiny, in the Providential scheme, or alternatively a token of God's inscrutable wisdom, was sacred and to be jealously preserved" (Greenfeld, 1992, p. 349).

This enhanced the importance of struggle in the moral imperative for self-realization, as part of God's will and one's duty, any compromise was a failure because it denied true self-realization. And since true being lay in the collective, one must therefore struggle to realize it (the whole), which was done by developing the individual as part of the embodiment of the whole.

The state consequently acquired a metaphysical role in self-realization, combining the whole and its parts, integrating them into a collective consciousness. By this process there would be a greater reciprocity of parts leading to a greater whole and to achieve this required the extension of rights and opportunities for citizens to increase their involvement in the state while the state acquired new rights and duties to direct its citizens. Democracy thus became instrumental to a universal consciousness, thereby increasing individual consciousness.

Struggle and suffering involved in improving this consciousness would then involve a growing sense of oneness within the state as all shared in a common suffering and self-realization (knowledge). A religious sense of destiny transcending one's present being is implied: "This phraseology would describe political matters in terms of development, fulfillment, self-determination, self-realization, and would then be indistinguishable from aesthetic or religious questions where power is not in question" (Kedourie, 1993, p. 40).

Collective destiny became a paramount concern; but the problem of defining the collective remained, partly resolved by what Kedourie (1993) described as "The Excellence of Diversity."

Since struggle was so important there needed to be differences or opposites to struggle against, making wars important for self-realization and holy. Struggle between states developed egos, passion, and consciousness; consequently, the world needed different states, religions, and languages as part of God's plan to overcome mediocrity and impel continual striving. Difference and diversity was moral and sacred, not uniformity, "and hence each state has its own peculiar colour and features. Each state stands for and embodies an idea, or to be more exact, each state embodies a particular phase of the universal Idea" (Stace, 1955, p. 438). Thus this solved the problem of state borders, and where there was dispute this stimulated struggle, part of God's design, the idea of world history.

This also helps to explain the importance of religion, whose fundamental concern is with the spirit, and language, through which the spirit and idea are expressed and revealed. Language provides consciousness and expression, amalgamating events and things with emotions creating a unique experience formative to an autonomous culture, part the divine plan. Further, the more primitive a language, the more it linked into an original spontaneity and purity, which defined "natural" boundaries, making religion and language especially important for Romantic nationalists (enlightened nationalists had sought to overcome differences via science and reason). Difference now defined the divine idea experientially via language: "The test, then, by which a nation is known to exist is that of a language. A group speaking the same language is known as a nation, and a nation ought to constitute a state" (Kedourie, 1993, p. 62). Meanwhile, Hegel had also given the state a divine imperative: "In Hegel's opinion the state was God's spirit as it is expressed on earth. Therefore it was the individual's duty to worship the state as a manifestation of the spirit of God" (Israel, 1979, p. 33).

The idea of the nation-state became a moral force and struggle in diversity was sanctified; whatever denies this is unholy and corrupting. Thus the Enlightenment values that ushered in modern nationalism now came to corrupt it and to be struggled against, while multi-national states became sinful and any harmony and prosperity resulting was corrupting and lacking passion. Civilization, as cosmopolitan order, rational principles, universal laws, science, and rationality, key concerns for the Enlightenment (Pagden, 2013) and associated with industrial standardization (products of division of labor) were equally sinful and unnatural because they denied uniqueness and diversity. Romantics invoked new concepts of nature: spontaneous, raw, non-contrived, authentic, uncorrupted by civilization, and different, "and spontaneity is the gift of those who retain their own peculiar character, who are not corrupted by the veneer of civilization" (Kedourie, 1993, p. 50).

Difference, spontaneity, the primordial, now represent purity and truth (authenticity) and become sacred: to lose one's culture or dilute it becomes sacrilegious and unnatural (the guiding ideology of modern Irish Nationalism, while Unionism was rooted in the Enlightenment).

But Romantic nationalism had great appeal in the nineteenth and twentieth centuries because it helped provide people with a sense of ontological security (Giddens, 1991a and b) at a time of great social and economic change brought about by the "unholy" forces of (Enlightenment) modernization, science, and industry. It helped create a political and psychological world of warmth, passion, and belonging to counter the calm, rational calculation of the Enlightenment that had disrupted the traditional harmony, social order, and its sense of belonging, thus helping respond to the loss of sacred mission, physical and psychological, and place in a scientific cosmos. Consequently, the ethnic idea became the basis of modern nationalism. However, as Eriksen (1993, p. 6) observes, ethnicity (cultural identity) only becomes nationalism when attached to political demands for statehood.

Eulogizing Romantic values, ethnic nationalism had a natural predilection for the arts, although usually third rate (Berlin, 2000). Thus culture became political, and novels, poems, and music developed revolutionary connotations where a truer and more exciting world existed in the imagination (Kedourie, 1993; Greenfeld, 1993; Berlin, 2000). Visionary worlds, unconstrained by civilization's "superficial" forces, can inspire men of passion to raise their consciousness. Thus Romantic visions founded on religion, passion, and original spontaneity (invariably backward looking) replaced rational, empirically founded analysis or, one could argue, complemented interests threatened by enlightened developments, as the true test of politics (what Durkheim argued against).

Perhaps the most successful and typical exponent of German Romantic politics was Herder (1744–1803) who overtly defined the linguistic group as the true nation. History, he claimed, was a progressive force of amelioration brought about by violence, revolution, and diversity as the divine will. He particularly opposed the use of French by Germany's state elites, advocating only German (authentic purity). Language was holy and words expressed self and being, the product of history, struggle, and a people's unique experiences; it was thus an expression of the senses and united those with shared experiences (Greenfeld, 1993; Kedourie, 1993; Lyon, 1994).

Language then bonds men with soil, creating a collective sense of being not shared with others. Each collective has unique traditions, values, and inner experiences that can only be known through it, which now negates Enlightenment ideals of universal and objective criteria for culturally specific values of truth and validity:

> Hence, Herder's final conclusion, namely that each human group must strive after that which lies in its bones, which is part of its tradition. Each man belongs to the group he belongs to; his business as a human being is to speak the truth as it appears to him; the truth as it appears to him is as valid as the truth as it appears to others. (Berlin, 2000, p. 66)

This makes truth collectively specific and asserts an incompatibility between different collectives, which has now become the basis for modern ethnic nationalism.

## Religion

Religion is a major theme in most nationalism (Hastings, 1997; Greenfeld, 1993; Smith, 2003; Colley, 1994; Dingley, 2011b; Ruthven, 2005) and classical sociology (Nisbet, 1996; Turner, 1991, 2013). In pre-industrial society, religion's role was central as the only organized body of knowledge, learning, literacy, and moral instruction. It was also the focal point of peasant society:

> In the days before newspapers, mass based political parties or television it was a major means of communication between the government and people. It was an important centre for communication at local level. It was a means by which moral and political values were inculcated and cultivated. It ensured in an age when contacts between even neighbouring localities were few that a common identity and world view were shared over wide territories. (Brooke, 1994, p. 24)

Religion was thus a major distributor of ideas and knowledge covering major aspects of man's social, political, and economic life. Pre-modern society had a concept of moral economy (Alder, 2002), where religion directly impacted on economic behavior and organization to restrict individual's ability to rationally manipulate economic behavior to take account of communal needs (Brown and Harrison, 1978, pp. 19–21). Religion directly impacted on man's material activities and consciousness and helped form his cultural identity: a superior being that existed over man and directed him in more ways than one, as Durkheim suggests.

Nearly all the major philosophers associated with nationalism were from a religious background and illustrate a natural continuum between religious ideas and nationalism, with most nationalisms invoking ideas of divine will: "The problem of nationalism is not about the intrusion of the sacred into the political (simply assumed to be inherently ethnic), but about the sacralization- proneness and salience of nations, in the modern world. They attract sacralization, and other real or potential objects do not" (Gellner, 1994, pp. 72–73).

Nation and religion coagulate just like Durkheim's society and religion. Nations carry a religious message, particularly the ethnic (cultural) ones that stress collective over the individual. The rational universalism of science found in Romantic nationalism a non-rational oppositional authority to challenge it. Perhaps this was the point as modern (particularly English) economics undermined local, non-modern communities, cultures, and economies: Enlightened rationalism became an economic and communal threat.

Yet even "English" economics invoked a religious message. Adam Smith's economics was a branch of moral philosophy (which also included theology; Lux, 1990, chapter 1) developed around Scottish Presbyterian principles taught to Smith by the Ulster Presbyterian philosopher Francis Hutcheson and imbued with Presbyterian individualist ideas of justice and fairness. Yet it was this religiously imbued, rational economics of radical individualism, that later posed a threat to the "traditional" economy and community in Catholic Ireland (and other emerging nations).

Hence the need for ways to resist modernity was often felt, seeking opposed values, communal rather than individual, mystical and religious rather than rational and material:

> Almost all historical instances of nationalism have been interwoven with religious predicates, the nation is consecrated, it is ultimately an holy entity. Service, even death, for the sake of the nation's cohesion, self-assertion and glory are elevated by national rhetoric to the level of sacrifice and martyrdom. National awakening in early nineteenth century Germany, and later in other countries was experienced as rites of intoxication and solidarity shared by an entire community. In nationalism, the religious is secularized and the national sanctified. (Alter, 1989, pp. 9–10)

Sacrifice for a nation (God) is now ordained because nationalism now refers to the same things as religion. Going beyond individual material interest, nationalism provides a greater being to which individuals can defer on matters moral and material. The social (relational) and cultural role that the churches played are now assumed by nation-states via national broadcasting, newspapers, transport, education, and other communication systems. The idea of man's being and identity, once clerically formed as a child of Christ, is now nationally formed as a child of the nation, which, nationalists tell us, has always existed and will continue to exist, just like God, as man's creator.

Nation and religion are thus highly congruent ideas and subsidiary national ideas are similarly formed and distributed by modern states, where schools and universities replace religious instruction and modern media replaces religious communication systems and the state replaces the church as social organizer. States construct and transmit the ideas of identity and belonging within a modernist framework to control and direct society just as the church did in medieval society. And for religion to survive it had to accommodate itself to this.

Thus, in the nineteenth century, religion starts to become national. Indeed the tie between the two increases as language (how one transmits the idea, or word, of God) becomes increasingly important as the idea. Ethnic identity as linguistically defined both utilizes and is the language it utilizes, just as the word of God is only realizable through the language (Dingley, 2011) and so spreading the word helps preserve the language.

Nationalism thus acquired a religious role in men's lives, nations acquire souls, utilizing symbols, myths, ceremony, and rituals in the same way religion did to recall worshippers in a similar way (Hobsbawm and Ranger, 1992, chapters 1 and 7). This in turn suggests the social (religious) construction of nations.

## The Social Construction of Nations

O'Boyle (1970) and Mayer (1975) suggest a major social problem in nineteenth-century Europe was of many more educated men, particularly arts and humanities graduates, than jobs available (Garvin, 1981; Hart, 1999, 2005; Joy, 2005; and Dingley, 2012; make similar points concerning Ireland). Meanwhile, there was a dearth of graduates in science and engineering for the modern industrial economies and as Berlin (2000), Greenfeld (1993), or Kedourie (1993) all indicate it was not them but the unemployed or under-employed educated who formed the core of nineteenth-century nationalists. Significantly, the only area of Ireland with a modern industrial economy was Protestant Ulster, while Roman Catholicism had a strong antipathy to science and industry (O'Leary, 2006; Remond, 1999; Chadwick, 1998).

Britain was the workshop of the world with a great empire and colonies to settle that could accommodate its excess educated, thus ensuring comparative political stability. In Europe the opposite was true: France, Italy, and Germany (Mayer, 1975; O'Boyle, 1970) had an excess of employable graduates, underdeveloped economies, and few colonies to export their unemployed to, consequently, great political instability. They needed an inner solution and were those countries most associated with developing enlightened, unification nationalism that opposed the ancien order. Germany, in particular, pre-1860s, had a large oversupply of graduates seeking state employment in a static economy and society (Greenfeld, 1993, pp. 293–303; Kedourie, 1993, pp. 35–36; Lyon, 1994). This then linked to solving personal socio-economic predicaments to nationalism as form of (state) job creation scheme.

Herder typified the Romantic nationalist, associating his lack of job opportunity with rule by a French speaking, absolutist German elite. Thus Herder campaigned for a German-speaking state bureaucracy, education, and cultural programs, opening up career paths for the likes of him:

> Having been exiled physically and culturally by the dominant elites, they needed to see this not as their personal failing but as an aberration foisted upon them by these elites who, in reality, had isolated themselves from the people in their countries and their cultural traditions. Blyden, Herder and Wang contended loudly and persistently that they were the true interpreters

and prophets of their cultures and that the ruling elites were the perverters of the faith. This justified to these three cultural nationalists their own pain and suffering, making it a personal sacrifice for the greater good of their people and their culture. (Lyon, 1994, p. 232)

Job opportunities and Romantic suffering and struggle: a simple vernacular explanation and solution for their failure and insecurities, with some truth. (Something similar also occurred in Ireland where a science-based elite left Catholics either excluded or having to enter a scientific-industrial culture Catholicism opposed.)

Equally these nationalists were not part of the traditional aristocratic elite: "They all came from what we would call the emerging middle class and were the sons of teachers. They were proud of their status and had raised expectations as a result. It is the frustration of these expectations that may explain the bitter alienation that inspired them" (Lyon, 1994, p. 226). Once again, they replicated Irish nationalism's provincial middle classes frustrated in their social aspirations by a cosmopolitan elite (Garvin, 1981; Hart, 1999, 2005; Joy, 2005; Dingley, 2012).

Over-educated, unemployed, or under-employed, a new middle class sought to establish its place in the world via ethnic nationalism, although once secured they often altered their opinions: "For the change of fortune was followed by a change of heart, complete in the case of Goethe, wavering but unmistakable in that of Herder" (Greenfeld, 1992, p. 344). Nationalism was therefore often a vehicle for disaffected intellectuals, but it also had to resonate with some reality to gain wider support and become successful, which requires some explanation.

The concept of nations is old enough, pre-existing the French Revolution: "Natio in ordinary speech originally meant a group of men belonging together by similarity of birth, larger than a family, but smaller than a clan or a people . . . Medieval universities were, it is well known, divided into nations" (Kedourie, 1993, p. 5).

Division into linguistic-cultural groups predates the Bible, but not as political units with fixed borders, territory, and defined self-consciousness. Until the radical socio-economic changes wrought by industrialization, the vast majority of the world's population lived, worked and died in small rural villages: "Pre-industrial agrarian society is one in which the overwhelming majority of the population lives the life of agricultural producers, and spends its life within the bounds of small self-contained communities ('the idiocy of rural life'—Karl Marx)" (Gellner, 1994, p. 38).

This was Durkheim's mechanical society, of self-sufficient parochial peasants, speaking vernacular dialects with little knowledge or consciousness beyond their local community. They may have acknowledged some distant sovereign and state, invariably different in language and culture, which often changed as a result of conquest or dynastic inter-marriage. It meant little to the average peasant for whom life continued in its traditional parochial way, as illustrated in former-Yugoslavia's regions: "You may find areas, in both Macedonia and Bulgaria, where the peasants do not really know whether they are Macedonians or Bulgarians (and in some places they think they may be Serbs)" (Glenny, 1992, p. 72).

Attitudes began to alter during the profound socio-economic changes of the nineteenth century, products of new religious thinking (the Reformation), secular speculation (science and the Enlightenment), and economic development (world trade and industrialization), which all impacted significantly on nineteenth-century Ireland. This forced men to comprehend their world differently, paving the way for nationalism, as new socio-economic relations produced new concepts of state legitimacy.

Industrialization initially only affected a few states but such was its impact that it enforced changes even in states and territories not directly involved. The new cheaper mass-produced goods and services, undercutting domestic producers, necessitated responses from non-industrialized regions and states, even if only to protect indigenous economies. It implied new socio-economic and political reorganization to adapt to industrialization or protect against it and its effects.

As Gellner observed, industrialism demands greater mobility and egalitarianism than traditional hierarchical society and a division of labor requiring a new social organization, knowledge, and values to make it effective:

> The difference is this: the major part of training in industrial society is generic training, not specifically connected with the highly specialized professional activity of the person in question, and preceding it. Industrial society may by most criteria be the most highly specialized ever; but its educational system is unquestionably the least specialized, the most universally standardized, that has ever existed. (Gellner, 1983, p. 27)

Industrialization required a homogenous society of standardized skills, knowledge, and culture, where everyone needs to read, write, and be numeric in the same way to integrate and coordinate between different specialists (division of labor). This permits internal mobility and exchange in much larger collective units where social cohesion is based upon reciprocity and exchange, as with Durkheim's organic solidarity. While agrarian society was composed of self-sufficient segments that required no standardization or exchange, their social cohesion being maintained via mechanical solidarity. But when confronted with modernizing disruption segmental societies required a new political organization (ethnic nationalism) to resist (Eriksen, 1993, p. 9) while industrial societies required a unification nationalism to compete.

## The Nation as Ethnic

In the nineteenth century, the national idea shifted from its enlightened, cosmopolitan origins to a Romantic, ethnic idea, a relatively clearly defined political philosophy that assumes the existence of nations as natural, either in being or coming into being and with unique characteristics:

> Linguistic, sartorial, gastronomic, ritual, doctrinal variety abounds. People express and recognise their identity in these idiosyncratic features of their social action . . . "Ethnicity" or "nationality" is simply the name for the condition which prevails when many of these boundaries converge and overlap, so that the boundaries of conversation, easy commensuality, shared pastimes, etc., are the same . . . Ethnicity becomes "political," it gives rise to a "nationalism," when the "ethnic" group defined by these overlapping cultural boundaries is not merely acutely conscious of its own existence, but also imbued with the conviction that the ethnic boundary ought to be a political one . . . and, above all, that the rulers within that unit should be of the same ethnicity as the ruled. (Gellner, 1994, p. 35)

And by the late nineteenth century even unification nationalisms began acquiring some ethnic trappings, such was its legitimizing force. Indeed, its appeal in France became a target for Durkheim's sociology, and, by extension, of his attacks on mysticism and Romanticism in contemporary socio-political thought (Hughes, 1961, pp. 35–36). This, not least because although often presented as primordial cultures, "ethnic organization and identity, rather than being 'primordial' phenomena radically opposed to modernity and the modern state, are frequently reactions to the processes of modernisation" (Eriksen, 1993, p. 9).

As Eriksen, further elaborates ethnicity is primarily about exchange relations and interactions leading to gain and loss, producing meaning and identity and so becomes political and economic, material benefit as well as cultural meaning: "ethnicity as an instrument for competition over scarce resources, which is nevertheless circumscribed by ideologies of shared culture, shared origins and metaphoric kinship" (Eriksen, 1993, p. 45).

Modernization and economics made culture and new social organizations politically relevant, as Durkheim argued. Ethnic nationalism creates barriers to keep "others" out and protects existing internal interests (relations) while unification nationalism extends relations and interests across cultural differences into new integrative exchanges utilizing cosmopolitan cultures. Culture alone may be important but acquires pre-eminence when it becomes a means to distribute important economic, social, and political rewards.

Culture as a tool to include or exclude from socio-economic organizations, such ethnic language use, gives it the political significance afforded by nationalism. Meanwhile modern democracy and industrial division of labor also give culture a unique significance, since participation in both requires the requisite culture.

Democracy creates an imperative to share the same language, cultural symbolism (frequently religiously derived), and economic interests to participate in it, otherwise individuals are not of the people and cannot share its rewards. Culture also helps define the morality that defines the legitimate community and democratic authority. Industrialization's division of labor required standardization and organization over extensive, distant, and abstract relations in a regularly recurring process and to participate one had to share in the relevant culture of exchange relations and abstract, scientific knowledge and authority, as opposed to the immediate experiential and religious authority in segmental societies.

In this sense nations are recent social constructions, responding to modern socio-economic changes:

> Moreover, with Gellner I would stress the element of artifact, invention and social engineering which enters into the making of nations. "Nations as a natural, god given way of classifying men, as an inherent . . . political destiny, are a myth; nationalism, which sometimes takes pre-existing cultures and turns them into nations, sometimes invents them and often obliterates pre-existing cultures: that is a reality." (Hobsbawm, 1992, p. 10)

This emphasis on social construction leads Anderson to define the nation as "an imagined community—and imagined as both inherently limited and sovereign" (Anderson, 1991, p. 6).

It is imagined in the minds of nationals who constitute the nation as a mental construct, akin to Hegel's "idea," but imagined in response to modern economic and political demands. The nation occurs in the mind, mental cognition of relations that produce a shared sense of collective interest expressed via a shared culture. This emphasis on imagination implies great significance for education in society, ideas, and the intellect, structures and patterns of thought, traditionally the role of religion, which still dominates Irish education.

However constructed, nations often did develop from some pre-existing ethnic or state identity in which the imagination was developed. Anderson (1991) emphasizes colonial structures that imposed a common reality via administrative systems and Hobsbawm (1992) argues that in Europe the old states provided a similar framework over their multi-ethnic populations. While Greenfeld (1993) even argues that some pre-industrial states had a genuine sense of national identity.

Smith (1986, 1991) argues that social groupings based on religion, race, ethnicity, language, and territory predate ancient Greece, having an organization, bonding traditions, and symbols that reflect a basic human need to belong and identify. However, many such groupings have existed, demised, merged, or transformed themselves, implying no reason to equate them with the precursors of modern nations. But, nations don't come from nowhere, the somewhere is ethnicity:

> Nationalism is about land, both in terms of possession and (literal) rebuilding, and of belonging where forefathers lived and where history demarcates a "homeland." Subjectively, therefore, locating a nation depends on a reading of ethnic history, which presupposes links between the generations of a community of history and destiny in particular places of the earth. This does not mean that the nation is ancient; only that, subjectively, there are premodern elements within many nations. (Smith, 1991, p. 70)

Ethnic groups are constellations of myths, memoirs, values, and symbols with a characteristic style and communication code separating "us" from "them." They produce different social processes affecting men's behavior and identity (culture) but are different from nations because, despite having an economic function, they imply no political imperative for their own state even if they become building blocks for them.

Such ethnic groups always existed as loose local collectives often only vaguely linked and aware of each other; their cultural and linguistic links often being so vague that they could easily have blended into other cultures. They were territorially poorly defined, often nomadic, with shifting boundaries that cut across state frontiers. But what grouped them together was a shared myth-symbol complex, traditions, folklore, cults, ideas of common descent, practices, language, and religion.

Ethnicity also seems to be a product of change. At times of pacific stability it is often little felt, but at times of change, such as industrialization, it can harden into overt forms:

> Ethnic symbolism referring to the ancient language, religion, kinship system or way of life is crucial for the maintenance of ethnic identity through periods

of change . . . migration, change in the demographic situation, industrialisation or other economic change, or integration into or encapsulation by a larger
political system. (Eriksen, 1993, p. 68)

Thus:

> Several authors have regarded utility as the master variable for the maintenance
> of ethnic identity, regarding identity as contingent on ethnic political organ-
> isation which is formed in situations of competition over scarce resources.
> However, notions of utility are themselves cultural creations, so the boundary
> between that which is useful and that which is meaningful becomes blurred.
> (Eriksen, 1993, p. 74)

This makes ethnicity highly utilitarian, drawing selectively on the past for
present use.

Pre-modern states were mostly indifferent to concepts of ethnicity and
cultural homogeneity and until the age of nationalism most elites distanced
themselves from those they ruled. They developed a "high culture" based
on courtly practice (Gellner, 1983, chapter 2) and often spoke a different
language from their subjects, thus keeping ignorant peasants in awe, as with
French in Germany or Latin in the Roman Catholic Church, which enhanced
the sense of mystery and power of church and state—the commands of God,
over illiterate peasants.

However, pre-1789 a core level of "national" (identification) sentiment
did exist in certain states, even if not culturally homogenous. Greenfeld,
(1993) argues that in all five of her case studies a national consciousness of
sorts existed. Gellner (1994) refers to Carr's four time zones of nations in
Europe (Atlantic seaboard, Central Europe, East Europe, and East Europe
after 1918), where different levels of "national" consciousness existed the further east one went. This corresponds to a regression in trade and economic
development the further one went from the Atlantic seaboard, reinforcing the
link between cultural homogeneity and economic development.

England and France were probably the first states to develop some form
of national consciousness in late medieval times, a product of perpetual wars
between the two and the development of indigenous vernacular as the official
language of state. By Tudor times, most Englishmen spoke some variation of
English, particularly after Caxton's introduction of printing (1476) helped
create a standardized English. But in France a less homogenous development
occurred: "French was essential to the concept of France, even though in
1789 50% of Frenchmen did not speak it at all, only 12–13% spoke it 'cor-
rectly'" (Hobsbawm, 1992, p. 60).

The role of language was important for both exchange relations and sharing the idea necessary for an imagined community. As Weber (1976, pp. 336–37) explains, many nineteenth-century French citizens did not feel French largely because they did not speak French.

Language also had another important aspect: pre-Reformation West European thought was a (Catholic) Church function (as was state adminis-tration), and conducted in Latin, emphasizing a transcendent authority. But the Reformation ushered in new thinking, rational and attacking the mystical other-worldliness of Catholicism, emphasizing a material here and now, in the vernacular and associated with science and in states autonomous from Rome. The word of revelation, truth, and rational inquiry that enlightened man now came down to earth in the vernacular (Shapin, 1995; Gaukroger, 2008; Burke, 2000). Rational relations were emphasized in a shared world of scien-tific knowledge, reasoned salvation, and new knowledge based on discovery as new trade routes and relations developed beyond Europe. This process was further reinforced by the invention of printing: cheap vernacular books greatly expanded the numbers able to read the word (truth) for themselves as indi-viduals outside of the Church (Eisenstein, 2005; Febvre and Martin, 2010).

Anderson's (1991) print-capitalism heavily affected language development by producing masses of cheap books in standard permanent languages, creat-ing standardized mass vernacular markets that sharply defined language blocs off from each other. It produced a common language through which a com-munity could imagine itself as a distinct collective and discern a real differ-ence from non-nationals, in an experiential manner:

> These print-languages laid the basis for national consciousnesses in three dis-tinct ways. First and foremost, they created unified fields of exchange and com-munication below Latin and above the spoken vernaculars . . .
>
> Second, print-capitalism gave a new fixity to language, which in the long run helped to build that image of antiquity so central to the subjective idea of the nation . . .
>
> Third, print-capitalism created languages-of-power of a kind different from the older administrative vernaculars. (Anderson, 1991, p. 44–45)

A new, real, national knowledge, in its own medium of expression, giving substance to Hegel and Herder's ideas was created.

The sixteenth and seventeenth centuries further increased national con-sciousness as warfare became more sophisticated and complex, requiring professional armies and navies and new state organs to oversee permanent logistic and administrative structures that involved new relations between state and its servants. As war grew bigger and more expensive so it affected more people and more directly (Montgomery, 2000; Holsti, 1996).

Greater use of the vernacular to ensure communication between state administration, officer corps, and ordinary soldiers and sailors was needed, while new administrative needs exceeded the church's ability to cope, particularly as new technical and scientific knowledge outstripped clerical learning. And in Reformation countries a separation between church and state occurred requiring states to recruit from a much wider circle. The old mainstays of state (church and nobility) saw themselves as part of an international caste separate from the masses; now states had to recruit from those masses and use their vernacular, effecting new relations and shared identities.

The new states were costly and required increased taxes, creating new demands from those taxed to participate in the state—people power—leading to closer relations between state and people, which distanced relations between state and church. Consequently, the state became more "national" (shared culture) in character. Cultural differences often remained, but were increasingly seen as threats to state authority, leading to conscious decisions to centralize and extend state control throughout its territory. Nation formation was at first, then, a deliberate process of state security and control that opposed ethnic, linguistic, and cultural diversity, as in eighteenth-century France:

> Who in the Departments of Haut-Rhin and Bas-Rhin, has joined with the traitors to call the Prussian and the Austrian on our invaded frontiers? It is the inhabitant of the [Alsatian] countryside, who speaks the same language as our enemies and who consequently feels himself their brother and fellow citizen. (Barere, quoted in, Hobsbawm, 1992, p. 21)

And, as Weber (1976) illustrates, such problems dogged France up to 1914.

Nations emerged, such as Britain or France, based on a centralizing state, with reasonably defined territories, that tried to develop a shared identity for pragmatic reasons, often acquiesced in by local elites where they saw economic opportunity, such as Scotland's unification with England (Colley, 1994).

In Carr's second time zone few modern nations existed: Italy and Germany were fragmentations of different states sharing only a loose cultural identity, while the Austrian and Ottoman Empires were ethnic, religious, and cultural mixes lacking any shared identity. And their location around the Mediterranean left them isolated from access to the new Atlantic and global trade routes.

Further East, in Carr's third time zone, there was little more than a mass of "ethnic" groups, frequently overlapping, and ruled over by states in medieval conditions. As Hobsbawm (1992, pp. 51–63 and 93–100) observes, Czechs and Slovaks spoke their own vernaculars although often ruled by a German-speaking nobility. The state language of the Austrian Empire covering Serbs, Slovaks, Hungarians, Germans, and others, was Latin. The Russian Empire, consisted of Poles, Russians, Ukrainians, Estonians, and more. The elites spoke mostly German or French, yet the peoples of these polyglot ethnicities lived as contentedly as poor peasants anywhere could without any idea of nationalism.

Meanwhile, Anderson (1991) emphasizes the "Creole" concept in the development of nationalism. Creoles were the colonial, non-native inhabitants of European colonies, particularly in the Americas, who were mentally and physically apart from their mother country. These colonies had sharply defined territories and internal relations (often the result of natural barriers or specific treaties drawing precise borders). Such creoles, by the eighteenth century, were the products of generations with no first-hand experience of the mother country, although ruled by its elite primarily for its interests.

Creoles felt looked down upon by mother countries and excluded from elite membership and consequently developed a separate sense of interest, in a bounded colony with close intra-relations, sharing similar experiences, time, and space. This was reinforced by a colonial print-capitalism that provided an internal communication network that informed internal relations, creating internal knowledge, close relations, and identity between people and territory. Meanwhile, territory, sharply defined, performed an imperative role in defining the people. This land was "our land," giving "us" "our" identity and common interest—clearing it, working it, fighting off natives— and "our" economic resource (O'Brien, 1988, "*God Land*"). A distinct set of bounded relationships and interest arose defining the "people" separately from the mother country:

> The "Mexican" or "Chilean" creole typically served only in the territories of colonial Mexico or Chile: his lateral movement was as cramped as his vertical ascent . . . Yet on this cramped pilgrimage he found travelling companions, who came to sense that their fellowship was based not only on that pilgrimage's particular stretch, but on the shared fatality of trans-Atlantic birth. (Anderson, 1991, pp. 56–57)

Creoles were specifically forced to look inward, thereby explicitly imagining themselves nationally, an idea exported back to Europe as a model for radical revolt against Europe's ancien régimes, static economies, polities, and exclusive elites ("throne and altar"; Burleigh, 2005). This revolt, following the French Revolution, provided the outlet for the Romantics and excluded the over-educated. However, its resonance in Britain was less, due to her progressive economic and political development over several hundred years, which negated a need to revolt; in addition she had new colonies to export her excess populations to as new creole states (Anderson, 1992, p. 25).

The imagined community further evolved via the nineteenth-century novel (another product of print-capitalism), which helped circulate the idea of an ideal type of man. A man of the people, as hero, as in the works of Stendhal, Schiller, or Balzac, or critiques the character of the old order in Jane Austen, or Tolstoy's eulogy of the simple peasant. Similarly, poets such as Byron, Shelley, and Wordsworth eulogized the French Revolution and national liberation.

Music similarly developed in public performances too big for private recitals, such as Beethoven's symphonies, which also expressed sentiments of national liberation and free expression, such as Beethoven's ninth symphony. Consequently, public performance and the mass reading of novels forged new abstract relations of collective experience to inspire shared imaginations among a growing class of educated and excluded young men.

The arts became both the medium and the message as artists created and transmitted the "idea" in the popular vernacular, and in an arts culture that slowly superseded science. Meanwhile, cheap print-capitalism made the message widely available for mass participation and forging mass consciousness: "The reading of books became a political, a revolutionary, activity . . . Mean provincial towns where nothing ever happens, dusty libraries, prosaic lecture rooms became the stage of an absorbing secret game . . . what started as a poetic dream would be enacted with inexorable logic as a living nightmare" (Kedourie, 1993, p. 98).

In unification nationalism, this correlated with industrialization and increased trade which necessitated larger, more stable states with unified administration, financial, and legal systems within defined territories. A single language enhanced economic relations, essential to industrial division of labor, making economic, political, and linguistic unity mutually reinforcing and generating shared identity and interests. It also increased economic opportunities for the newly under-employed in state services to facilitate economic and industrial development and in managing the new industries, thereby helping develop a collective consciousness via shared knowledge and relations applicable to modern economies and transcending old differences.

Significantly, nationalism first occurred along both sides of the Atlantic seaboard, where the growth of world trade meant rapid development and new economic relations, particularly for Britain, given its strategic position astride major trade routes: "How indeed could the economic functions and even benefits of the nation-state be denied. The existence of states with a monopoly of currency and with public finances and therefore fiscal policies and activities was a fact . . . For the state . . . after all guaranteed the security of property and contracts" (Hobsbawm, 1992, p. 28).

These factors helped transform concepts of state and polity to forge a wider concept of "the people." The state no longer represented exclusive elites ruling over self-sufficient localities and regions with their own customs and cultures. Developing states now found themselves ruling over people defined via extended, cross-cultural economic relations and interests (class for one) where the newly educated and traders were developing a new consciousness. As Alder (2002) explains, previously economies had been static, self-sufficient, parochial, and self-regulating, rarely trading outside of local guild areas and with weights, measures, and currencies often fixed locally, not by the state. In Germany before *Zollverein* (customs union, 1834) 18 states all had their own customs and tariffs, while Prussia, pre-1818, had separate customs between town and country (Fulbrook, 1990). Ancien states were not unified culturally, economically, or legally.

But industrialization and world trade forged new relations, first in the Atlantic seaboard states, which already had stable state structures and nascent capitalist economies. They made the message—that nations, particularly big ones, were good for trade. Consequently, the original focus was to create large homogenous units with standardized fiscal policies, weights, measures, and laws and to overcome ethno-cultural differences in pursuit of rational (scientific) economic interest, a key to British unification (Colley, 1994).

The social and cultural nature of pre-industrial, peasant society was based on "low culture," that is, parochial knowledge, consciousness, and skills responding to local needs, unchanging in a static world of tradition and custom, invariably acquired by emulation of one's forebears, which needs no formal education and leaves one tied to a locality.

However, in modern socio-economic systems a new "high culture" is required. "High" refers to an ability to extrapolate and abstract knowledge and reason beyond one's locality, which requires a formal education to develop a consciousness of extended relations and abstract knowledge one can apply in a variety of situations. Such a high culture enables one to think beyond the sensate and experiential, it also requires a shared education and culture on universalizing principles to enable extended exchange. In addition modern industrial economies, predicated upon division of labor, require increased specialization; specializations that are interactive and compatible and where work involves the manipulation of shared cognitive signs and symbols across distances. This in turn requires that entire populations be educated in the same high culture, honing specializations that develop in-depth different aspects of the shared high culture—differences that are compatible, complimentary, and enable rapid mobility and change, hence also a less rigidly structured and more democratic, inclusive society (Gellner, 1983, 1997).

Shared high culture enables industrial division of labor, which created an imperative for unification nations, as Durkheim observed. And while Ulster was part of the British unification process, Southern Ireland was not. But significantly, while British classical economics emphasized laissez-faire processes of industrialization, downplaying the role of the state, Europeans emphasized the opposite (often to catch up with Britain) that states should promote economic development, which gave an overt economic dimension to their nationalism. Particularly influential here was the German economist List, for whom the nation was an economic unit directed by the state:

> List was enormously perceptive about a number of things crucial to the history of the nineteenth and twentieth centuries and of economic growth—the importance of the polity, of formal education and training, and of the administrative and cultural infrastructure of the economy. Knowledge, education, the cultural infrastructure and bureaucratic support all are crucial, and excessive concentration on labour and capital obscures it. Forging the political and cultural (hence eventually ethnic) framework is the key to late industrialism. (Gellner, 1994, p. 19)

List, Muller, and Roscher were prominent "national economists" who greatly influenced German and European thought in opposition to British hegemony, with its cosmopolitan economics and free trade (Berdahl, 1972), which later also influenced Irish nationalism via Sinn Fein.

Significantly, national economics appealed to Romantic nationalists who thrived in times of economic depression and fears, whereas rational ideas, reason, and scientific inquiry appear to accompany economic optimism and prosperity. Romantic irrationalism accompanies economic depression and German interest in national economics declined as it became an industrial power (post-1871):

> Reason, scientific enquiry, and the atmosphere of freedom in which alone these can flourish must be abolished in the literal sense if illusion is to consolidate its power over men's minds. The economic development of the nineteenth century which made Germany into an industrialist and capitalist country also liberalised its political and social structure and created the institutional environment which made possible a rational analysis of economic processes. (Roll, 1973, p. 213)

This was also the period when Southern Ireland's rural economy went into relative depression and Romantic nationalism gripped Irish politics. Romantic ideas now combined with Catholic Irish economic interests that opposed British free trade and world markets. Concurrently, social-Darwinian ideas of competition between nations, part of a natural order of struggle between different peoples, also entered into politics, combining well with German national economics and Romantic nationalism in Ireland (Cronin, 2000, pp. 148–49).

Unification nations now found an ethnic imperative to match economic development, the planning and integrative mandarin roles for unemployed graduates to effect better social relations and (high) cultural integration required in modern economies:

> Thus in the perspective of liberal ideology, the nation (i.e. the viable large nation) was the stage of evolution reached in the mid-nineteenth century. As we have seen, the other face of the coin "nation and progress" was therefore, logically, the assimilation of smaller communities and peoples to larger ones. This did not necessarily imply the abandonment of old loyalties and sentiments, though of course it could. The geographically and socially mobile, who had nothing very desirable to look back upon in their past, might be quite ready to do so. (Hobsbawm, 1992, p. 39)

Ethnic and unification nationalism now mixed, combining Romantic with rational imperatives, as in Italy, France, and Germany, industrializing nations seeking an integrating culture to aid economic development and compete internationally (often in defiance of the Catholic Church; Remond, 1999; Burleigh, 2005). They created clear national borders, defined national interests and consciously integrated diverse states and ethnic identities into new nations, often sponsoring as an aid socio-political integration. Durkheim was specifically sponsored by France to visit Germany to study her successful unification (Giddens, 1996, pp. 11–12; Thompson, 1982, p. 36). Thus, "the success of Durkheimian sociology in achieving institutional pre-eminence within the French university system . . . had much to do with its compatibility with the ideological needs of the Third Republic" (Hickox, 1976, p. 205).

Indeed, central to Hickox's argument is that the European "mandarins" role was highly compatible with that of sociology. The idea of the state as an abstract entity over and above society, constructing and directing it (nationally) as an intelligent force, was dominant in Europe and corresponded with ideas of societies as abstract wholes requiring abstract analysis and construction. Thus when state becomes nation-state, nation conflates with society as the object of sociology, to create an integrated nation and reified whole.

Meanwhile, the British intellectual and mandarin tradition was different, its ideology reflected utilitarian individualism, competing interests, and classical economics, while Empire focused state attention outward. Thus Britain never developed a classical school of sociology since it implied an alien view of society as an abstract force; only market forces had an abstract existence. Nor did Britain experience a cathartic period of rapid national transformation/unification; state development was gradual, involving a sense of un-thought out "naturalness" devoid of abstract theorizing (Anderson, 1992, pp. 51–59 and 205–31). Consequently Britain never developed a national idea.

European nation-states were mostly modern constructs, needing careful planning and construction, where, as in Germany, a variety of independent states united (1871) into a single state, although some local autonomy was retained (Blackbourn, 1997, pp. 243–59). A similar process occurred in Italy, where 12 states were united into one, although only 2.5 percent of the population spoke Italian (Hobsbawm, 1992, pp. 37–38). They represent the second stage of Carr's time zone of unification nationalism, industrializing to compete with Britain.

Here, language was increasingly stressed in national identity, leading to a plethora of linguistic institutions and studies to codify and standardize language to facilitate extended relations and homogeneity. But this also created many problems of national definition, thus the Catalan vernacular in Spain was closer to French than Spanish.

A single language became increasingly important as government centralization, administrative, and military needs developed pragmatically alongside ideological ones, thus German was chosen for the multi-linguistic Austro-Hungarian Empire in the 1860s. Meanwhile, national languages, particularly those used to advance separatist claims were often used retrospectively to create a nationalist myth, deliberate constructs from a variety of local idioms or even inventions: "National languages are therefore almost always semi-artificial constructs and occasionally, like modern Hebrew, virtually invented" (Hobsbawm, 1992, p. 54).

Similarly, new disciplines such as archaeology were utilized to manufacture national pasts and continuity, while history was frequently usurped by nationalists to invent a story with moral and political imperatives (Hobsbawm and Ranger's *Invention of Tradition*, 1992).

Into national histories the findings of antiquarian interest are poured, classified, and displayed in museums and galleries, codified, recorded, and labeled to provide an image, a mental vision of truth on permanent display, constructing relations between past and present: "The census, the map, and the museum: together, they profoundly shaped the way in which the colonial state imagined its dominion—the nature of the human beings it ruled, the geography of its domain, and the legitimacy of its ancestry" (Anderson, 1991, pp. 163–64).

Thus a retrospective reality is often constructed for national claims that would have been unknown to the original actors but suits current needs. It also enables the new mandarin ranks to absorb the newly educated in an ethnic-national project supportive of economic interests, presumably the role O'Dowd (1996) identified for the Irish intellectual.

Historical record is then supplemented by current record as governments collect more data on their populations for administrative, economic, and military needs. What almost became a mania for statistics emerged in mid-nineteenth-century Europe, thus the first census of England and Wales (1801), the first registration of births, deaths, and marriages (1837), and first International Statistical Congress (1853) as populations were increasingly counted, grouped, and codified. This helped solidify impressions of national being, characteristics, and relations within often arbitrary borders while also reflecting a real economic and political need for social knowledge and, by implication, sociology.

In Ireland government statistics were collected on an all-Ireland basis thus developing an impression of Ireland as a single unit administratively centered on Dublin. However, as economic histories suggest (O'Grada, 1995; Hoppen, 1999) industrial development was almost exclusively restricted to Ulster. Thus a simple reading of "Irish" statistics could give a misleading impression of "Irish trends" when there were actually two economic trajectories. And it is economic interest and organization that impels nationalism.

All-Ireland statistics also illustrate the problems of experiential and sensory knowledge Durkheim associated with crude empiricism and positivism, as against scientific analysis, which seeks deeper, less obvious explanation. Social facts were not easy to know and their real essence was often different from that perceived (Schmauss, 1994, pp. 62–63). Image and reality were often different. Thus the image presented by statistical categories (such as an arbitrary all-Ireland) can miss important divergences that would reveal distinct differences. Thus, "A knowledge of Ulster history would have made it plain that partition was inevitable in any event" (Lee, 1989b, p. 153).

In Europe conscription also helped turn peasants and workers into nationals via national armies constructing new shared experiences and consciousness (Weber, 1977, chapter 17, illustrates this in France). People were now educated, taxed, policed, and administered by nation states, and national officials, who claimed their loyalty and service, which then imposed reciprocal state relations to admit nationals (the people) into the state by extending the franchise and introducing welfare programs, essential to gain working-class loyalty. Bismarck's "Kulturkampf" and social welfare reforms in Germany aimed to do just this (Blackbourn, 1997), especially against a hostile Catholic Church (Remond, 1999).

But most vital in nation construction was education (Durkheim's sociology was central to French educational reforms; Giddens, 1996, p. 15). Through it, impressionable young minds were collected together in a shared closed environment and taught a common syllabus, language, myths, symbols, and beliefs by commonly trained teachers. (In Ireland education was resolutely denominational.) Thus were inculcated common national ideas, which, with military service, proved ideal in socializing entire populations, transforming ignorant peasants into nationals:

> The introduction of popular, state-controlled education in Europe or of extensive mission education in colonial territories can have a major impact on popular attitudes. Mass literacy, "print capitalism," and the construction of a "standard, national culture" provide the basis for new popular political attitudes and demands. (Breuilly, 1993, p. 21)

In France, commentators literally looked upon their own citizens as the educational objects of missionary and colonial intent:

> "They are sending colonists to faraway lands to cultivate the desert," complained a Breton, "and the desert is here!" "They are building railway lines in Africa," wrote the *Revue du Limousin* in 1862. "If only they would treat us like Arabs!" An agricultural revue took up the cry: "There is in the heart of France a region to be colonized that asks only to be accorded the same working conditions . . . as the colonies." (Weber, 1977, p. 489)

Unsurprisingly, barely half the population spoke French.

Nations may be mental constructs but once formed the imagined community becomes real enough—the idea that really influences behavior, identity, and attitudes, forming "national characteristics." Thus one learns to identify with certain symbols that represent valued or idealized forms of behavior that one should emulate and maintain.

Given education's importance it became a major battleground for control between state, church, and nationalists: whose idea triumphed made the nation. If education could combine with religion, as in Ireland, the message provided gave a pre-existing legitimacy to nationalism, a ready-made past and history, once suitably adapted. Since church and state were the only recorded past it was important for nationalism to appropriate at least one, if not both, for substance.

This new social construction was largely the work of a specific social stratum, the middle classes and mandarins, themselves increasingly a creation of industrialization, which manufactured a significant professional middle class who were paid to think—industrial society's cultural elite. The same strata as O'Boyle's (1970) "Excess of Educated Men":

> What is striking, however, is the depth of involvement by the educated middle classes; by comparison the commercial and industrial bourgeoisie was far less active in national movements . . . The background of the majority of Risorgimento politicians and "awakeners" of the European peoples was . . . writers, journalists, lawyers, clerics, teachers, low-ranking civil servants, academics and members of the liberal professions in the widest sense of the word. (Alter, 1989, pp. 69–70)

However, while middle-class intellectuals may create the idea of the nation, it only succeeds if it meets the material conditions pertinent to time and place. "The characteristic differences evident in the social make-up of every national movement depended, in other words, on specific conditions and circumstances; the level of economic development in the region was not the least important among them" (Alter, 1989, p. 71).

Unification nationalism was relevant to the socio-economic needs of industrialization and division of labor and a new culture built on mass education:

> The citizen of modern society owes his employability, his cultural participation, his moral citizenship, his capacity to deal with the all pervasive bureaucracy, not to skills acquired at his mother's knee or on the village green, or even from his master in the course of a workshop apprenticeship: he owes it to skills which can only be acquired by passing through a pervasive, all-embracing educational system, operating in a standardised linguistic medium, transmitting information contained in manuals rather than in cultural context, and depending on the well-diffused ability to receive, understand, react to and transmit messages to anonymous interlocutors, independently of context. (Gellner, 1994, p. 41)

Modern man needs an extensive abstract, literate high culture (cognitive and moral knowledge) to enter into the modern industrial nation, without which he is isolated and dysfunctional. And the economic function of that culture makes nationalism a uniquely viable form of political organization.

Prior to the 1870s, nationalism is regarded as liberal, progressive, and unifying (Hobsbawm, 1992; Alter, 1989; Gellner, 1983; Smith, 1998). Thus the Italian nationalist Mazzini thought Ireland too small to be a viable nation and saw her future as part of Britain. However, after the 1870s, the nature of nationalism altered, emphasizing a fragmenting conservatism, anti-change and glorifying low ethnic cultures espousing cultural separation, not integration.

This change was partly a by-product of unification processes and mass participation: "Bureaucratic expansion, which also meant bureaucratic specialisation, opened the gates of official preferment to much greater numbers and of far more varied social origins than hitherto" (Anderson, 1991, p. 76).

The intimate elites who comprised the old state functionaries were being replaced by the middle-classes, the purveyors of national consciousness whose only linking relationship was speaking the same language. Consequently, language acquires an even greater importance as a source of identity.

Advancement in the state apparatus required proficiency in state language and high culture, consequently the non-proficient suffer exclusion. This was the case for many local officials in multi-ethnic state bureaucracies, such as post-masters, station-masters and school teachers (whose custom supported many local shopkeepers, professionals, and tradesmen) who found their own vernacular culture limited their bureaucratic progress. Equally, vernacular culture invariably implied only limited and often low-culture knowledge and skills, redundant in modern industrial society. Such a situation invariably invoked a defensive response and the erection of barriers to protect the vernacular culture and promote opportunities within it.

As each vernacular population became more literate, it opened new print-capitalism markets, constructing a new permanence and reality to vernacular differences. These are given a new reality by anthropological, sociological, and historical studies that establish lineages. Vernacular communities become ethnic—nations with a history and form of their own who acquire territorial significance on new maps, followed by transport and communications systems with an internal focus to develop ethnic relations and awareness, which becomes nationalism when it successfully links with an economic interest.

Democratic politics also gave language new values. To address and transmit one's message to the people and identify with them utilizing people's own language, beliefs, and symbols makes politicians part of the imagined community and collective destiny. But they must also communicate messages that resonate with dominant interests:

> The national integration of the Irish tenants and agricultural labourers was achieved less by the force of rational argument than by the emotional appeal to real individual sentiment and worries. Tenant farmers and agricultural labourers were largely unimpressed by speeches they heard at nationalist meetings on the English system of oppression in Ireland, or the political advantages of Home Rule. "But when they heard speeches about the land and landlordism and the rights of the people to the soil". . . their deepest feelings were stirred. (Alter, 1989, pp. 81–82)

Romantic ideals and economic interest blended. In Catholic Ireland this meant addressing concerns of peasant-proprietor farmers, small-town professionals, and the "over-educated and under-employed."

After 1870, rapid social, economic, and demographic change began disrupting Europe's old, stable communities and identities, with their defined sense of order and place. Men felt lost and confused (Giddens, 1991a and b; ontological insecurity), which was particularly the case in rural Ireland (Connolly, 1985, p. 60) and Europe, where sociology, with its concern for order, sought to address such problems (Nisbet, 1996).

Industrialism created severe socio-economic dislocation in many non-industrial areas, as in Ireland, and undermined local elite's, especially religion and aristocracy (Burleigh, 2005; Nisbet, 1996; Hughes, 1961). Modern, industrial states' transport and international markets made local political, religious, and economic elite's redundant, as happened in Ireland where rail networks led to imports that undermined local industries (Lee, 1989, p. 35). This prompted a conservative interest in nationalism as a form of regional protection. Breuilly (1993) divides these into two main categories: first, those led by local elite's threatened by modernizing reforms who therefore found it convenient to claim (or manufacture) ancient rights and privileges, such as the Magyars of the Austro-Hungarian Empire. Second, oppositional to the metropolitan state, subordinate language, and cultural groups:

> which deprived of institutional privileges through which to express their ambitions, came to base them simply upon language, religion and other forms of cultural identity. The organizational basis of these movements was much simpler. They appealed to a territorially more concentrated group and lacked the elite diversity or economic development of the more dominant cultural groups. Again the ideology, with its greater concentration upon history and language, appeared to reflect and help the self-understanding of the developing national movement. It also depended much more on popular support and this tended to make a land reform programme and appeal to democratic principles more central. (Breuilly, 1993, p. 145)

Such would appear to equate with Irish nationalism.

Nationalism, was also its own vested interest, creating and providing the answer to O'Boyle's (1970) and Mayer's (1975) lower middle class excess of educated men:

> In contemporary nationalist movements, cultural nationalists are usually drawn from the education world or the creative arts, especially writing and broadcasting. Here we can see that a "vested interest" in nationalism is involved, for the livelihood of such people is bound up with the nation's identity. Teaching

a national language, writing it, and broadcasting it brings such people eco-nomic gains and a reason to favour nationalist political behaviour, though not always to the point of supporting a nationalist party. Usually nations possess educational and cultural institutions, even if they do not have statehood or autonomy. Workers in such institutions are the backbone of nationalist move-ments. They are not recognisable as being economically deprived but may be considered part of a "segmental cultural division of labour" . . . This means that their occupations are identified with the nation, and that they defend their economic interests in a way which can be described as nationalist political behaviour. (Kellas, 1991, p. 80)

Concurrently, nationalism also provides status and identity for such "workers" as guardians of the nation and even as the nation. This was pre-cisely the starting point for Ringer's (1969) German mandarins, Greenfeld's (1993) Romantics, and Garvin's (1981) revolutionary Irish nationalists.

The simple peasant was now eulogized as content, humble, sturdy, moral, religious, and pure. And the creators of this image formed their own sectional interest as defenders and interpreters of its idea. These are usually the same men that Kellas (1991) identified whose descendants now form the backbone of the nation and eulogize its pre-modern virtues, De Valera in Ireland being a classic example (Brown, 1981; Lyons, 1982).

But why look back "nationally" if nations are so new? Because we look back through what we know today, the "modern" nation, that helped destroy the real past that is mourned, also an idea that has modern legitimacy and moral sanction. Additionally, nations are often built upon pre-existing ethnic identities that did have some historical validity. The nation is thus often part construction to defend modern interests under a historic cloak, making revi-sionist historians very suspect.

Socially, the nation also replaces the old, stable close-knit communities with a new larger community and identity, retrospectively given a timeless-ness and continuity, while also often helping to preserve traditional commu-nities and relations within it from external dislocation by creating national barriers. This provides ontological security to the threatened masses, a sense of meaning, place, and purpose as part of a (new) communal identity with a past, present, and future in a reordered cosmos. The articulators of this were those educated enough to be aware but lacking the skills and knowledge for advancement in contemporary modernizing states. They had nowhere else to look but a past that they re-imagined as a basis for a new present and of neces-sity this had to offer an alternative to the Enlightenment values on which modernity was founded.

Culture then was given substance via pre-unification traditions, folklore, music, arts, and literature, presented as non-material interests and hence morally superior as well as ancient and timeless. Meanwhile, current lack of statehood is presented as resulting from tragedy, betrayal, or conquest, such as British "oppression" in Ireland. This is a project for the excess of educated men, such as Herder, men of letters not equipped for industrial society:

> The leaders of the burgeoning Finnish nationalist movement were "persons whose profession largely consisted of the handling of language: writers, teachers, pastors and lawyers. The study of folklore epic poetry went together with the publication of grammars and dictionaries, and led to the appearance of periodicals which served to standardise Finnish literary [i.e. print-] language, on behalf of which stronger political demands could be advanced. (Anderson, 1991, pp. 74–75)

Humanities triumphed over science, as with Irish nationalism.

A major dimension of this nationalist construction is of national reawakening. This was often retrospective and invention to present the nation as part of a natural, divine order, creating a veritable industry in the discovery, creation, and invention of traditions, which have important functions for nations in three overlapping ways:

> (a) those establishing or symbolising social cohesion or the membership of groups, real or artificial communities, (b) those establishing or legitimising institutions, status or relations of authority, and (c) those whose main purpose was socialisation, the inculcation of beliefs, values and conceptions of behaviour. (Hobsbawm and Ranger, 1992, p. 9)

Thus did O'Dowd (1996) identify modern Irish intellectuals as state constructors. And to effect this role nations need their own educational system to ensure the inculcation of the idea, exclude foreign imports (cultural, religious, and material) and enable the nation to imagine itself (Durkheim's collective consciousness).

Meanwhile, independence was an opportunity for either economic development or protection, hence the appeal of List's economics to Ireland's Sinn Fein. Consequently, when existing ethnic differences can be tied to economic differences, ethnicity can be re-identified in ruling class/subordinate class terms:

> Under conditions of capitalism or the free market, backward regions cannot easily develop, being thwarted by the effective competition of more advanced areas. They need to insulate themselves. If already possessed of an effective centralized leadership, such development will be pursued by means of economic or political and cultural insulation and protection, in the interest of securing the

desired political and military strength for the elite in question and the unit over which it presides. If the backward area in question has been incorporated in a colonial or a territorially continuous empire, the local elites perceive the advantage of setting up a separate unit, within which they will possess the monopoly of access to political and other positions, instead of needing to compete in a larger unit, with rivals favoured by a better established educational tradition. (Gellner, 1994, p. 43)

Thus local elites advance their interests under an image of radical anti-imperialism, as in Ireland (Howe, 2000, pp. 72–75).

However, land-less peasants, now eulogized as the ancient repository of national purity, were often quite uninterested in the decline of their own local elites and culture, while established ruling classes were fairly pragmatic about which language they used, although tending to see vernaculars as barbaric. And here control over education was vital, not only to generate a common identity but also knowledge for real economic interests. Irish peasants supported nationalism because it claimed economic benefits, nationalists from O'Connell to Griffith presenting Irish poverty as a result of being tied to British metropolitan interests (Unionists claimed the opposite) an idea socialized into the population through a Catholic education deeply opposed to modernity (Remond, 1999; Chadwick, 1998).

As Breuilly illustrates with the success of modern Scottish nationalism: "Whatever its historic concern with Scottish identity and independence, the message it has put before the electorate has stressed bread-and-butter issues" (Breuilly, 1993, p. 321).

Nationalism is successful for functional socio-economic reasons, which applies as much to the masses as the educated middle class (Hobsbawm, 1992, p. 125). Consequently, nationalists must discard their imperialist shackles to gain independence via an ethnic claim to the land. But it is mostly a middle-class (usually petit-bourgeois) view, representing their interests:

> The socialists of the period who rarely used the word "nationalism" without the premise "petty-bourgeois," knew what they were talking about. The battle lines of linguistic nationalism were drawn by provincial journalists, schoolteachers and aspiring subaltern officials. The battles of Habsburg politics, when national strife made the Austrian half of the empire virtually ungovernable, were fought about the language of instruction in secondary schools or the nationality of station-masters jobs. (Hobsbawm, 1992, p. 117)

The same applied to Ireland (Garvin, 1987; Augusteijn, 2002).

Post-1870 also saw theories of race applied to nationalism, suggesting a comparable genetic to cultural purity within a pseudo-scientific framework.

This now helped develop a conservative, inward looking nationalism as racial protector to "our" nation, which of course was superior to others (Hobsbawm, 1992, pp. 107–8). Further, it helped develop nationalism as a defense against socialism, a threat to all property interests, cosmopolitan or parochial (Hobsbawm, 1992, pp. 122–23) it was also godless and international, perceived as "scientific" and consequently a threat to Romantics and religion. The nation now became a protector of land, race, and God against revolutionary modernity, a key concern in Durkheim.

However constructed, the nation works and has established itself as the universal political unit, serving a function in which social belonging and culture play vital roles:

> A modern society is a mass, an anonymous one, in which work is semantic not physical, and in which men can only claim effective economic and political citizenship if they can operate the language and culture of the bureaucracies which surround them. The socioeconomic processes which helped establish a liberal consumerist society in the West also engendered nationalism, for men can now only live comfortably in political units dedicated to the maintenance of the same culture as their own. (Gellner, 1994, p. 177)

In this way nations connect men at an abstract and metaphysical level that accords with prevailing material conditions, in a religious type of belonging and identity, which creates its own objective, social reality.

Nationalism's development thus closely mirrors Durkheim's sociology both in terms of social forms and historical development as a response to economic and industrial development, with its integral division of labor. Most important, nationalism was an idea—the nation—which implicitly reflects Durkheim's concept of society, with clear religious roots as an abstract force standing over the individual and impelling their social identities and behavior. The idea must have material utility to translate into a social movement (nationalism) but still has a relative autonomy as a force in itself, over and above the individual. In this way it acts as the moral force Durkheim identified in religion and society.

Nationalism now becomes a system of moral and cognitive knowledge (the idea) constraining the individual to behave socially (collectively) which also implies that different collectives will have different moral and cognitive imperatives (knowledge) of their collective good that differs from others. This difference will vary largely according to degrees of economic development, extended and exchange relations, mechanic versus organic society. And these differences will then be symbolized in the nature and role of religion in society and the status of science as useful knowledge. Religious versus scientific knowledge becomes a dividing line between ethno-separatist (mechanical) and enlightened-unification (organic) nationalisms. The more scientific the social knowledge, the lower the ethnic identification and tendency to unification ideals, the more religious the knowledge the closer to ethnic-separatism.

In Ireland the only industrial division of labor occurred in (predominantly Protestant) Ulster, the rest of Ireland was predominantly rural-peasant and Catholic, which indicates an incompatibility and inability to develop a shared national idea. A further complicating factor was Ulster's self-identification as British, rather than develop its own national identity, while Britain palpably failed to develop an idea of itself as a nation, identifying with Empire.

British ideas, attacked by Durkheim (1984) were individualist and attached to classical economics and utilitarianism that saw society as epiphenomenal, a series of individual contracts and not an external force over the individual. Consequently, Britain had no "idea" or knowledge of itself as a nation, leaving unanswered questions about what it meant to be British, except in rather negative terms. This leaves Ulster Unionists floundering and Irish nationalists as the only ones with an "idea" in Ireland.

# CHAPTER 4

# Ireland, the Revisionist Debate

Revisionism is an attempt to analyze Irish history from a more empirical, scientific, stance, testing long-held beliefs and ideas about the course of Irish history and its interpretation. Its main tools in this have been recourse to documentary evidence, contemporary witnesses, and statistical analysis and records to assess the assumptions and accepted discourse of traditional Irish (nationalist) history. In brief, it has resorted to an empirical methodology that stresses the need for objectivity in both method and output, which has challenged much of the accepted discourse of Irish history. As a result revisionists have tended to "debunk" as myth or exaggeration much traditional Irish history.

However, debunking myth is politically dangerous in the field of nationalism as so much of it is bound up with myth, such as myths of descent in national consciousness, hero and founding father myths, and myths of sacrifice and eternal struggle and their religious relationship (Smith, 1991, 2003; Anderson, 1991; Hobsbawm and Ranger, 1992). Most nations rely on myths, to a certain extent, to bind and help develop cosmological maps that provide social (political) bonding and purpose.

Revisionists are now attacked by the anti-revisionists, defenders of the traditional Catholic nationalist history; most prominently they include arts and literary writers such as Fennell and Deane, historians such as Bradshaw and Murphy (Brady, 1994; Boyce and O'Day, 1996), and sociologists such as Rolston, O'Dowd, Tomlinson, and Munck (Miller, 1998). However, as Howe (2000, p. 90) observes, the high ground of Irish history is now revisionist, while the anti-revisionists are dominated by literary and cultural theorists (p. 76).

The defense of traditional history is based not so much on a rejection of revisionism's empirical data but the claimed failure of revisionists to comprehend the narrative and structure of Irish history. Thus, while revisionists are good deconstructionists they fail to produce a satisfactory narrative that itself explains the course of Irish history (assumed as the nationalist version) and gives it meaning. That revisionist objectivity produced a history that lacked humanity and emotion and thus failed to respond to the human, social, and political needs its subject matter aroused. This is then represented as part of an attack on traditional nationalism, claiming that objective, or neutral, history is just part of a thinly veiled attack on the Irish nation (Boyce and O'Day, 1996, chapter 1; Brady, 1994, chapter 1). Thus, objectivity is undermining the "idea" of the nation.

What revisionists particularly attack, and central to the nationalist core "idea," is the concept of an Irish history of struggle, suffering, and catastrophe, of an ancient Gaelic and Catholic nation fighting to assert itself against an imperialistic England/Britain (Connolly, in Boyce and O'Day, 1996, p. 15). By their attention to empirical data and evidence and by developing a more politically detached approach, revisionists question this version of events and proffer a less catastrophic and more Britain-friendly version of events:

> Broadly, while Ellis advances a view of history as aiming for the high ground of critical detachment and dispassionate engagement with events, Bradshaw believes that it is the job of the historian to attend to the catastrophic dimension of Irish history. On one level it is a question of whether "objective" or "subjective" approaches can best do justice to Irish history. (Maley, in Brewster et al., 1999, p. 13)

The origin of revisionism lies in the journal *Irish Historical Studies*, founded in 1938 (Brewster et al., 1999, p. 13; Whyte, 1991, p. 122), and Whyte quotes the Irish historian J. J. Lee's succinct and approving summation of the journal's import:

> Irish Historical Studies (I.H.S.) took history out of politics. In its pages it is virtually impossible to identify authors as catholic or protestant, nationalist or unionist, southern or northern. In the context of the centuries long polemical tradition, it would be difficult to exaggerate the significance of this achievement. (Whyte, 1991, p. 122)

"This achievement," however, was limited to a small number of scholars, often educated outside of Ireland, such as T. W. Moody and O. D. Edwards who helped found the journal. Later these scholars were followed by a generation of students heavily influenced by them, such as F. L. S. Lyons, Ruth Dudley Edwards, Roy Foster, Oliver MacDonagh, Steven Ellis, and George Boyce. But revisionists only really began to have any impact in the

1960s and 1970s when students influenced by their ideas graduated in large numbers (Boyce and O'Day, 1996, pp. 6–7). It was this later period that saw the establishment of revisionism as a serious challenge to popular nationalist history when a newly educated generation of Irish graduates found themselves in key positions in society. These were the first generation to have fully evolved after Irish independence (1921), entering into middle and senior positions in society without any direct experience of the "struggle" for independence.

Of particular importance here is what anti-revisionists, often sneeringly, refer to as the Dublin 4 elite. Dublin 4 is a smart area in the Republic of Ireland's capital wherein live senior civil servants, journalists, and media executives (particularly from RTE, the Republic's broadcasting authority and the Anglo-Irish *Irish Times*), senior academics, and successful business and professional people. (Before independence it was also the most strongly Unionist area in Southern Ireland.) Dublin 4 appeared to exemplify Hughes (1961) "mandarin class" or London's "chattering class" in Hampstead.

One of the severest critics of Dublin 4 and revisionism is Desmond Fennell who identifies Dublin 4 thus:

> As synonymous with the people who frequented certain pubs and restaurants between the Shelbourne Hotel and Jury's Hotel, "the equivalent of what in London were known as the 'chattering classes': people who, through their jobs in the media, civil service and the professions, were in the position to influence the direction of society in an intravenous manner." (Fennell, 1993, p. 188)

These people Fennell further describes negatively as "liberals" and as such: "much about them can be better understood if it is viewed as a secular religion, competing with and trying to replace Ireland's other two main religions, Catholicism and nationalism" (Fennell, 1993, p. 207).

Revisionism is thus not just an abstract set of ideas it is also perceived as an attack on the nation and religion (noticeably excluding Protestants), a nation that, according to Fennell, exists only in the less fashionable parts of North Dublin and rural Ireland. These Fennell extols as the plain people of Ireland, the "rednecks," who exhibit all the truly national characteristics, as opposed to the liberal, enlightened, secularizing, individualistic, material, and consumerist instincts of Dublin 4. It is Dublin 4 that Fennell associates with forsaking the Republics traditional neutrality, joining the European Union, dropping the Catholic Church's special constitutional position, abandoning bans on contraception, divorce, and abortion, and undermining the traditional wisdom that made the nation (Fennell, 1993, chapter 10).

Similarly Deane excoriates liberals and empiricists closely associated with Dublin 4:

> Empiricists make good liberals . . . The kindest view of liberalism in present day Ireland would credit it with the wish to improve the existing politico-economic system in such a manner that people would be as economically secure and as free as possible from all the demonic influences of "ideologies," religious and political. Its buzz word is "pluralism"; it's the idea of the best of all possible worlds is based on the hope of depoliticizing the society to the point where it is essentially a consumerist organism, absorbing the whole array of goods that can be produced within the free market. No doubt there is a suspicion that the market is, in some sense of the word, a system and that consumption is allied in particular ways to production and distribution. But the emphasis is on the idea of the individual and his/her liberty within a system that is junior to the individual itself. Systems change, but individuals—as an idea, not, thank heaven, as individuals—go on for ever. The full realization of the individual self is regarded as an ambition that institutions exist to serve. Those that do not—religion, education, the 1937 constitution, for example—are to be liberalized, gentrified or abolished. (Deane, in Brady, 199, pp. 238–39)

Revisionism is thus seen as essentially reflecting "modern" trends that attack what Irish nationalism stood for and appeals mainly to Dublin 4's wealthy elite who can afford its pluralist life style. Meanwhile, in the rest of his article, Deane overtly defends the "poetic," "mystic," Catholic, and Gaelic elements of the Irish soul (the national and religious "idea"), the opposite of the corrupting revisionist values.

However, part of the appeal of revisionism to Dublin 4, it is claimed, is the lack of a truly native and revolutionary model for themselves as an educated social elite, consequently:

> The educated Catholic middle class that came to affluence in Dublin in the sixties had no option but to become old-fashioned people with old-fashioned, pre-revolutionary attitudes, rendered in sixties swingers' guise. They had little recourse but to express their sense of difference and their snobbery in terms that were largely a throwback to Protestant-colonial and English precedents, and consequently antagonistic to the Irish nation. It was no accident that the newspaper that first gave them ideological affirmation, and that rose to life again through them, was Dublin's only surviving "Protestant" newspaper, which still to this day, out of piety to its past, prints the "Church Notes" of the Protestant Church's weekly. (Fennell, 1993, p. 201)

The Protestant newspaper being the aforementioned *Irish Times*: while Protestantism is now inextricably linked with all of Deane and Fennell's demons, un-Irish and outside of the "idea."

In Fennell one also sees the riposte to J. J. Lee's idea that revisionist history is religiously or nationally blind. Nationalists see revisionism as inherently opposed to the very things Irish nationalism stood for. Indeed, this is emphasized by another of revisionism's severest critics (Brendan Bradshaw) who calls attention to the English/British origin and training of most revisionists. After revising the observation of Ellis, that most revisionists were either English or members of the old Anglo-Irish Protestant elite, Bradshaw exposes more telling traits about the revisionists:

> However, the decisive development, as it now seems, was the training of the leaders of a new generation of Irish historians in England in the early 1930's, at first, mainly at the London Institute of Historical Research and later at Cambridge . . . Two features of this exercise must be emphasised as decisively influencing the course of future developments. One is the cultural mix represented by the group: closely associated with Trinity, University College, Dublin, and Queen's, Belfast, it reflected in social terms the middle class milieux of the three confessional communities of the island, Protestant, Catholic and dissenting. This goes far to explain the pervasive influence of the approach to the history of Ireland which they came to promote. On the completion of their training all four were soon ensconced in academic posts at their old colleges and with remarkable rapidity came to dominate teaching and research at the main centres of historical studies in Ireland. This feature also holds a special significance for the nature of the ideology which they came to promote as practicing historians. Their shared experience of professional training—fostered a sense of a common professional identity and a common commitment to professional values transcending the diversity of cultural backgrounds. Henceforth, there would be neither protestant, catholic nor dissenter *qua* historian but a common academic profession. (Bradshaw, in Brady, 199 pp. 197–98)

For Bradshaw, and other anti-revisionists, to be professional, seeking underlying consensus based on universal technical and scientific criteria of objectivity ("the principle of a scientific research technique," p. 198), was to deny the national history.

Revisionism also denied Irish history by posing empirical questions and scientific analysis, making it Anglo-centric. Thus the revisionist Roy Foster's *Modern Ireland* (1989a) is criticized for producing an English view and emphasizing English relations, or relations that merely place Ireland within a totalizing network of British relationships: "The relationships he describes are more complex than simple, more assimilationist than confrontational, more symbiotic than predatory; but still these Anglo-Irish relationships dominate" (O'Neill, in Brady, 199, p. 218). Thus revisionist history becomes conflated with English views and interpretations, as well as English practitioners, which implies the denial of an alternative (real?) Irish history. It also implies the extended relations of Durkheim's organic society and of a unification nationalism that is accompanied by a universalizing science and objectivity.

Presumably, given the conflation of English and Protestant with revisionism, anti-revisionists would prefer a history based solely on one of Bradshaw's three cultural/religious traditions: one assumes the Catholic (traditionally anti-science and objectivity). History then becomes no more than the maintenance and eulogy of a tradition (idea). But why choose one tradition and not another?

This question is rarely addressed; Irish nationalism just assumes the Catholic tradition, and this is one of the points that revisionism raises—why that assumption? But this then raises the question of whether or not science and objectivity also represent a tradition, perhaps of a different, even higher order (in the sense of Gellner's high culture, 1983, or as implied in Durkheim's sociology of knowledge), a universalizing tradition. It also links in with the philosophy behind ethnic-separatist and unification nationalism. The battle between revisionist and anti-revisionist reflects not only the fundamental differences between the ideas of Enlightened unification and Romantic separatism but also the opposed forms of scientific and religious knowledge and their relationship to Durkheim's organic and mechanical society.

While Bradshaw is a more traditional academic (Cambridge), Fennell is perhaps more polemically outspoken. He was a respected academic (history and politics, University College Galway) and art critic and journalist. His writing exhibits a classic anti-revisionist style with few empirical references and little statistical data to support what is essentially an impressionistic narrative and arguments that simply accept and assert the rectitude of his nationalism. And it is the basic reliance on narrative, as against empirical analysis, which lies at the heart of anti-revisionism.

The narrative reliance of anti-revisionism is perhaps better illustrated in the less polemical arguments of Deane:

> So, no system, no meta-narrative, just discreet issues discreetly interlinked now and then . . . Revisionism attacks the notion of a single narrative and pretends to supplant it with a plurality of narratives. It downplays the oppression the Rising sought to overthrow and upgrades the oppression the Rising itself inaugurated in the name of freedom. The rewriting of modern history has, as its terminus, the Northern problem and this explains its present intransigence by criticizing those who did not anticipate or recognize its inevitability and

its depth . . . But history is discourse, events and conditions are not. They are outside discourse, but can only be reached through it—to paraphrase Barthes . . . Historians do not write about the past; they create the past in writing about it. And, when they do that, they are also writing in and of the present. It says a good deal about historians that so many of them still believe in their capacity to be "objective." (Deane, in Brady, 1994, pp. 241–42)

Deane dismisses revisionism as pseudo-scientific and (p. 234) finds that he can dismiss one of the foremost revisionist claims to "value-free" history (Connor Cruise O'Brien) as nothing more than polemic (although this does raise the question of whether any enterprise can ever be "value-free"). This, because O'Brien (a Southern Catholic, former cabinet minister in the Republic, and academic of repute) had declared himself to be a Unionist. Thus if a historian revises his political views to support revisionist arguments, he can now be dismissed as a polemicist and his objectivity dismissed without reference to analysis of its factual or analytical content.

Effectively this places subjectivity on the same level as objectivity and places truth beyond empirical evidence, thus placing nationalism's alternative subjective reality, at least, on a par with revisionist objectivity. Of course all history and social science involves constructing a narrative and selecting and interpreting facts and events. But in the revisionist debate two problems in particular arise; first, the generally poor quality of analysis (by objective and scientific standards) that afflicts the anti-revisionist arguments (the essence of Howe's entire book; 2000).

Second, that important sections of Southern Irish society appear to reject core tenets of traditional Irish and anti-revisionist narrative (hence Fennell's diatribe against Dublin 4) as do the entire Unionist population of Ulster. Yet it is a narrative that claims authority over the entire island of Ireland. Thus as a narrative it fails to provide a unifying myth, or "idea," for the anti-revisionist, nationalist project. Consequently, while myth sustaining narratives may well have a real function, they at least have to accord with relevant people's sense of reality or relevance, which in turn implies some degree of objectivity.

What Deane comes down to is a defense of the established (nationalist) meta-narrative against almost any type of revision, irrespective of empirical evidence, which, for inclusion, must conform to the nationalist narrative. Meanwhile, conflicting evidence can be dismissed as polemical because it leads people to revise their political stance. Simply maintaining the meta-narrative is not polemical for Deane, which reflects a thoroughly scholastic frame of mind and Durkheim's argument that the categories of the mind reflect the structure of society.

O'Brien also becomes just another narrative because he too has selected facts, according to canons of objectivity that presumably can be equated with the traditional narrative's canons of subjectivity, which places subjectivity on a par with objectivity simply because both involve human choice. But it fails to grasp the qualitative difference between the two approaches or to understand the wider political implications of historically informed political and policy decisions based on empirically informed truth, as against merely maintaining an emotive narrative as truth. Truth becomes more closely related to questions of reality and real needs in a real world, while concepts of reality begin to require objective clarification.

Of course both revisionist and anti-revisionist claim a truth, but of a different kind. Anti-revisionists see their truth lying in the narrative as a whole and its maintenance (the "idea," as in scholastic philosophy), which revisionists then deconstruct. The references to truth and objectivity in anti-revisionism lie in their use of analogy to support their narrative as against the revisionist use of empirical data to analyze the narrative (Howe, 2000, p. 148). This is particularly the case where anti-revisionists rely on arguments of colonialism and imperialism or invoke cultural theory to defend their nationalism (Howe, 2000, chapter 7).

Both objectivity and subjectivity may inform their own narratives. However, there are important practical implications for actions and policies based on narrative myths as against narratives based on objective analysis. When dealing with practical problems, an analysis built on myth tends not to have the same efficacy as one built on evidence and scientific analysis. However, such an analysis may well undermine myths that meet an important national need, which appears to be the main defense of anti-revisionism (Howe, 2000, p. 93), which suggests the original "idea" may have been fundamentally flawed.

Problems of reality may well be why it is Dublin 4 and not the other nationalists that are revisionist: They are those most likely to encounter the "real" objective problems of nation and statehood most sharply. These tend to find the tools of enlightened analysis more useful than romantic myth: the educated and governing elite and its immediate agents and advisers:

> The gathering debate over the practice of academic history has been related by commentators to the operation of several external forces, to the "intractable" troubles in the North, to the unexpected re-examination of Irish identity that followed upon Ireland's sudden encounter with Europe, to the collapse of consensus in the light of successive governments' inability to resolve the Republic's chronic social and economic problems. (Brady, 1994, p. 23)

To maintain a narrative might be emotionally comforting and politically convenient for those who accept or have a vested interest in the narrative, but: does it help solve real-world problems? (Conversely, the whole point of the narrative may be to avoid dealing with the real world—a form of escapism that helps explain Deane's approval of mysticism and poetry in place of empiricism.)

Given that Dublin 4 is most likely to have to confront the problems of the real world, this begs the old question, particularly acute in the social sciences, of: what constitutes the real world and objective reality? This becomes especially important in nationalism, given the recent origins of many nations. The reality, truth, and construction of nations goes to the core of the study of nationalism, while for governments the problem is one of: whither the nation and what is its real interest? Similar problems confronted Durkheim's France and were explored in his sociology.

Deane is probably correct in implying that much of the revisionist argument has Northern Ireland as its terminus (the real issue). The troubles from the late 1960s onward prompted people to reflect much more critically on Ireland, its history, and its nationalist narrative. This narrative, while impelling nationalist activists in Northern Ireland, provided them with no unifying "idea" able to entice the Unionists into the traditional nationalist idea. In fact, traditional nationalism offered no real solution or clear understanding of Northern Ireland at all, which became a major theme for one of the foremost revisionist historians, T. W. Moody:

> Here he identified nine popular myths that needed demolition by historians, myths being defined as "received views" which combined "elements of fact and fiction." Amongst these were the "dogma that the true Irishman was both Catholic and Gaelic," and the Anglican myth that the Church of Ireland was descended from the Celtic Church of St Patrick. But Moody singled out for special attention the notion that there was a kind of Irish predestiny that linked past with present, and that saw the only valid theme in Irish history as the struggle, the long, enduring struggle, between Ireland and England. This was to telescope Irish history; and few would disagree. But Moody was particularly anxious because this myth was used by the Provisional Irish Republican Army as the primary justification of its "irredentist" war to abolish partition. (Boyce, in Boyce and O'Day, 1996 pp. 219–20)

Meanwhile, the anti-revisionist riposte was almost predictable:

> But some revisionists are perfectly happy to acknowledge the place of the Troubles in forming their views . . . A reaction rather than a response to violence, revisionism is concerned as much with concealing as with healing the wounds of Irish history, with dissolving conflict into consensus. It has its body, which is now slimmer and fitter and healthier, purged of its propensities for violence and signs of suffering. (Maley, in Brewster et al., 1999, p. 18)

The revisionist attempt to point out that it may be the myths of traditional Irish history that cause the violence and suffering are dismissed as efforts to conceal them (Rolston, in Miller, 1998, chapter 13, illustrates such a dismissal).

Implicitly, for revisionists, attempts at being scientific and objective become "un-Irish," but some, such as Deane, take the argument onto a higher level by confronting some genuine problems related to scientific objectivity, although already well appreciated, such as Carr's *What Is History* (1964). History does involve the selection of facts and making judgments and even objectivity has its selective biases with many political ramifications. Science is a human endeavor and not just an abstract reality, therefore it does need some examination of what facts, by whom, and into what theoretical schema they are to be placed. Science can be used and abused just like any other technique.

But, having dismissed science because it also responds to human needs, what Deane appears to imply is an uncritical acceptance of his (nationalist) meta-narrative as the only valid version of being Irish. For a nationalist this may well be the case, however, if nationalism and national identity is about sharing a set of ideas (such as Anderson's, 1991, *Imagined Communities*), then only by accepting those ideas can one share in the national identity. If it is ideas based on subjectivity and emotions, not objectivity and science, which shape nationalism, then Deane and Fennell have some validity. Indeed, if one's primary focus becomes facts and a universal and unifying professional scientific technique, no matter how objectively imperfect, then one inherently becomes either non- or anti-nationalist. The crux of nationalism is often the claim to a culturally unique and specific ordering and interpretation of facts—its truth and idea (often missing in British thought).

Part of the reality of any nation lies in its shared, subjective dimension, which raises the problem as to what and how one creates a shared subjective reality, certainly Unionists appear unable to share one with anti-revisionist nationalists. This may imply that even subjectivity requires a certain level of reality and objectivity for it to achieve nationalist goals.

The anti-revisionists do have a valid point in the importance of narrative. Facts by themselves are often just a jumble of data that need order and narrative interpretation placed upon them before they have any meaning (scientific method addresses this via causal analysis; Ravetz, 1971; Shapin, 1998; Sokal, 2010). And shared meaning is important for social stability, ontological security, and individual emotional well-being, a central concern in the development of sociology (Nisbet, 1996). However, what is questionable is whether the anti-revisionists insistence on their narrative as the sole legitimate one is valid, or, whether critiques of it can be dismissed just because they are politically or emotionally destabilizing.

Fennell saw the origins of revisionism in the hedonistic interests of the socially aspirant residents of Dublin 4. Deane, however, places revisionism in the context of the academics' role and function as a producer of knowledge (not necessarily unrelated to socially aspirant groups' hedonistic interests). However, the two can easily combine as the knowledge produced by anti-revisionists can just as easily be seen as a corollary to the interests of those excluded from the socially aspirant group.

Indeed, an important aspect of revisionist history has been to argue that traditional Irish history was a specific construction to legitimate the rise to power of the socially aspirant group of the late nineteenth century, the Catholic peasant-proprietor and his ally the small-town tradesman: "As Fitzpatrick observed, Garvin oscillates between decrying the baneful effects of the Gaelic revival and interpreting Gaelicism as just the vehicle of a reactionary and threatened bourgeoisie in search of power" (Hutchinson, in Boyce and O'Day, 1996, p. 115). Following the same reasoning it is just as easy to link anti-revisionism to the status quo: the current socially dominant group threatened by a new aspirant group linked to the revisionist narrative.

Deane argues for the importance of narrative as a major determinant of facts, how they are selected and what they mean, but tends to ignore the role of facts as a determinant of narrative, a scientific narrative of causal relations. Equally, he overlooks the question of whose narrative and how it got to be accepted or imposed in the first place and its testability. Thus the facts that the socially aspirant, or governing strata, confront may lead them to revise their existing narratives or construct new ones. The new one may even be regarded as superior in terms of explaining events and guiding action.

Deane also points to the importance of contemporary issues and political concerns as initiating historical trends. In other words all science is selective, biased in its selection of facts (why and how they are selected and to what purpose they are put). Thus, for Deane, one narrative can be equated with another without considering that they can be tested and possibly superseded by better narratives as new facts become available and old narratives cease to offer explanation or adequate guides for social and political action. This, of course, may well undermine the idea(s) on which the nation is built and its legitimate claim to existence, or a social groups claim to power within the nation.

Here the revisionist debate becomes slightly obfuscated as revisionism broadly diverges along two paths—ideas. The first is a multi-tradition, multi-ethnic, but still inclusively Irish, theme that sees an Irish nation inclusive of many traditions and histories. The second is characterized by the idea of two nations or meta-narratives in Ireland. Both are responses to the troubles, but while the former seeks to amend the traditional narrative for an inclusive multi-cultural unity the latter argues that partition is natural and reflects the reality of two separate narratives.

Thus there is a brand of revisionism that is still nationalist in that it pursues the idea of a united Ireland, a single nation, but recognizes that the old nationalist narrative was too narrow and exclusive to include all the people of Ireland. This kind of revisionism represents a new and possibly more liberal nationalism, emphasizing varieties of Irish-ness and traditions, Gaelic and non-Gaelic, Anglo-Irish and Unionist, Protestant, Anglican, or Dissenter along with more modern cultural cleavages of women's experience and "travelers."

Typical of multi-cultural revisionism is the Field Day project. Originally a theatre project in Londonderry it tried to develop a pre-partition bringing together and debate between different perspectives and traditions in Ireland (Brown, in Keogh and Haltzel, 1993). It was founded in 1980 by the playwright Brian Friel and the actor Stephen Rea and has become a permanent arts foundation with an editorial board that includes Seamus Deane, Seamus Heaney, and Tom Paulin, all literary figures.

Interestingly, Field Day's focus is nearly totally literary and defines culture accordingly, although recently it has published historical monographs by authors such as Terry Eagleton and Luke Gibbons. But while it proclaims a pluralist and inclusive ethos, it is largely guided by a traditional nationalist orientation that rejects a British identity and associates itself with contemporary narratives of British cultural colonialism in Ireland (Howe, 2000, pp. 110–20).

In a similar vein to Field Day several other organizations, such as the Cultural Traditions Group and the John Hewitt International Summer School, have also expounded a general theme of "varieties of Irish-ness." These in turn have been closely associated with the Institute of Irish Studies (Queen's University, Belfast). But Field Day, and by implication similar projects, has been summarized by one of its sternest critics as merely reconstructed nationalism:

> My own conclusion is that Field Day is reconstructed rather than unreconstructed Catholic nationalism . . . There is no scientific or nature writing that, coincidentally or not, does not traditionally satisfy any nationalist desires. Low church evangelism is on cautionary exhibition, but Catholic apologetics are missing, probably because, as Edna Longley (1992) alleges, they are taken

as read, needless of mention because Ireland is assumed to be an overwhelmingly Catholic country; as soon need to mention camels in the Koran (to borrow from Borges). Unionism has a token, merely implied presence in the guise of Protestantism (the aforesaid evangelicalism), whereas nationalism is regarded as a philosophy with a respectable literature. (Foster, in O'Dowd, 1996, p. 87)

In the cultural traditions branch of revisionism a dominant Catholic nationalism is reconstructed to allow a minority role for Unionist/Protestant traditions. A similar theme is played out in traditional history, where attempts to pour Unionists and Protestants into the nationalist mold, or narrative, have also become fashionable. Thus a new emphasis is placed on the role of Protestants in the formation of the Irish nation, such as the role of Grattan and Flood (1780s Ascendancy politicians) in trying to gain legislative independence for the Irish Parliament. Similarly, Protestants who figured prominently in modern nationalist and Home Rule movements (Davis, Mitchel, and Parnell) or the Gaelic revival (O'Grady, Hyde, or Hobson) are given prominence.

Multi-cultural revisionist history has an air of wishful thinking about it as the traditional narrative is revised, or broadened, to try and include as many Protestants as possible within it. One such example is the United Irishmen movement and their abortive "rising" of 1798, and the prominent role played in it by the Protestant Wolf Tone, commonly held up as an example of cultural and religious inclusiveness. Tone is particularly praised as the model of new, tolerant, multi-denominational nationalism:

> He redefined the Irish nation on an inclusive, non-religious, basis, rejecting outright the confessional nature of Protestant patriotism. In 1796 Tone explained that, as the means towards furthering the cause of reform in Ireland his objective was "to unite the whole people of Ireland, to abolish the memory of all past dissensions, and to substitute the common name of Irishman, in place of the denominations of Protestant, Catholic and Dissenter." (McNally, in Brewster et al., 1999, p. 37)

This has an air of liberality about it that implies anyone not now conforming to the new multi-cultural nationalism is guilty of sectarian sentiments. Republicans, in particular, have been quick to identify themselves with Tone and his ideas. The commemoration of Tone's death at the Bodenstown cemetery, where he is buried, has become a major event in the Republican calendar. That the staunchly anti-revisionist Republicans should attach such importance to Tone and his ideas as many multi-cultural revisionists perhaps illustrates Foster's (above) argument that this branch of revisionism is merely reconstructed nationalism. A more thorough-going revisionism casts the legacy of Tone in a different light:

> Tone's movement even before he died in 1798 had already developed characteristics he could hardly approve of: "His ideas were of an age which had already passed, and one suspects that his own militant republicanism might not have outlived that recognition. For his reputation as nationalist hero, his death was perhaps timely." (Boyce, in Boyce and O'Day, 1996, pp. 227–28)

As most of the revisionist histories of Tone and the United Irish show, the majority of Protestants were hostile toward him and the movement. Also, once the United Irish moved outside of small Presbyterian areas in Ulster, it rapidly degenerated into a (Catholic) sectarian uprising (Boyce, 1991, p. 131; or Foster, 1989a, p. 279).

The attempt to rewrite nationalism, its culture, and its history may indicate a more liberal attitude on the part of nationalists, but for the pure revisionist it raises the same old questions of truth and objectivity. For as Stewart (1989) constantly stresses, Ulster Protestants are perpetually haunted by a recurring nightmare of Catholic uprising, slaughter, and loss of property. Consequently, whatever the liberal gloss or newly reconstructed narrative he is presented with, the Unionist still recoils from any idea of a united Ireland. After 40 years of the troubles and attempts to rewrite nationalism, the Ulster Unionist support for the Union is as strong as ever (Hennessey, 1997, pp. 248–49; Mitchell and Wilford, 1999, p. 61).

Attempts at constructing a history and culture and their apparent failure to affect people's attitudes and behavior must then raise the question of how valid an exercise it is. This in turn raises the whole question of the empirical reality of culture and history. Are they just constructs that can be foisted on a dumb population to get them to think acceptable thoughts? Or, do culture and history, to successfully affect men's thoughts and behavior, need to reflect at least a basic reality? Put more crudely: Is there a real world or is it all just narrative? This, in turn, reflects the core debate between Enlightenment and Romantic philosophy. Does a real world exist to be uncovered by science or is the world a construct of striving wills, dark forces, and consciousness creating acts? (Berlin, 2000a).

The concept of a real world implicitly allies itself to the ideas of the most committed revisionists (and Durkheim) of an objective reality that is open to analysis using scientific method and empirical data. History can now start to be seen as part of an exercise in revealing reality, cause, and effect in human affairs. These give a course and structure to human behavior and decisions as men respond to real interests. For sociologists this implies such ideas as empirical analysis, positivism, and structural-functionalism and the kind of analysis associated with Durkheim or Marx; and Marxists have been at the forefront of revisionism (Whyte, 1991, pp. 182–93).

However, Marxism itself divides into revisionist and anti-revisionist camps. The anti-revisionists claim a lineage from the Marxist James Connolly and his participation in the Easter uprising to assert a natural conflation between revolutionary socialism and Irish nationalism. They are termed *Green Marxists* by McGarry and O'Leary (1995, chapters 2 and 4) and are now heavily identified with the colonial and British imperialism interpretation of Irish history so roundly condemned for its lack of analytic rigor by Howe (2000). Such Marxists include McCann (1974, 1980), Farrell (1976, 1980), and Munck (1985), while the less overtly Marxist, but generally sympathetic, include Rolston, Tomlinson, and O'Dowd (see Miller, 1998).

Green Marxists stress an Irish national context, the use of religion to divide and the malignant influence of the British presence (the Union) on the troubles in Ulster. British capitalism and imperialism is still held up as a cause of division in Ulster and in Ireland as a whole, which inevitably implies that Unionist separate identity is a form of false-consciousness (while Irish nationalism is not). The nationalist schema is maintained but the divisions and troubles are explained in largely economic terms of British exploitation and capitalist manipulation of religion to divide the working class. One could describe the traditional Marxists as nationalists trying to squeeze Marx into their narrative.

But traditional Marxist interpretations have become increasingly difficult to maintain:

> Traditional Marxism, like traditional nationalism, was being eroded, not just by the tides of historical scholarship, but also by the course of events. The theories which had comforted Marxists and nationalists—that Protestant workers did not really believe in Unionist ideology, but had been bamboozled by the bosses (as Marxists would say) or by the British (as nationalists would put it)—became increasingly implausible in view of the fury shown by unionist workers at the civil rights movement and, later, the IRA campaign. (Whyte, 1991, p. 182)

Not surprisingly Whyte (p. 190) found this group one of the most conservative on Northern Ireland and in a previous publication concluded: "Those who adopt the traditional Marxist analysis in Ireland are Green before they are Red" (Whyte, 1978, p. 261). However, Whyte does imply the possibility of testing theory or narrative against real events, making him a revisionist.

This has been an important theme for revisionist Marxists as it led them to conceptualize Irish history and Northern Ireland outside of the traditional narratives. Most important, it has led them to accept Ulster Unionism as a real, autonomous phenomenon. Hence instead of trying to concoct a meta-narrative embracing everyone on the island they accept two narratives as reflecting the objective presence of two peoples, or nations.

Partition, for Marxist revisionists, merely reflects an objective reality, the basis for a two nations' theory. Northern Ireland's religious divide is regarded as reflecting a false consciousness fostered by nationalists who mislead Catholics as to their "true" material interests (Whyte, 1991, pp. 182–87), although elements of Protestant exclusiveness are also acknowledged. This argument is now so associated with the acceptance of partition that the modern literature often refers to revisionist Marxists as Orange Marxists (McGarry and O'Leary, 1995, chapter 4).

The crux of revisionist Marxism lies in a structural-functional analysis that stresses the emergence of two separate economies in nineteenth-century Ireland (Probert, 1978; Clifford, 1992; BICO, 1971, 1972; McGarry and O'Leary, 1995, chapter 4). The first was a Southern peasant proprietor and small-town economy dominated by Catholics. The second was a Northern industrial economy dominated by Protestants, but complicated by a sizable minority of Catholics. Thus two economies emerged with no reciprocal or symbiotic relationships and consequently formed two separate socio-economic structures of relationships, which accords with a Durkheimian analysis and most theories of nationalism in its socio-economic structural-functionalism.

There is thus an objective reality in socio-economic structures; culture and history reflect these different structures producing different meanings and responding to different needs. While this affirms the legitimacy of the Republic it is not acceptable to traditional nationalists because it also legitimates partition and thus contradicts the nationalist narrative of a natural all-Ireland nation.

Revisionist Marxists further go on to explain the troubles in terms of the failure to fully integrate Catholics (mostly nationalist) into Northern Ireland. Indeed it even suggests that the tolerance of two separate cultural identities is less than liberal and a cause of the troubles. That, by allowing the Catholic community to maintain a separate existence and identity, it has led to the creation of two competing socio-economic structures, cultures, and interests within the Province. This argument was strongly developed by the BICO group and has also been strongly associated with Bew, Gibbon, and Patterson (1979, 1996) and Bew and Patterson (1985). Their arguments, again, are akin to Durkheim's and nation creation.

However, the revisionist Marxists empiricism is most probably best reflected in "the inability of its practitioners to agree on their conclusions . . . There is no agreement among them on the nature of the British presence, or the best future for Northern Ireland" (Whyte, 1991, p. 193). This probably reflects their empirical nature that seeks to search for an objective reality and possible trajectory of "real" historical development. This can be compared with the traditional Marxist (and non-Marxist) nationalist history that seeks to maintain an existing meta-narrative and force all history and facts into it (Whyte, 1978, p. 261).

Culture is seen by Marxist revisionists not as some benign variable that can be manipulated to achieve integration but as a product of real (material) forces (such as Gibbon, 1975). And the more sophisticated introduce Althusserian ideas of relative autonomy (such as Probert, 1978), to counter a crude determinism, but rarely is Durkheim mentioned.

However, while offering major insights, revisionist Marxism also has its detractors, not least because of their economic determinism: "Rose's key claim is that the conflict is so intractable because it is not economic. Economic conflicts, about the share out of material benefits, are bargainable: conflicts about religion and nationality are non-bargainable and therefore much harder to resolve" (Whyte, 1991, p. 192). Such would have been a crucial observation for Durkheim, with his emphasis on the social–moral dimension and the role of religion in addition to economic function.

However, at least positivism and economic determinism acknowledge the need and relevance for empirical testing and real material interests in the formation of national identity. And it was a critique of economic determinism that led to the interest in Althusser's semi-autonomous superstructure (culture) theory. It also implies that Unionists are more than just anti-Catholic bigots while at the same time admitting a real material interest behind Catholic nationalism. This latter point also helps explain revisionism in Dublin 4 as their particular socio-economic position may have led them to new material appreciations. The important point is that narrative becomes functional to structural relationships, primarily, but not exclusively, economic. Narrative, to be successfully taken up and accepted by people, needs a positive basis in terms of relating to real, material, aspects of men's lives.

However, Marxism is not the only structural-functionalist, empirical, or positivist school of thought, although non-Marxist applications of them are comparatively rare. One rarity is an interesting study by Ruane and Todd (1996) where they analyze Northern Ireland's conflict in terms of structures of power and Protestant domination: "The conflict is also generated by a distinctive structure of dominance, dependence and inequality" (Ruane and

Todd, 1996, p. 309). They then discuss ways to dismantle this structure, assuming this will solve the troubles:

> The first is the further confirmation and more positive expression of the British government's declared position that it has no selfish interests in Ireland and that it seeks genuinely to facilitate reconciliation and agreement on the island of Ireland.
>
> A second prerequisite for disassembling the nexus of dominance and dependence is the construction of an alternative source of security for Northern Protestants on the island of Ireland.
>
> A third requirement in disassembling the structure of dominance is the establishment of full economic, political and cultural equality between Northern Catholics and Northern Protestants in whatever future geo-political unit they find themselves. (Ruane and Todd, 1996, pp. 309–11)

While the structural analysis is clear, as is the consociational thinking, the solutions implied assume that structural relations are non-functionally related to positive factors. Again, one gets the impression of new attempts at solutions within a nationalist framework, which conveniently ignores future problems of Catholic domination. One finds no recognition of the need for empirical investigation into the validity of any of the narratives and where an all-Ireland context is assumed as the only frame of reference, not tested. That there might be a functional basis to the Union and Unionists position built on positive (objective) criteria is ignored.

Critical structural-functional analysis appears to be a preoccupation of non-nationalists, even if they started off as nationalists. Thus the revisionist Marxists such as Bew, Patterson, and Gibbon, or BICO (British and Irish Communist Organisation) originally began in the Republican family. Their metamorphosis into pro-Union closely mirrors the split among Republicans in the early 1970s between the Marxist Officials and the non-Marxist Provisionals who stuck to the traditional narrative. The split was based heavily on empirical analysis and functionalist arguments. Marxist Officials argued that de facto Catholic and Protestant workers were materially better off in Northern Ireland and that its industrial economy created a real difference of interest from the South, making it economically dependent on British capital and markets. An empirical and functional reality lay behind partition that traditional nationalists ignored.

Meanwhile, other positivist and structural-functionalist perspectives, such as Durkheim's, whose work was predicated upon the reality of society, the conscience collective (translatable as national consciousness), and the role of religion, are virtually ignored. And, given the importance of religion in Ireland, his positivism and structural-functionalism should offer important insights into both partition and the troubles in Northern Ireland.

However, Durkheim's positivism would probably immediately place it in the revisionist camp, given nationalism's virulent anti-revisionism and because in seeking to establish the structural reality of society Durkheim was intent on deconstructing narratives to find a positive basis for their social construction. This then reflects the conflict between Enlightenment and Romantic thought as Romantics sought to build nations or societies around alternative values to that of the Enlightenment (Berlin, 1990, pp. 36–37, and 2000a, p. 55).

Durkheim also has relevance to Ireland in that he lived and worked (1856–1917) at the same time that modern nationalism arose in Ireland, and in most modern European nations/states, such as the unification of Germany (1870s), Italy (1860s), or Republican France (1870s). Durkheim was largely inspired by French nation building (Thompson, 1982, pp. 145–47; Giddens, 1996, pp. 22–26) and his positivism led him to reject the Romantic anti-revisionist type arguments used to defend traditional Irish nationalism.

The anti-revisionists also often have a self-perceived political role of national maintenance, maintaining the all-Ireland ideal, meta-narrative, and myth(s). This is not surprising as it was very much part of the academic role in the nineteenth century (Durkheim in France or Weber in Germany are examples). However, while the Enlightenment tradition sought an objective basis to their nation and unification, Romantics looked the other way.

This period saw the modern nation-state become the dominant form of political organization (society or "bounded unity"; Giddens, 1987, p. 22) in the Western world and many academics, particularly the anti-revisionists, would still see themselves having an important national(ist) role (Fennell or Bradshaw in Brady, 1994, for example). As the literature on nationalism (such as Hobsbawm, 1992; Gellner, 1983; Kedourie, 1993) indicates, nations were often largely constructed by academics and teachers. Frequently they had a vested interest in nation construction and there was a strong correlation between the abstract idea of a nation and the role and function of all intellectuals, "mandarins," and "wordsmiths" (Hughes, 1961; Anderson, 1991; Greenfeld, 1993).

Intellectuals were important in constructing a national narrative and in including what they wanted to see, as against what there was empirical evidence for. And conspicuous in the formation of Romantic nationalism was the role of artists and humanities graduates (Greenfeld, 1993; Kedourie, 1993) even if, usually, not very good ones (Berlin, 2000a, pp. 55 and 111).

Revisionists in pursuing the idea of "value-free" history and emphasizing empirical data, may be implicitly attacking major vested interests of a national narrative constructed on non-empirical grounds. Empirical study would undermine legitimizing national narratives and myths, consequently challenging the moral authority of the state and other pillars of it, such as academics. Hence, revisionists cannot be quite as neutral as they see themselves, giving some truth to anti-revisionist claims that revisionists just swap one value-laden, political position for another, for by denigrating a national narrative one implies legitimacy to its opposition. Thus, "Revisionists are despite themselves; by refusing to be Irish nationalists, they simply become defenders of Ulster or British nationalism, thereby switching sides in the dispute while believing themselves to be switching the terms of it" (Deane, in Brady, 1994, p. 242). Deane is correct but ignores the point that the revisionists accept the legitimacy of Ulster "nationalism" in a way that anti-revisionists don't because their empirical research leads them to acknowledge realities that anti-revisionism doesn't: nationalism based on different principles, narrative or empirical, Romantic or Enlightenment, and political positions based on reality or myth.

Revisionism versus anti-revisionism returns one to nineteenth-century arguments (largely resolved by the late twentieth century, therefore no longer regarded as political) as to what constitutes the proper bounds of the nation. Also, it recalls questions of positivism versus mysticism and the defense of Enlightenment values. These were problems central to Durkheim's work as he sought a scientific and positivist basis for society (nation), that there were rational principles for societies, which had a real existence. He attacked the "mystical abstractions, the literary and dilettante" (Hughes, 1961, p. 279) and the tendencies of ethnic, Romantic ideas then current.

In this way Durkheim relates to contemporary Ireland and the revisionist debate by seeking a positive basis for society (nation) in a manner reflecting key revisionist concerns. Not non-political, but a rational basis for political action rather than myth and emotion. Thus it may be controversial and political but only because it is new knowledge challenging old, new truth opposed to old truth, but on a more verifiable basis (science).

In nineteenth-century France, Durkheim addressed similar problems, making his sociology very pertinent to an objective analysis of Irish or British identities and definitions of the nation via his positivism, where he defines society (nation) via its structure of relations binding individuals. What makes relationships and structure so binding is their functional character, which Durkheim then analyzed as the basis of a "conscience collective," holding a super-ordinate position over individuals, affecting their behavior, thoughts, and sentiments, culturally binding them to the collective structure. However, he also recognized the need for a narrative to help bind that structure, this being part of his reasoning in *Professional Ethics and Civil Morals* (1992) but a narrative that reflected real structural needs.

Durkheim thus helps provide positivist insights into the revisionist debate. Rarely is even the concept of nation creation (such as a unifying social structure) addressed, even by revisionists:

> Revisionists largely fail to explain Irish nationalism . . . For revisionism itself, despite an apparently nationalist agenda, is vitiated by the fact that it operates within nationalist assumptions about the organization of knowledge and research. Whether they are aware of it or not, most Irish historians are methodological nationalists since they tend to take for granted the nation as the proper unit of analysis. (Hutchinson, in Boyce and O'Day, 1996, p. 101)

This reflects the success of nationalism as a political doctrine since 1789 and the role academics play in defining the political world. However, it fails to distinguish between nations built on different principles, particularly Enlightened as against Romantic. It may also explain the antipathy of Marxists (such as Hobsbawm, 1992) to the very concept of nationalism, which they see as an artificial construct.

Many of the constructors were artists, teachers, academics, historians, or sociologists, who had a vested interest in the construction. As Anderson (1991, pp. 176–85) demonstrates, the construction of Indonesia was a product of an educated middle class who built upon a colonial administrative structure a historical and social-cultural "superstructure" that had little indigenous substance. Eugen Weber (1976) shows how a similar process occurred in France: "A complex of territories conquered, annexed, and integrated in a political and administrative whole, many of them with strongly developed national or regional personalities, some of them with traditions that were specifically un- or anti-French" (Weber, 1976, p. 485).

However, Weber also observes that the peasants, at least partly, chose to become Frenchmen as France not only had a political reality as an overarching state structure constraining them but also real economic advantages and opportunities. Nation construction was a two-way process, as modern Breton Nationalism or Ulster Unionism indicates. A local populace can also resist national integration if it sees advantages in doing so.

In modern France the growth of a transport and communications structure enabled the peasant to extend his local economic and social relations and develop new "national" extended opportunities, although national communication and transport structures also bounded them within new national limits. Construction built upon real conditions in which men consciously negotiated their social and political attachments as well as had them framed: They also chose their nation.

While nationalists claimed a historic inevitability to the nation state, to help legitimate it, historians and sociologists often had the task of supplying the legitimating past, present, and context. This is not only what many of them did but what many, particularly anti-revisionists, still see as a prime role:

> In that continuous pattern they saw the nation, presented by great men, women and movements, righteous insurgents, and brave soldiers, inspired by right ideas and acting rightly. They saw this with pride. They cherished songs, poems and other writings emanating from this inheritance, and they revered countless places, buildings and relics which it had imbued with value. The revisionist historians, instead of maintaining this framework of meaning, moral interpretation, and anchored value, and reviewing it through industrious and creative vision, set about demolishing it . . .
>
> In short, the revisionists provided a history which, far from sustaining, energising and bonding the nation, tended to cripple, disintegrate and paralyse it. (Fennell, in Brady, 1994, p. 189)

A moral and a political mission becomes part of the academic's role—to help make and sustain the nation. A similar nationalist role was also accepted by sociologists such as Durkheim, and it was part of Marx's pariah status and that of international socialists and anarchists that they were internationalist in an age of nationalism. This suggests a lack of total naturalness to nations, that should require such active maintenance, particularly by academics from the "over-educated and under-employed" with their vested interests.

However, in a socially constructed world it is naive for social scientists to think that their work has no political implications. The crux of revisionist debates is precisely what political mission is to be pursued in academia. The anti-revisionists fall into the Romantic mold, intent on manufacturing an anti-Enlightenment nation hostile to ideas of science and structure, regarded as anti-liberation (Berlin, 2000a, p. 114). Whereas the revisionist "objective" history is built on Enlightenment ideas of science and rationalism opposed by Romantics:

> In claiming that their methods were justified as an attempt to create a "value-free" historical science, Moody and Edwards were, Bradshaw claimed, at best intellectually and politically naive . . . Under the pretence of objectivity their followers had distorted or buried the heritage which the community had received from the past. The fashionably sardonic tone, the narrow, calculating mode of argument and the cynical mode of assessment which the university history schools had encouraged, had served to de-sensitise modern historical

writing to the sufferings and injustices of Ireland's past. This implicit desire to evade the essential catastrophic character of Irish history had been compounded by an overt attack on the idea that a clear sense of national consciousness had been deeply rooted in Irish history and was not just a recent or accidental creation. (Brady, 1994, pp. 10–11)

This returns one to the Sturm und Drang school of the German Romantics that Berlin (2000a), Greenfeld (1993), and Kedourie (1993) observe, the product of artists and poets.

This was an issue that Durkheim addressed, he also tried to synthesize the competing Romantic and Enlightenment ideas by seeking a scientific basis for the emotional and mystical (recognizing these needs to be met) by scientifically analyzing the community and the "psychic" or subjective needs that it met. Equally, for Durkheim, God did not exist as such but did exist as a real symbolic representation. Construction based on reality is a core theme of Durkheim's.

This returns one to the problem of defining the nation. For how one defines it will have important political implications in assessing the reality and legitimacy of its existence and its territorial and moral claims, as well as the academics' mission in it. And defining initial criteria can create major hostages to fortune for both academic and political activists alike. It also implies scientific criteria that would probably count against the Romantic anti-revisionist arguments, assuming that one can scientifically define a nation.

Science, with its empirical emphasis on causal relations, implies structural and functional relations that would fit in with the positivist tradition of Durkheim, relations that also imply a relative autonomy to certain collectives. If this is correct it has important implications for the revisionist debate as it may, or may not, imply a real (in Durkheimian terms) political legitimacy to Northern Ireland.

If nations follow on from a real structure of internal relations and respond to structures of real external relations then it should be possible to establish their reality. There now exists a positivist basis for identifying nations and criteria established beforehand to test political claims. For Durkheim the social-political world may have been man-made, but made in response to real external facts, forces, and relations.

Consequently one inevitably addresses a key concern of Irish nationalism—partition and Northern Ireland:

More generally, there has been a proliferation of commentary on the politics and history of Northern Ireland, as scholars respond to the demands of heightened political awareness and of political discussion . . . Naturally these works address issues of contemporary political concern (economic performance, employment practice, security policy), and thereby become themselves part of the political agenda, informing and provoking debate. Writing history becomes making history: historiography becomes once again, as in 1886 or 1912, part of the historical process. (Jackson, in Boyce and O'Day, 1996, p. 136)

Jackson could well have added "part of the political process" as well. Here Durkheim can both help in understanding this unresolved problem by posing the question of "the nation" in positivist terms and help illuminate important aspects of the conflict in Northern Ireland and partition.

By posing nation as society and utilizing the idea of structures of relations (collectives) creating specific forms of consciousness one may be able to deduce the formation of national identities as different forms of knowledge creating different knowledge of self and identity, correlating with the different sets of relations. In this way different types of consciousness, equating with national identity, may be seen to exist in Ireland leading to different national identities.

Do different consciousnesses exist in Ireland? Can one identify networks of knowledge producing relations that support a consciousness that clearly separates Ireland off from Great Britain? Also, can one identify similar relations and consciousness defining Ulster Unionists off from the rest of Ireland? These then become the pertinent questions for a Durkheimian analysis of nationalism in Ireland. As such, questions of the rights and wrongs of "British rule," or absentee landlords, the relative wealth or deprivation of the population, and the other questions of revisionist history become rather secondary.

The primary Durkheimian question would be the existence, or not, of separate collective consciousness, built upon unique structures of relations that reflect real interests of collective existence. One does not have to imply any pejorative interpretation to their separate existence, merely their existence and reality. If they exist(ed) then there also exists the basis for separate nations, whose origins are irrelevant, pejoratively, to the reality of their existence.

This does not ignore the fact that relations and identities often overlap and blur, or that people may be part of multiple sets of relations and identities. One of the problems posed by nationalism is frequently the lack of clear boundaries and precise definitions of national identity that nationalism seeks to imply. But what it does suggest is that there are core relations that dominate individual lives and impel them to accept or become part of a primary collective and share its consciousness.

Ireland, it will be argued, provides an example of where rural relations were being redefined and defended against the encroaching reality and knowledge of an external industrial world. The Southern Catholic nationalist Ireland had a rural economy and social relations (the nationalist reality they knew and understood) facing severe disruption from the industrial knowledge and relations of both the United Kingdom (UK) and an emerging world economy. New knowledge, based on industrial and global relations, encroached on rural relations and disrupted them, creating a new national consciousness, a nationalist reaction to protect rural society. The relevant relations and interests could be compared to those of a segmental peasant society, where industrial, capitalist, organization, relations and consciousness, central to the British identity (Loughlin, 1995) were not relevant to the productive mode and social structure that dominated Catholic Ireland.

This latter point is very significant as it is fundamental to the partition of Ireland. Ulster had evolved a productive mode, industrial organization, and socio-economic structure at odds with the rest of Ireland but close to Britain. Thus the consciousness and identity (self-knowledge) of the majority in Ulster were fundamentally different from the rest of Ireland and part of what Irish nationalism defined itself against. Equally, the different historical experiences and relationships formed by Protestants during and after the plantation created a different sense of historical identity and continuity.

Consequently, Ulster Unionists developed a consciousness founded upon a set of relations different in nature from the rest of Ireland. They had a unique knowledge and consciousness of themselves and their interests that was not shared by the rest of Ireland. This consciousness was founded upon a set of relations Durkheim associated with organic structures and division of labor.

The mechanical structure and segmental relations of Catholic nationalist Ireland made independence a proposition that accorded with maintaining a known reality for them against British modernization. For the dominant group in Ulster the opposite was true as many of their most important relations were increasingly British, extended, and organic (a unification "United Kingdom" British identity). Equally, their internal Protestant industrial relations passed on a different consciousness to that of the Catholic nationalist.

Ulster Unionists could afford to ignore the rest of Ireland; their vital interests and relations were not linked to internal Irish relations but to Britain, making their identity and self-knowledge Unionist and British, which also built on a past knowledge (consciousness) that was different from the rest of Ireland. This also explains how they could afford to form their own Unionist organization, separate from that of Southern Unionists (Gibbon, 1975; Buckland, 1973), which for Durkheim would imply their separate national being.

# CHAPTER 5

# Science and the Arts in Ireland

There is also a deeper edge to the revisionist debate with important implications for the sociology of knowledge and the existence of the nation; the very status of science itself. The revisionist argument is based heavily on the application of "scientific" concepts of objectivity and empirical data. As recent research on the history of science in Ireland indicates, such scientific ideas have a clear national, political bias (Brett, 1999; Bowler and Whyte, 1997; Foley and Ryder, 1998; Kearney, 1985; O'Dowd, 1996). Such a bias also appears to support Durkheim's association of scientific knowledge with industrial relations and consciousness, thus furthering the relevance of a Durkheimian analysis of Ireland.

Contemporary research on Irish science appears to place it firmly in the Protestant and Unionist ideological camp, as an interest, or consciousness. This in turn refers back to Merton's argument that relates the rise of science to the Puritan ethic in Protestantism:

> Puritan sentiments and beliefs prompting, tireless industry were such as to aid economic success. The same considerations apply equally to the close connection between Puritanism and science: the religious movement partly "adapted" itself to the growing prestige of science but it initially involved deep-seated sentiments which inspired its followers to a profound and consistent interest in the pursuit of science. (Merton, 1973, p. 229)

As such the very idea of revisionist history with its scientific methodology becomes a politically Protestant idea. In Ireland, the "low" nature of even the Anglican Church has often been remarked upon and in Ulster the Calvinistic Presbyterians provide the dominant ethos (Brett, 1999, p. 31). To be scientific is to be Protestant (Burke, 2000, pp. 37–38) and, in Ireland, Unionist. This has an implication that Irish (Catholic) nationalism was founded upon non-scientific principles, which when "scientifically" analyzed would antagonistically deconstruct the nation.

Science, thus, becomes a source of Protestant authority and legitimacy, part of their culture. Scientific truth represents a Unionist attack on Irish (Catholic) nationalism and truth. This argument would be supported by Irish nationalism's emphasis on Gaelic culture, with its stress on literature, arts, folklore, and pre-industrial attributes (Brown, 1981, chapters 2 and 3; Lyons, 1982, chapter 3; Boyce, 1991, chapter 8): specifically, themes that denied the rationalizing and utilitarian values associated with science and raised the idea of an alternative, arts-based culture. This would also blend in with Catholicism's emphasis on scholastic philosophy.

Ever since the late nineteenth century, such an antiscientific culture has achieved a remarkable degree of political authority. It derives from the same German Romanticism that informed most ethnic nationalism in Europe and appeared to establish itself around the 1870s (Hobsbawm, 1992, pp. 101–4). In Ireland such anti-science attitudes followed a similar vein:

> Furthermore, ever, since Arnold and his neo-Hellenism, neo-Romanticism, anti-scientism, anti-industrialism and anti-nonconformism academics in the humanities have discountenanced the kind of culture inherited and generated by Ulster Protestantism, and unionism has been identified almost exclusively with this culture. It is a culture regarded as having no charisma, seductiveness or mystique, and as deeply philistine, given its important components of industrialism, commerce, technology, and low-church Protestantism. (Foster, in O'Dowd, 1996, p. 90)

This science-based culture also carried the further disadvantage of being identified as British: "And since much of it is a dialect version of British culture, to celebrate it is to appear to celebrate Britishism and therefore by implication to appear triumphalist, anti-Catholic, anti-Irish" (Foster, in O'Dowd, 1996, pp. 90–91).

Another disadvantage of science was that its very precepts are regarded as universal and not national. This was precisely why the first wave of unification nationalisms were regarded as so revolutionary. They closely followed the ideals of the French Revolution and Tom Paine's *Rights of Man* that joined Enlightenment values of science, individualism, and rationalism with industry and universality into a universal high culture. The Union of Britain and Ireland was unification nationalism, and the separation of Ireland from it had to be a denial of its principles for it to gain legitimacy.

Hence, there is the emphasis in Irish nationalism on a literary and folk culture and narrative that denigrated rationalism and science with their associated industrial, commercial, and material values; hence also the reference to alternative spiritual and mystic values that posed an (ascetic) alternative to the modernizing and utilitarian ethos of a commercial society:

A persistent theme in late nineteenth century Irish Catholic and nationalist thought was the opposition between a materialistic, corrupt and "unspiritual" England and a suffering, poor but spiritually superior, Ireland. Asceticism and dislike of commercial civilization were common themes in Catholic social thought of the period, expressed well, for example, in the writing of Belloc . . . In the writings of Canon Sheehan, London was rather similarly portrayed as the centre of imperial and moneyed evil. Father Peter O'Leary supplied the Gaelic League and a wider public with similar images of an English bloated plutocracy v's an Irish virtuous asceticism. Romantic images of selflessness and asceticism in a corrupt world abounded in the nationalist literature of the period, echoing not only the priestly sub-culture so conspicuous at the time in Ireland, but also an international zeitgeist. (Garvin, in Boyce, 1988, p. 107)

Irish Nationalism provided an alternative truth, not to be found in universal science and utilitarian values, but in religion and arts, culture that is specific. Consequently, Irish Romantic nationalism blended well with the Catholic Church's struggle against liberalism, materialism, irreligion, and other forms of modernism (MacDonagh, 1983, p. 103; Connolly, 1985, p. 27).

The role of science in Ireland is an area only just starting to be explored but the role of culture has long been a key area of study (Boyce, 1988; Lyons, 1982; Brown, 1981). Culture in Ireland has almost exclusively been seen in terms of the Anglo-Irish and Gaelic-Irish literary revivals of the nineteenth century, which provided the basis for a separate Irish identity and nationhood. Both cultural schools posed themselves in the Arnold and Leavis tradition of what is now regarded as cultural studies (Jenks, 1993, chapter 1; Milner, 1994, chapter 2). However, since the Anglo-Irish literary revival reflected an Ascendancy "high" and cosmopolitan culture, it failed to dominate the literary revival of the time and was supplanted by the "low" culture of the Gaelic revival (Brown, 1981, pp. 117–34; Lyons, 1982, chapter 3).

This cultural studies perspective tends to see culture as an autonomous set of ideas and also as something anti-science, anti-technology, anti-industry and anti-modernity. In both its autonomy and anti-science guises, cultural studies thus replicates core Romantic values of autonomous will and independent spirit along with an artistic vision of reality (Berlin, 2000a and b, p. 121). Science gets dismissed as culture, which is to ignore the structural-functionalist view of culture, at the heart of Durkheim. Only the literary, arts, and humanities concept of culture is interpreted as true culture. This takes one back to the Romantics both in cultural theory and in ethnic nationalism; artistic creation alone is accorded the accolade of true authority and legitimacy. Sciencebased, unification nationalisms are not accorded the accolade of (national) legitimacy, having been superseded by Romanticism.

Further the universal basis of science and its authority and legitimacy become the basis for attacking it as imperialist and oppressive, since they allow little room for local diversity or spontaneity. Because science was almost exclusively Protestant in Ireland it would become identified with both Unionism and imperialism in the nationalist's mind. Science was British and cosmopolitan, which nationalists opposed. The German Romantic nationalist Muller could just as easily been speaking for any Irish nationalist: "Science, he says, can reproduce only a lifeless political state; death cannot represent life, nor can stagnation (that is, the social contract, the liberal state, the English state in particular) represent movement" (Berlin, 2000a, p. 124). Science was also critical, "bottom up," and more democratic; it thus posed a threat to the idea of an ethnic nationalism that emphasized a group dependency and authority over the individual and the hierarchical authority of Roman Catholicism.

This dichotomy between science and arts culture has important implications for it poses serious problems of ultimate truths, morals, legitimacy, and authority, at all levels of political and communal authority and autonomy, of what is real. These were also central to the origins of sociology in the nineteenth century, which addressed the same problems of social reality, which were often at the core of nationalist movements. Truth and a moral claim:

> An example of the nationalist use of history and the nationalist's desire to return to a golden age is provided by the Gaelic revival of the 1890's. The vision was as much pagan as Catholic . . . The vision of an ethnic golden age told modern Irish men and women what was "authentically theirs," and how to be "themselves" once again in a free Ireland. (Smith, 1991, p. 66–67)

Scientific deconstruction of such a vision seriously undermines its authenticity and any pagan golden age was pre-science. Catholicism was also rooted in the prescient intellectual schema of scholasticism, an Aristotelian as against a Platonic order (MacCulloch, 2004, pp. 78–80) on which its theory of transubstantiation rested (Brooke, 1991, pp. 141–42) and which had been the basis for Papal denunciations of Bruno, Copernicus, and Galileo (MacCulloch, 2004, pp. 686–88).

Indeed, insistence on instruction for Catholics in scholastic philosophy lay behind many of the difficulties of integrating Catholics into Northern Ireland's University and teaching training system after 1921 (Harris, 1993, pp. 216 and 226). And as Russell (1996, p. 428) observes scholasticism's chief faults lay in an "indifference to facts and science." Science was an intellectual associate of the Reformation, particularly of its more Puritan and Calvinist wings (Brooke, 1991, chapter III) and rejection of Aristotelian scholasticism (Shapin, 1995; Gaukroger, 2008). Reformation emphasis is on individual thought and rational scrutiny, and its attacks on the worship of images (idolatry) for analysis is reflected in the structure and plainness of its churches (Brett, 1999, chapter 3). False images should not be allowed to interfere with the contemplation of a truth that transcended the here and now, the objective and utilitarian.

As Brett (1999) argues, this is the essence of the Ulster culture and identity, as revealed in the style of its churches, plain and austere, where no images distract the mind and the simple structure of the unadorned building is left to display its own unique architectural style and internal structural beauty, the laws of science (of God). Quoting Frances Yates, Brett observes:

> No more will places in churches or other buildings be visibly impressed upon the imagination. And, above all, gone in the ramist system are the images, the emotionally striking and stimulating images the use of which had come down through the centuries from the art of the classical rhetor. The "natural" stimulus for memory is not the emotionally exciting image; it is the abstract order of dialectical analysis which is yet, for Ramus, "natural" since dialectical order is natural to the mind. (Brett, 1999, p. 46)

If one associates imagination with the arts and the construction of a vision and images, as Romantics do (Berlin, 2000, chapter 5), and compares it with science, which deconstructs in search of formal structure, one arrives at opposed views, purposes, and truths. Both were products of Christian thought, but in radically opposed directions; inner Romantic vision is posed against external objective fact. Science implies submission to facts and structures, discipline, and conformity to rules and laws, in that way freedom lies through understanding empirical data, process, and structure. Romantic knowledge denies these for the freedom of the will to create whatever, for it claims no structure to things, no reality beyond the will and its creations (Berlin, 2000, pp. 118 19).

Science also implied a shift from image to abstract and a shift from top down, central authority to a bottom up dispersed authority; from papacy and episcopacy to democratic presbytery (Brett, 1999, p. 12). In Irish terms from Catholicism to Protestantism, from icon rich and mystical to minimalist and knowable, from emotion, passion, and excitement to rational, disciplined, and utilitarian. Thought was no longer to be employed in composing knowledge and images (constructing and art) but in rational analysis to unveil knowledge and an ultimate form (deconstructing and science): "The newly whitened walls of the buildings were lit by new uncoloured glass letting in daylight, which in the great ministers revealed for the very first time the structural logic of their architecture" (Brett, 1999, p. 39).

From merely surrendering oneself to the mystical (narrative) of the nation or church, to revealing the truth of political constructs like nations via critical inquiry become the immediate analogy in the revisionist debate. And if form and structure are immanent in the object, as in the architecture, to be revealed by careful analysis, this also implies a universalism and cosmopolitanism (Pagden, 2013). With this new learning one also sees the rise of the printed word as a medium. The "word" is not only central to the Reformation where the truth is to be revealed via study of the printed, vernacular text in the bible, but also in science. Science based itself in printed texts, in plain intelligible vernacular language that was very precise (between 1475 and 1640 10 percent of printed books were scientific; Brett, 1999, p. 93); indeed science was impossible without print, which restructures the mind (Ong, 2002; Eisenstein, 2005; Febvre and Martin, 2010).

For Protestants a utilitarian and scientific culture can pose particular problems in relation to national identity. First, its universalizing characteristics make it difficult to assert a cultural specificity normally central to nationalist ideas. Second, culture, particularly since the days of Arnold, Leavis, and Elliot, has become defined purely in arts terms so that utilitarian values and systems get dismissed as non-culture:

> Utilitarianism has typically been the intellectual property, however, of organic rather than traditional intellectuals, whereas it has been the latter who have typically organized the teaching of cultural theory in both the old and the new universities. Hence the peculiar mismatch by which an actually dominant paradigm is persistently misrepresented as either marginal, archaic, or even simply non-existent. (Milner, 1994, p. 8)

As Herbison (2000, pp. 12–13) notes, for Ulster Protestants, culture also implies ideas of individualism, self-help, and knowledge, democratic and anti-authoritarian ideals that are difficult to equate with Romantic concepts of culture. Neither does individualism blend well with the communalism of many modern nationalisms.

This creates specific problems for Ulster Protestants since it tends to deny them a legitimate cultural identity, making Irish nationalism the only real cultural identity in Ireland. This then casts Ulster Unionists as reactionary and uncultured bigots and/or part of a colonial presence. Thus

Aughey (quoted in Howe, 2000, p. 201) complains that culture is simply equated with cultural nationalism in Ireland, a complaint supported by O'Dowd who claims that Unionists are devoid of all culture and intellectualism (p. 176). Meanwhile, another anti-revisionist, McVeigh, can equate analytic academic work with British imperialism (p. 217). A similar position is also taken by the "green" Marxist, Rolston, who equates objective history with ignoring British imperialism and oppression in Ireland (in Miller, 1998, p. 262).

Here one can identify an immediate analogy with Durkheim's sociology of knowledge and his account of the rise of science. A knowledge that is at first fixed and mystical, yet also shifting, ethereal, and local gives way to a universal knowledge (science) that is abstract but more permanent and based on a knowledge of underlying causes and laws. Science, for Durkheim, strips away the image and mystery to reveal deeper structures and inner forms that are more fixed than the image (Jones, 2001, pp. 32–36). Such an advance he also correlates with the rise of individualism and the decline of the power and authority of religion.

Durkheim also dismissed Romantic claims to individualism as superficial. Romantics' image and emotion-laden knowledge makes them more dependent on their collective; their identity is more bound to it and this makes them more subject to authority. Examples of this can be seen in the anti-revisionist denigration of individualist and liberal ideas associated with Dublin 4, the very people who break away from submission to nationalist narratives. In this way revisionism and science can be identified by Romantics as imperialist since they are part of an external, universalizing culture that supersedes local ones.

Science unlocked mystery and secrecy and revealed the often unseen, it thus gave holders of scientific knowledge power and authority in a revealed truth, undermining established narratives, analytically deconstructing them. It therefore had important political consequences that were felt, in Ireland, as aids to Protestant power:

> Nineteenth century Ireland as a whole might be called a "secret society"—not in the sense that the majority of Irish were bound by oath to agrarian movements, and attended nocturnal meetings to plot the assassination of their landlords, but that secrecy and strategic silence became mechanisms of survival, and alternative spaces for enacting social and political power. As W.E.H. Lecky noted, "Ireland's Catholics learned the lesson which . . . rulers should dread to teach. They became [adept] in the arts of conspiracy and disguise. Secrets known to hundreds were preserved inviolable from authority. (Murphy, in Foley and Ryder, 1998, p. 46)

Science thus became an important aid to "British rule." In fact part of their claim to authority in Ireland was its civilizing, scientific, and enlightenment mission (MacLeod, chapter 1, in Bowler and Whyte 1997).

But perhaps one of the greatest scientific claims of a civilizing mission and legitimacy was the importation of political economy into Ireland. As Bolan and MacDonough (in Foley and Ryder, 1998) observe, it was claimed as scientific and particularly associated with Britain (Howe, 2000, p. 61) and associated with the decline of native industries and economic disruption, beyond Protestant Ulster. Scientific economics conflated with "national" loss echoed another nineteenth-century Romantic theme, of an alternative economy:

> There is even such a thing as Romantic economics, particularly in Germany, in the form, for example, of the economics of men like Fichte and Friederich List, who believed in the necessity of creating an isolated State, *der geschlossene Handelsstaat,* in which the true spiritual force of the nation can exercise itself without being buffeted by other nations: that is to say, where the purpose of economics, the purpose of money and trade, is the spiritual self-perfection of man, and does not obey the so-called unbreakable laws of economics . . . you must not make the mistake of supposing that there are external laws, that there are objective, given laws of economics which are beyond human control. (Berlin, 2000, p. 126)

Irish nationalism thus found in Romantic anti-Enlightenment thought alternative knowledge to Britain's by emphasizing spiritual values as against scientific. Indeed, Griffith, Sinn Fein's founder, was particularly influenced by the Romantic German economist List (Cronin and Regan, 2000, pp. 148–49).

Political economy and being part of the UK were associated with the opening of Irish markets to British goods, manufactures, and economic hegemony. Even the products were scientifically produced (industry as against local craft) and distributed via the technology of modernity (railways and steamships). Consequently, science and technology were viewed by nationalists as negative and destructive of the nation, stripping away mystery and autonomy for Enlightenment and integration.

Catholic Ireland thus developed a deep suspicion of science, which largely helps explain the schism in Irish education over denominational control. Science was only acceptable for nationalists if it was under the control of the Catholic Church, and even then it was not wholly encouraged (O'Leary, 2006). As Bennett observes, both Protestant and Catholic had their reservations about the teaching of science in nondenominational colleges, as proposed in Peel's 1845 "Godless Colleges" (Lyons, 1973, pp. 90–98), "that the educational structure of the colleges allowed revealed religion to be undermined through the teaching of science outside any denominational framework" (Bennett, in Bowler and Whyte, 1997, p. 43).

The Catholic Church preferred to establish a separate Catholic University (University College Dublin—UCD) that could control science. While science was not regarded as wholly un-Catholic it was regarded as requiring its own Catholic ethos, which moved it away from the universalizing and Protestant connotations acquired in Ireland. An example of this was the thought of a major Catholic scientist of the nineteenth century, W. K. Sullivan: "He believes that science should be taught to Catholic students in institutions with a Catholic ethos and staff, so as to eschew secularity and godlessness, and to give science a new cultural identity in Ireland" (Bennett, in Bowler and Whyte, 1997, p. 46). Even so, science was not popular in UCD (Bowler and Whyte, p. 108) and engineering was not taught there until 1909 (Bowler and Whyte, p. 93).

The situation in schools was not dissimilar: "By 1895, while English science schools enrolled 145,000 students, Irish schools taught only 6,500 (fewer than Wales)" (Jarrell, in Bowler and Whyte, 1997, p. 109). As Jarrell further notes (p. 110) 63 percent of Irish science students were located in Ulster (with a third of Ireland's population).

Further, most scientists in Ireland were either Protestant or British imports (Davies, in Kearney, 1985; Bennett, in Bowler and Whyte, 1997). In his survey of nineteenth-century eminent Irish scientists, Bennett states:

> 25% were born in Britain, 8% on the continent and 3% elsewhere. Of those born in Ireland, or of Irish parents temporarily abroad, 11% were wholly and a further 25% partly educated in Britain.
>   Of the members of the sample born in Ireland I have been able to establish the faiths of 87% and of these 62% were church of Ireland, 10% Nonconformists, 17% Protestants about whom I could not be more precise and 10% were Roman Catholics. (Bennett, in Bowler and Whyte, 1997, pp. 37–38)

And as Davies (Kearney, 1985) articulates ideas of Catholic socio-economic or political disadvantage offer little explanation. Many eminent scientists rose from humble origins, but the only examples in Ireland were two Ulster Protestants (Kearney, 1985, p. 306).

The importation of scientists also had ideological implications as science became associated with the British Government who tried to promote it in Ireland, while many of the individual institutions used to foster science in Ireland were also British, such as the Royal Society or the Science Museum in Kensington. As Bennett (Bowler and Whyte, 1997) notes, not only was much Irish science driven by Government but it was also driven by concepts of science as enlightened, nondenominational, and therefore integrative and Unionist in ethos.

Science in Ireland thus had major British and Protestant connotations that made it ideologically alien to Catholic nationalists and as strengthening Unionist control and British cultural penetration and identity. It was seen as anti-religious, anti-Catholic and non-Irish:

> Science itself was in danger of being ethnicised as foreign (not truly Irish), categorised as anti-religious (not acceptably Catholic) and classified as socially distant. The Anglo-Irish had their "places of knowledge" (to borrow Ophir and Shapin again)—estates, gentlemen's houses, observatories, botanical gardens, rooms of curiositie—and so what Ophir and Shapin say would seem vividly to apply to the Irish case: "the place of knowledge is implicated in the network of relations between knowledge and power, in the distribution of knowledge in society, in perceptions of validity and legitimacy. (Foster, in Bowler and Whyte, 1997, p. 124)

As Foster further argues, this also struck at the source of the Catholic Church's power in Ireland, which was the control of social relationships, very pertinent to Durkheim's sociology.

However, broad attitudes to science apply mostly to Southern Ireland (Foster, in Bowler and Whyte, 1997, p. 131) with a consequent tendency to overlook Ulster: "Still, the history of intellectual Belfast—continuous with intellectual cities in Britain, especially with those in the industrialised midlands and North of England and lowlands of Scotland . . . has been driven underground" (Foster, in Bowler and Whyte, 1997, p. 131). Here the social locus and dominant relations were industrial, urban, middle class, and Presbyterian, mostly non-conformists who had previously been excluded from professional occupations and had to turn to engineering and mechanics as alternative occupations. Also, much of Ulster's scientific and technological knowledge was imported from Scotland and hence not included in either the ascendancy or nationalist consciousness.

The Ulster Scottish connection is particularly important here, since until the late eighteenth century Presbyterians were barred from Ireland's only university (Trinity College, Dublin, an Anglican institution). Scotland was also closer to Ulster, easier to access and part of a traditional link going back to the fourteenth century. Thus the majority of Ulster students went to Scotland, especially Glasgow, where the established church was Presbyterian. Thus formal education in Ulster was dominated by Scots Presbyterian thought (Erskine and Lucy, 1997; Herbison, 2000). Equally many teachers in Scottish universities were from Ulster, the most famous being Francis Hutcheson, who held the chair of moral philosophy at Glasgow from 1729–46 and taught both Adam Smith and Carlyle as well as being a major influence on Hume (Erskine and Lucy, 1997, p. 38; Broadie, 2007).

Consequently, Ulster was intellectually part of the Scottish Enlightenment:

> The heady mixture of democratic consensus and schism inherent in Presbyterianism combined with the intellectual climate of the scientific revolution and the Age of Reason to produce the Scottish Enlightenment. It was an atmosphere that Ulster students at their most impressionable age came into their own and discovered that, however oppressed at home, in Scotland they were an accepted part of a vigorous intellectual establishment. (Erskine and Lucy, 1997, p. 37)

One should think of an Ulster-Scots intellectual tradition symbolized by the late nineteenth century Ulster physicist Lord Kelvin who spent 50 years at Glasgow University and gained a peerage. This found a non-academic corollary in the industrial and manufacturing centers of Belfast and Glasgow, built on science and technology, engineering and international trade, market economics and liberal individualism (the very things Irish nationalism revolted against). As Lucy (1995, p. ix, 26, and 89) observes, both liberal and industrialist fears were central to Ulster opposition to Home Rule.

Ulster was part of the Scottish Enlightenment tradition:

> By the late eighteenth century, a strong material basis had developed for sustained cultural and intellectual cross-fertilization between Ulster and Scotland. Against the general background of demographic growth and industrial expansion, the communications infrastructure improved and business relationships flourished. A tangible product of increasing contact was migration. Again, this was a reciprocal process with Scottish mechanics engaged for Ulster firms, and Ulster weavers and bleachers imported into the Scottish linen industry. (Erskine and Lucy, 1997, p. 67)

This helps to isolate out Ulster Protestants from both a Catholic nationalist and a Hellenistic Anglo-Irish (that England can empathize with) culture. It also helps deny an Ulster culture to many outsiders, excepting Scotland, for, as Loughlin (1995, p. 98 and 201) observes, Britain began to redefine itself in the 1930s in an arcadian England fashion (partly influenced by Leavis and Eliot), which helped isolate Ulster out as non-British. Contemporaneously, the same process helped to gain English, but not Scottish, sympathy for Irish nationalist ideals that saw Ulster Unionists as uncultured: "For

Irish intellectuals, Ulster Unionists are the Hebraists and the Philistines of the island, neither the Hellenists of the Anglo-Irish nor the artistic Celts of the native Irish. They are assumed to lead sub-intellectual lives" (Foster, in O'Dowd, 1996, p. 89).

This reflects both the way that culture became associated with art and the difficulty that arts-based culture has in recognizing science as culture. It also reflects the way that Irish studies and culture has become infused with purely nationalist concepts that write out science as culture and implicitly discriminates against Ulster unionism. It also indicates how a dominant (nationalist) narrative blots out less fashionable, or numerous, ones. Empirical reality is first denied (the nationalist dismissal of Unionism) but it continually re-emerges to disrupt the nationalist narrative as reality reasserts itself (unionism and revisionism).

As O'Dowd (1996, pp. 1–21) observes, science was associated with a "natural" British state building that grew out of a core pre-existing identity to encompass backward peripheral regions such as Ireland. It was, in its own image, and that of early sociologists, modernizing, progressive, and civilizing and regarded as a natural process. Building nations in opposition to the state required an opposite kind of intellectual activity and the assertion of non-science identities. It therefore requires considerable effort to construct a nation able to ward off scientific deconstruction.

This brings one back to anti-revisionism in Irish history. The function of the intellectual and cultural (arts) theorist was to construct the image or vision of a nation to ward off the structures and strictures of scientific analysis associated with (British) statehood. Science, unless strictly controlled, was an enemy of Romantic nationalism and the existence of a science-based culture (Ulster) within its territory could hardly be dealt with by scientific means. Hence, better merely to denigrate it from the perspective of cultural aesthetics, alternative values or merely ignore it.

Thus, as Howe (2000, pp. 44, 121, 138, 182–83) observes, the Irish nationalist claims of imperialism and colonization are built on literary attacks, or, in social science, by analogy, but not by scientific analysis. Where attempts are made at serious analysis using specific models of imperialism, such as Lenin's, the Marxist authors Bew, Gibbon, and Patterson (1979) found the arguments did not stand up to testing (Patterson writes a particularly damning critique of Republican claims to socialism, 1989).

Also, partly because Ulster Unionists saw themselves in a "natural," "all-British" mode, they never thought to mount a serious intellectual challenge to defend their culture, their idea. Consequently, they could neither effectively assert their separate identity nor ward off nationalist hegemony in Ireland. Only their stubborn refusal to be absorbed into a nationalist Ireland, for reasons they may well not have been fully conscious of, reminded outsiders of their separate existence.

This was further exacerbated for Ulster Unionists by the disappearance of Southern Unionists (most simply left Ireland or kept quiet due to intimidation; Hart, 1999, chapter 12) in the new Irish nation. But while Southern Protestants were dominated by Ascendancy figures, for whom science was often a disinterested past-time, applied, if at all, mainly to government, in Ulster it was applied as the basis of economic life and industry (Foster, in O'Dowd, 1996), a working culture lived out in daily life not as an elite aristocratic interest.

## The Romantics in Ireland

As many historians of nationalism observe, after its early unification stages it quickly became associated with an anti-science, anti-industry and anti-modernity assertion of alternative values. A return to the soil, nature, and mystic religion and rejection of material and industrial values became the vogue (Kedourie, 1993, pp. 97–98; Greenfeld, 1993, pp. 386–95; Hobsbawm, 1992, pp. 101–4). Not only did this occur among ethnic nationalisms but also among the unification elites. A high (Hellenistic) culture of literature, arts and crafts, rural idylls, and an idealization of medieval life established itself, led in Britain by Arnold, Leavis, Eliot, and William Morris (Milner, 1994, chapter 2).

A particularly strong influence were the German Romantics (Berlin, 2000, chapter 5; Greenfeld, 1993, chapter 4) who rejected modern civilization as represented in the French Revolutionary School of progress and Enlightenment (which Durkheim championed) or English economics and utilitarianism. These were seen as superficial, lacking in soul, and also destructive of the interests of German arts and humanities graduates (Berlin, 2000; Greenfeld, 1993; Mayer, 1975; O'Boyle, 1970). Romantics turned to a "deeper" inner knowledge built on reflection and spiritual development, not utilitarian or rational knowledge.

The Romantic tradition derived from Kant, Fichte, and Hegel was given its most overt expression in the works of German philosophers such as Lessing, Feuerbach, and Herder. They were the catalyst for a non-scientific concept of the nation built on images not easily deniable and open to easy experience (the things that Durkheim's attacked). Most important here was the existence of distinct (to them) language groups, customs, folklore, costumes, and fairy tales (such as the Grimm brothers were busy collecting). These helped to create "natural" borders in the minds of Romantics, not artificially fixed as in French civilization.

Such folk groups and customs were to be found mostly among the peasant populations of Europe who were now interpreted as containing an alternative knowledge and wisdom. Their knowledge was of the soil, and local, and their commitment to religion indicated a spiritual message that provided the basis for a non-material (non-industrial) and natural way of life. Concomitant with this was an asceticism that equated virtue with lack of material wealth, emotion over calculation (rational thought), and even a tolerance of violence:

> To be thoroughly satisfactory, the emotion must be direct and violent and quite uninformed by thought. The man of sensibility would be moved to tears by the sight of a single destitute peasant family, but would be cold to well thought out schemes for ameliorating the lot of peasants as a class. The poor were supposed to possess more virtue than the rich; the sage was thought of as a man who retires from the corruption of courts to enjoy the peaceful pleasures of an unambitious rural existence. (Russell, 1996, p. 651)

A way of life that equated with peasant society and was now threatened by Enlightenment civilization and industrial progress became the basis for much ethnic nationalism.

An alternative world was posited where science, universalism, and unifying norms and values are replaced by artistic and unique ones—Romantic: "The whole movement is an attempt to impose an aesthetic model upon reality, to say that everything should obey the rules of art" (Berlin, 2000a, p. 146). In this world, to understand and to know in the scientific sense was to deny and destroy life itself and useless folly:

> When Wordsworth said that to dissect is to murder, this is approximately what he meant: and he was much the mildest of those who expressed this view.
> To ignore this, to evade it, to attempt to see things as submissive to some kind of intellectualisation, some sort of plan, to attempt to draw up a set of rules, or a set of laws, or a formula, is a form of self-indulgence, and in the end suicidal stupidity. (Berlin, 2000a, p. 120)

The essence of life as ephemeral was a key message, with deep forces and spiritual expression, inexhaustible and not reducible to scientific knowledge, which merely killed the life giving vitality of the subject—its will. This will or force could only be known via its outward images or symbols, which left an impression on the mind. Just as dissecting a butterfly tells you nothing about its living vitality and essence, only its dead form, so science could tell you nothing about a nation's being. So, only the living expression of the nation, symbolized in its culture, and its will to impose itself gave anyone a feeling for what it was.

For Romantics, the most important cultural criterion was language, the peasant vernacular, representing a unique culture with its own inherent meanings and value, not the universalizing languages of Enlightenment (French) or industry and political economy (English). Vernaculars were clear and distinct, different in words and construction and in expressing different meanings, local and of an esoteric (mystical) nature (Lyon, 1994; Greenfeld, 1993, p. 319). Within the language was then contained all the folk-tales, myths, and other expressions of nationhood, which in turn are supposed to express deep, inner meanings reflecting the soul of the nation, its vital being (Berlin, 2000a, p. 60–61; Greenfeld, 1993, p. 369).

This was not the original basis of Irish Catholic national consciousness, often equated with O'Connell, but became its foundation under Parnell and the literary revival of the late nineteenth century (Boyce, 1991; Foster, 1989a; Lyons, 1973):

> For the early nineteenth century saw the emergence of the Irish Roman Catholics as a political entity, and the development of their political consciousness inspired by their very real and keenly felt social and economic grievances. Catholic needs and aspirations were given organization and direction by Daniel O'Connell . . . no single minded nationalist, desiring self-government above good government; on the contrary, he dreaded the separation of Great Britain and Ireland that he feared must come if the Catholics did not participate in the benefits of the Union. (Boyce, 1991, p. 132)

The man responsible for mobilizing Catholic political consciousness in the first half of the nineteenth century was thus in the universalizing camp of nationalism, seeking integration not separation. He was keen to modernize and industrialize Ireland, to catch up with Britain: "His nationalism was largely modernizing, Enlightenment project . . . he emphasised the calm rationality of his own political arguments" (Howes, in Foley and Ryder, 1998, p. 155).

The critical shift in Catholic/nationalist sentiment appears to begin around the Famine (1845–47) and the events following when the Irish economy was radically transformed in Ulster and the rest of Ireland. The most important input here is from Young Ireland in the 1840s and its newspaper *The Nation*, which grew out of O'Connell's movement:

> The mid-nineteenth century movement known as Young Ireland marked the emergence of an Irish nationalism that was more ethnic and cultural than civic and constitutional. Although the movement fizzled out in the abortive rising

of 1848, its cultural and political legacies were extensive. The poetry of Young Ireland was arguably the most popular body of literature in Ireland for the rest of the century, and Young Ireland's nationalism played a key role in structuring later movements. (Howes, in Foley and Ryder, 1998, p. 151)

Associated most famously with figures such as Thomas Davis, John Dillon, Gavan Duffy, Smith O'Brien, James Mangan, and Lady Wilde, Young Ireland provided the basis for a cultural nationalism built on literature and the arts and openly espousing Romantic nationalist concepts: "It was to be realized not by politics but by cultural regeneration; it was to find its salvation, not in a modern industrial state, but in those parts of Ireland which had remained, as Davis put it, 'faithful and romantic'" (Boyce, 1991, p. 169).

For Davis, the most prominent Young Irelander, cultural regeneration implied the use of Gaelic, as the soul of the nation. Art was to be national and to serve a national purpose and consciousness, a distinct culture. In this he introduced into Irish life the strands of thought that emerged later in the century in both the Anglo-Irish and the Gaelic-Irish literary revival, so strongly associated with the triumph of Irish nationalism (Boyce, 1991, chapter 8; Lyons, 1982, chapter 3). Davis speaks of rejection of all things English, such as science, and an inward-looking protectionism of traditional Ireland:

> Thomas Davis wrote in 1845 that "the fairies and the banshee, the poor scholar and the ribbonman, the Orange Lodge, the illicit still, and the faction fight are disappearing into history." Much indeed was disappearing, and many concluded that malevolent English influence obliterated "historic" Ireland. (Lee, 1989a, p. 165)

Thus it should come as no surprise that a scientific history or sociology should be seen as a threat to Irish Nationalism. The inspiration for this outlook was provided by Germany: "Young Ireland was more idealistic, more influenced by German romanticism, less shaped by Irish Catholicism, and tended to conceptualize the nation in cultural rather than constitutional terms" (Howes, in Foley and Ryder, 1998, p. 152). Davis's own conversion to nationalism was typically Germanic:

> He fell under the influence of German romanticism . . . He fulminated against: "modern Anglicanism, i.e. utilitarianism . . . which measures prosperity by exchangeable value, measures duty by gain, and limits desire to clothes, food, and respectability" . . .
>
> A nation had a unique character . . . A nation was defined by its culture, by which Davis meant its literature, its history, and above all, embodying these, its language. (Boyce, 1991, p. 155)

As Stoter (Foley and Ryder, 1998) indicates, Herder, Lessing and the Grimm Brothers all had a powerful influence on Young Ireland's thinking. Davis conflated biblical with political images in the same way that Lessing did and spoke of a chosen people wherein, significantly, Christianity became nation. Davis's emphasis on the importance of language is borrowed directly from Herder, as is his association of people with the soil, and also his belief that there exists a natural being to the nation that politically implies self-determination for spiritual fulfillment.

Davis frequently held German Romantics up as Ireland's model, particularly in its pedagogical developments of both the heart and the mind:

> Exactly what kind of education Davis had in mind becomes apparent right from the start of his speech when he asserts to his audience: "the power of self-education, self-conduct, is yours: "Think wrongly if you will—but think for yourselves." What is demanded here is an independence from structures and a maturity of thought. The second part of this sentence . . . is taken directly from Lessing . . . Another literary borrowing made by Davis, this time from Herder: "Calling for the revival of the Irish language," O'Neill writes, "he [Davis] pointed to Germany's success in stopping "the incipient creeping progress of French" for "no sooner had she succeeded than her genius, which had tossed her in a hot trance, sprang up fresh and triumphant." (Stoter, in Foley and Ryder, 1998, p. 176)

This provided an important role model for Ireland against England (invariably implying Britain as a whole), not only in keeping out linguistic impurities but also structural (science) impurities that corrupt the soul.

And, just as Davis borrowed from Herder in language and literary matters so Gavan Duffy borrowed from Herder and Goethe when publishing his collection of folk songs and ballads (Foley and Ryder, 1998, p. 178). Duffy believed that they contained the spirit of the people and were the vehicle of cultural transmission as did the Grimm Brothers who corresponded directly with one of the other great Irish folklore collectors T. C. Croker (Foley and Ryder, 1998, p. 179).

Young Ireland also borrowed from the Sturm und Drang school of Romanticism (Berlin, 2000, pp. 55–57) that turned struggle and strife, suffering and violence, emotion and feeling into noble things: action mediated by the heart and feeling, visions and images to stir imaginations, not scientific analysis or underlying structures and causes. Thus Lady Wilde (Mother of Oscar): "In her works tears constitute a spectacle of suffering capable of generating national feeling and spurring nationalist action: they also signify that a viewer is reacting properly to that spectacle" (Howes, in Foley and Ryder, 1998, p. 158).

These were images of suffering that later informed the blood sacrifice of Patrick Pearse in 1916 (MacDonagh, 1983, pp. 85–88). Spectacle and emotive feeling, not rational analysis, were central to Romantic Ireland. As MacDonagh's (1983) title *States of Mind* aptly implies, there were two different casts of mind at work in Ireland, a Protestant Unionist one based on science and a Catholic nationalist one based on Romantic feeling.

In the Romantic vision the purpose of national independence was not measured in quantifiable, scientific terms of good government, but in terms of cultural and spiritual development and expression. For Romantics the same applied to laws, they were not to be judged in terms of happiness, harmony, or even justice, but in terms of unleashing primeval forces and creative wills, of spiritual expression, thus:

> Law is the product of the beating force within the nation, of dark traditional forces, of its organic sap which flows through its body as through a tree, of something which we cannot identify and cannot analyse, but which everyone who is true to his country feels coursing through his veins. Law is a traditional growth, partly a matter of circumstances, but partly the inner soul of the nation . . . every nation has its own law, every nation has its own shape; this shape goes far into the misty past, its roots are somewhere in the darkness, and unless its roots are in the darkness it is too easily overthrown. (Berlin, 2000a, p. 125)

Nothing further from scientific government could be imagined; this government was premised on a world in which morals, politics, and aesthetics are subjective and not objective, feeling not analysis. This German Romantic ideal was incorporated into Irish nationalism as the perfect foil to British science and utilitarianism:

> That science should figure as an element in the Irish Cultural Revival of the late nineteenth- and early twentieth-century appears at first view paradoxical, since many of the premises of that revival were anti-scientific. The familiar anatomy of the movement led by Yeats, Gregory and Synge, with its roots in romantic and symbolist anti-materialism, need not be reiterated here. (Lysaght, in Bowler and Whyte, 1997, p. 153)

They probably do need reiterating to explain modern hostility toward revisionist Irish history. Nationalist Ireland was largely a cultural and subjective construct, against scientific rationalism. As such the Irish state now had a vested interest in preserving its (Romantic) national integrity, and, as O'Dowd observes, intellectuals are often employed by states precisely to do this: "Of course, once a national state is established nationalist intellectuals take on the additional role of legitimising a particular political and social order. In this context the intellegentsia become legislators of social and cultural values." (O'Dowd, 1996, p. 18) Durkheim would have understood the point well, given his close association with the French Third Republic. Revisionist history goes to the heart of the nation-state's existence and the role of intellectuals in it.

## Literary Revivals, Gaelic and Anglo

Cultural specificity, particularly literary, was the basis of nationalist claims for an independent Ireland (Kiberd, in Foster, 1992; Lyons, 1982, chapter 4), which had to be clearly demarcated from English literature to legitimate their claim and Irish nationalists went to great lengths to do this. Most important was using Gaelic and a uniquely Irish expression, distinctly un-English, even if a copy: "For every English action, there must be an equal and opposite Irish reaction—for soccer, Gaelic football; for hockey, hurling; for trousers, a kilt" (Kiberd, in Foster, 1992, p. 267).

Simply being literary was inadequate, it must be uniquely Irish, expressing specific Irish values and qualities that implied Romantic, eulogizing peasant values and life, preferably in Gaelic, but English where the majority no longer spoke Gaelic. And this did act to spur on a Gaelic language revival (the Gaelic League, founded in 1893, following on from the Gaelic Athletic Association, founded 1884).

The Gaelic revival went far beyond language and expressed through literature all aspects of "authentic" Irish life and culture, including music, where "the Irish idiom expresses deep things that have not been expressed by Beethoven, Bach, Brahms, Elgar or Sibelius—by any of the great composers" (Brown, 1981, p. 147).

This was something that the Anglo-Irish literary revival could not offer, for not only was it written in English but its "Anglo essence implied an English idiom and view of Ireland, associated then as now as cosmopolitan, oppressive, and imperialistic: "The Celt and the Irish language were the new orthodoxies comprising an ethnic dogmatism that cast Anglo-Ireland in the role of alien persecutor of the one true faith" (Brown, 1981, p. 107).

The Anglo-Irish tradition, associated with writers such as Yeats, Synge, and Joyce did produce artists of international caliber, an arts corollary to the Ascendancy's Hellenistic science, a high literary cultural effort to understand and critically analyze Ireland. Yeats specifically sought to make an Irish contribution to European culture (Lyons, 1982, p. 39) making him cosmopolitan and modern, the very things Irish Nationalism opposed. His aesthetics were an attempt to enlighten, which he defended as just as much service to Ireland as anything else. Arthur Griffith, of Sinn Fein, was unimpressed: "Griffith had no difficulty in disposing of such equivocation, opening the way as it seemed to do towards the dreaded cosmopolitan heresy. 'Cosmopolitanism,' he replied, 'never produced a great artist nor a good man yet nor ever will'" (Lyons, 1982, p. 67).

A similar fate befell Synge whose play, "In the Shadow of the Glen," provoked riots in Dublin when performed (1907), since it attacked the prudery, sexual repression, and social relations of rural, Catholic Ireland:

> For daughters, especially, premarital virginity was not only a moral but also a social imperative, since their marriageability was an important element in the tortuous but life-long endeavour to add field to field. To destroy a girls "character" by intercourse outside wedlock was regarded in peasant eyes as "murder" and actually so called in some parts of the country. (Lyons, 1982, p. 157)

What nationalist Ireland wanted was a eulogy of Catholic, peasant values not a critical appraisal of such "unique" characteristics. Gaelic Ireland reflected an anti-intellectualism that reflected the dominance of small farmers, shopkeepers, and the Catholic priests recruited from their ranks that confirmed rural values (Brown, 1981, p. 30). As such it represents an example of Gellner's (1983) low culture, threatened by science and cosmopolitanism, just as traditional religion was. Thus:

> The symbol system of the new nationalism was parallel with that of Irish Catholicism and was a translation of the latter into political terms. Neo-Gaelic nationalism retained the values of self-sacrifice for the group, religious communalism, purity, respect for women, fear of external evils and idealism which were taught by the Irish Catholicism of the period. (Garvin, 1981, p. 104)

It was for this reason that Gaelic-Ireland triumphed over Anglo-Ireland (Lyons, 1982, chapters 3 and 4): It reconfirmed the values and interests of the dominant social relations, even though its major authors are mostly forgotten now (such as Canon Sheehan or Daniel Corkery) reflecting Berlin's (2000a, p. 111) dismissal of Romantic art as third rate. It helped defend established rural interests and relations against all that threatened it in modernization and cosmopolitanism by projecting an arcadian vision of a uniquely Gaelic peasant life and alternative values superior to those of corrupt England and modernity.

> In the writings of Canon Sheehan, London was rather similarly portrayed as the centre of imperial and moneyed evil. Father Peter O'Leary supplied the Gaelic League and a wider public with similar images of an English bloated plutocracy vs an Irish virtuous asceticism. Romantic images of selflessness and asceticism in a corrupt world abounded in the nationalist literature of the

period, echoing not only the priestly subculture so conspicuous at the time in Ireland, but also an international zeitgeist. (Garvin, in Boyce, 1988, p. 107)

De-Anglicizing Ireland was the essence of the Gaelic cultural appeal because England was regarded as threatening its traditional way of life:

> Irish Catholic culture and traditional rural life were under grave and rapidly mounting threat from anglicisation. Croke had sounded the toxin as early as 1884: "England's accents," he declaimed, "her vicious literature, her music, her dances, and her manifold mannerisms . . . (are) not racy of the soil, but rather alien, on the contrary to it, as are, for the most part, the men and women who first imported and still continued to patronise them." Over the next three decades, the polarisation of "alien" and "native" intensified, as did the double identification of "native" with Catholic and Irish speaking. (MacDonagh, 1983, p. 114)

Anglo-Ireland represented the alien, English values critically dissecting Gaelic life.

Given the rejection of cosmopolitan criteria anti-revisionists had to resort to assertion and analogy to defend nationalism, even in culture, which, in turn, helps explain the resort to imperialist and colonial arguments. These are "external" and thus claimed to be an imposition over the national. Once again, one returns to the revisionist debate and identifies the claim to an exception for Irish literature, as with Irish history, from external or universal standards since it has its own inner standards and values from which alone it should be judged.

On the latter point it is instructive to note the anti-revisionist objection to revisionist historians educated outside of Ireland. A similar point may be made about many of Ulster's Presbyterians, but could not be made against most anti-revisionists. Even in the nineteenth century, Brown (1981, p. 30) has observed how the Catholic seminaries of Ireland produced a homegrown priesthood that dominated the education of Catholic Ireland as education became increasingly denominational. A parochial self-defense may be identified as the core of an Irish nationalism that cannot be defended via international and rational standards.

Gaelic and Catholicism became a way of defining Ireland off from England, which was the important legacy of Davis and Young Ireland:

> Whereas O'Connell opposed the retention of the Irish language as a barrier to economic development, constitutional advance and modernisation, Davis was anxious to retain it precisely because it was a barrier—to English influence. It was a short step from denouncing this influence because it was "alien" to

denouncing it per se, for its supposed characteristics of utilitarianism, urban-isation and the like. Sooner or later, Gaelic would be seen as an offensive as well as a defensive weapon in the armoury of Irish nationalism; and sooner or later some would see that nationalism as essentially dependent on the Irish language. (MacDonagh, 1983, p. 111)

At a time of great social change and confusion over identity in nineteenth-century Ireland Gaelic responded well to an ontological need for place and continuity in response to the rapid modernization associated with (Protes-tant) England. Gaelic and Catholic provided an identity and difference that was comforting for many Irishmen (Connolly, 1985, p. 60) making them the bedrock of Irish nationalist identity. It told a good story that satisfied popular needs.

From this one might say that revisionists fail to tell a good story that satisfies popular needs. Unlike a good poem or novel they don't inspire their readers to Romantic visions and action. Rather, they suggest a critical dis-tance from heroic deeds and mystical missions, scientific caution as against emotional mobilization.

However, even if Gaelic Ireland represented only a third-rate Romantic ideal, it won because it had popular resonance with a Catholic population who could associate with a Gaelic heritage. It provided self-pride and in Romanticism found a philosophical base from which to legitimize it. This legitimacy was enhanced by the cultural studies legacy of Arnold and his followers, of anti-science with all its implications, of in-built bias for arts-cultural constructs, even if low ones (Foster, in O'Dowd, 1996). And it is this cultural vision of the nation as a spiritual and social union that dom-inates modern nationalism and stands in stark contrast to Durkheimian ideals.

This favors Irish nationalism and severely handicaps Ulster Unionists, whose intellectual case may be as good as nationalism's but less fashionable (Foster, in O'Dowd, 1996). Ulster Protestants' science culture, if accepted at all, is deemed of a lesser status, certainly not one that permits nationalists to accept its autonomous existence. Nor does it allow Unionists to sufficiently distance themselves from "English" concepts and associations that invoke spurious claims of imperialism.

Thus science has major political implications as a basis for knowledge, reality, and truth; it is posed as the opposite of culture, a threat to Ireland's identity, interests, and legitimacy. The partition of Ireland now represents a fundamental divide between an Enlightenment and a Romantic culture, two different moral schemas and concepts of truth that deny a shared "imagined community" or "conscience collective" and oppose each other's legitimacy.

Also, it helps to explain the lack of empathy for Ulster Protestants from an outside world that is possibly more attuned to Romantic nationalism.

An arts-based Romantic culture also blends well with Catholicism and its scholasticism. Both emphasize image, attacked by Protestants. Science was an essential tool to get beneath the image and deconstruct to find a more fundamental truth, as Durkheim observed. Thus both culture and Catholicism have a vested interest in rejecting science as a legitimate political base (one is now back at the kind of problems Durkheim addressed in France). This helps explain the Protestants alienation from Irish nationalism and the resistance of nationalism to granting Unionism an equal political legitimacy. But what now needs explaining is the origin of this divide in Ireland.

# CHAPTER 6

# Ireland and Nationalism

Nationalists claim a history of eight hundred years of Irish national struggle against British/English oppression or imperialism (Howe, 2000, chapter 1), which few modern historians would accept (McGarry, 2011). First, it was Normans who invaded twelfth-century Ireland; second, as Riordan (1990) reminds us, in pre-seventeenth-century Ireland, warfare was endemic and a Gaelic way of life, against each other as much as the Crown (who were accepted as legitimate rulers). Further, nationalism is a recent concept and irrelevant to judging anything in Ireland until the last two hundred years. In addition, the idea of natural borders is new (Heslinga, 1979, chapter 4) and the Irish Sea can as easily imply unity between Ireland and Britain as division.

However, the Anglo-Norman Crown did impose some kind of administrative-political unity over an island culture recognized as Gaelic, and by the fourteenth century there was a Parliament in Dublin with nominal authority over the whole island; although, in reality, large tracts of Ireland were beyond its control and Gaelic chiefs indulged themselves in their internecine warfare (Riordan, 1990). Only under the Tudors and Stuarts was Crown authority extended over the whole island.

The seventeenth century was crucial, since the wars in Ireland (often extensions of wider European struggles over religion and dynastic supremacy) resulted in the replacement of the Catholic aristocracy with a Protestant English-speaking one, imported from England, and several "plantations" of settlers. The largest plantation was in Ulster, of Scots and English, later added to by Scots fleeing Famine in Scotland and Huguenots fleeing religious persecution in France. Ulster, before plantation, was the least populated (around twenty thousand covering nine counties) and most economically backward region in Ireland (Connolly, 2008, 2009; Bardon, 2011). Indeed, a major purpose was economic development; civility, order, and religion being regarded as by-products of this, while many Catholics (planters and natives) were also granted lands (Elliott, 2001; Bardon 2011).

During this period, an English, Protestant (Anglican—Church of Ireland) Ascendancy replaced the previous Catholic aristocracy. An Anglican elite with a political and legal monopoly now ruled over a population of Catholic peasants who were politically and legally disenfranchised under the Penal Laws, progressively introduced after 1695 (Foster, 1989; Connolly, 2008). The Catholics formed a traditional subsistence peasantry whose Church was tolerated only at the village priest and parochial structure level, where they also maintained a network of rudimentary schools, from which future priests were recruited (Foster, 1989, p. 208). The Church of Ireland became the established church and only its members were allowed full legal, political, and civil rights (a situation in accord with post–Treaty of Westphalia European norms).

Meanwhile in Ulster the majority were Protestant (mostly Presbyterian Dissenters) working farmers and tenants of an Anglican aristocracy. They were also traders and imbued with the Calvinist ideals and commercial outlook of early modern capitalism (Bardon, 2011; Connolly, 2009; Greenfeld, 2003). As Dissenters they were also legally and politically excluded, although with slightly better property rights than Catholics:

> The Ulster plantation provided a new and un-assimilable element to the Irish population . . . From that point on, the population was sharply divided into planters and Gaels . . . the planters, it is argued, changed the face of Ulster by the end of the seventeenth century, building the plantation towns, clearing the woodlands and replacing the Irish pastoral habits with intensive cultivation. A thriving and industrious community with the puritan ethic that hard work was a virtue, they laid the foundations of Ulster's future industrial development, and also of the partition of Ireland in the twentieth century. (Stewart, 1989, pp. 23–24)

Put in Durkheimian terms, they brought about new social relations and consciousness.

However, seventeenth century wars had left a strong legacy: the Catholic uprising (1641) "massacre of the Protestants"; Cromwell's revenge and subjugation of Ireland (1649–51); and King William's triumph over (Catholic) King James that secured the Protestant Ascendancy (1689–91) (Connolly, 2008; Foster, 1989) created the basis for future resentments, divisions, fear, and distrust: "Sooner or later in each successive crisis the cry is raised of, '1641 come again.' The fear which it inspired survives in the Protestant subconscious as the memory of the Penal Laws or the Famine persists in the Catholic" (Stewart, 1989, p. 49).

This fear of massacre, a distinct economic ethos, and Calvinist theology combined to create a distinct and aggressive Protestantism in Ireland, especially in Ulster, with "that uncompromising Calvinism that was to influence so much of its subsequent history. These Presbyterians brought with them a characteristic tendency towards individualism and heterodoxy, both in matters of doctrine and of organization" (Lyons, 1982, pp. 124–25). That is to say,

> The aggressive and vivacious drives of early capitalism and imperialism were at work, immensely destructive of traditional cultures, but also creative and productive. What was perceived in Ireland was that one nation within the country had developed a tendency which was proving to be destructive of the social fabric of the other. (de Paor, 1986, p. 137)

The Ascendancy, meanwhile, contentedly maintained their traditional aristocratic role of presiding over the normal relationships of landlord and peasant: "The English ambition was, after all, to create a stable landowning aristocracy as well as English law and a docile church" (Foster, 1989, p. 32). Eventually, they would see themselves as Irish: "Those who in the 1690's called themselves 'the Protestants of Ireland' or even 'the English of this Kingdom' could see themselves as 'Irish Gentlemen' by the 1720's" (Foster, 1989, p. 178).

Linked, however, into their exclusive Anglican diocesan and parochial relationships, which also formed the governmental structure of Ireland, they exercised an exclusive control of administrative and political machinery whose end was to rule and protect their property and privileges. However, as the eighteenth century wore on, the Penal Laws (against Catholics) and Test Acts (against Dissenters) were relaxed and Catholics and Dissenters advanced in public life, especially following the growth of Catholic and Presbyterian mercantile middle classes. The economy prospered and political stability was established. However, ordinary Catholic peasants "sank to the position of mere cottiers, holding a few acres of land from year to year and depending upon their wages to make up the rent, wages were low and rents high, and the cottier lived at a bare subsistence level" (Beckett, 1969, p. 173).

However, in 1798 rebellion broke out, led primarily by Ulster Presbyterian radicals with some middle-class Catholic support in Dublin. This was inspired by Enlightenment (particularly Scottish) ideals, the American and French Revolutions, Parliamentary reform movements in Ireland and Britain, and new economic imperatives. Its organizational structure was built around the 1780s Volunteer (local militia) movement, which recruited heavily from Dissenters and was especially strong in Ulster (Foster, 1989).

Their enlightened radicalism culminated in the 1798 United Irish rebellion, which despite the shock it gave the "establishment" was eventually put down after it had degenerated into sectarian atrocities that indicated a less than united Ireland (Foster, 1989; Connolly, 2008; Elliott, 2001) and renewed sectarian fears. However, its real import is that modern nationalists date their nationalism from 1798 and its leaders, Wolf Tone and Robert Emmet.

In addition, the 1790s also revealed new forms of social organization of future significance. First was the Orange Order (1795): initially a band of Anglican laborers clashing with Catholics over jobs in Ulster, significant for an emerging industrial economy. Second was the social basis of Ulster's United Irish, almost exclusively Presbyterian and largely restricted to a particular class, again significant for an emerging industrial economy of linen merchants, weavers, and spinners:

> The vast majority of weavers in mid- and north Antrim and mid- and north Down were independent rather than proletarian. Their economic independence was coupled with a vigorous ideological independence. As a group they constituted the core of the oral and literary cultures of the communities in which they lived. In most areas independent weavers had formed reading societies which bought and distributed books, often supported by subscription, a local vernacular "bard," and acted as centres of political, economic and theological debate. (Gibbon, 1975, p. 30)

However, the sectarian nature of 1798 created an all-Protestant sense of self-defense against a commonly perceived Catholic threat. Self-taught, independent in religion, politics, and economics, non-Ascendancy and Dissenting Protestant ideals helped inform an all-Protestant and distinct Ulster consciousness and structure of relations. Meanwhile the Catholic world remained largely concealed and looked down upon, maintaining their own internal relations and conscious separation: "We clearly have here a people already learning the art of concealment" (Corrish, 1985, p. 70).

After the rebellion, the Irish Parliament was abolished and merged into an all United Kingdom Parliament (Act of Union, 1800) in London, with Irish MPs and Peers. For many Ascendancy this spelled loss of exclusive control but greater security as an integrated part of a major Protestant power; Dissenters accepted it because it provided greater economic opportunities; the Catholic hierarchy even supported it as part of a bulwark against French Revolutionary forces and, as a Catholic minority within the (Protestant) UK, they would appear less threatening and therefore gain greater toleration. Meanwhile ordinary Catholics, peasants and cottiers, were apathetic and indifferent; Parliaments meant little to them, landlords (Anglican), tithes, and rents were their problem.

Thus by the late eighteenth century there existed three consciousnesses in Ireland with their own exclusive relations, built around religion and economic interests, although Protestants shared a sense of insecurity.

## After the Union, in an Age of Nationalism

The Act of Union was a defining event since it integrated Irish political life into Britain's (England, Scotland, and Wales) as part of the UK. There was moderate goodwill toward it, so this was consequently a time when old divisions might have been overcome but were not (Foster, 1989; Beckett, 1969; Boyce, 1991).

The Ascendancy, however, retained a monopoly in the new Irish administration and forged new ruling relations with British aristocrats in London, while Catholics, throughout the UK, remained excluded from Parliament. Meanwhile Ulster Protestants shared the Ascendancy's new sense of security, plus new industrial and trading opportunities in the burgeoning markets of Britain and her Empire. They rapidly developed reciprocal economic relations within the Union, particularly with the industrializing north of England and Scotland (Kennedy and Ollerenshaw, 1985, p. 62), which boosted their prosperity, hence positively informing their consciousness. Of necessity, though, the new relationships were more abstract, responding to UK and international exchange relations.

These new market forces of (scientific) economics reciprocated the abstract knowledge of science in industrial production and helped develop a political (liberal) consciousness, extant from 1798. Important here was the "Scottish Enlightenment" (notably Adam Smith and David Hume; Broadie, 2007) in which many Ulster Presbyterians were involved (Francis Hutcheson, 1694–1746, regarded as its Father, was an Ulsterman).

For ordinary Catholics, things were different. Although the final Penal Laws were removed, they still remained unable to enter Parliament, which bred resentment especially among a growing Catholic middle class, also benefiting economically from the Union (Corrish, 1985). This denied them full integration and a future as equal citizens in the new Empire and forced them back into pan-Catholic relations and grievances. The Union thus became symbolically linked in Catholic consciousness, as Protestant, especially as the Church of Ireland, remained the established Church.

Significantly, this occurred just when the "nation" was being redefined as "the people," who alone constituted legitimate moral authority (Hobsbawm, 1992, p. 22), unlike the ancien régime, which was based on property. And in Ireland the majority were Catholic and alone identified as "The Irish, properly so called" (Boyce, 1991, p. 123).

And the radical changes of the nineteenth century would play upon these pre-existing consciousnesses to create new political imperatives that were far from unitary. These imperatives, economic and industrial development, would coalesce around new relations for and against modernity, preserving traditional Irish peasant socio-economic relations against the new industrial relations of Ulster (Hoppen, 1999, chapter 2; O'Grada, 1995, chapter 2; Clark, 1979) and the UK, which built on religious divisions that symbolized Durkheim's mechanical versus organic relations, which could not co-exist. Based on existing religious identities with a history of conflict and already linked to different forms of knowledge (traditional religion versus science, peasant versus industrial), the development of a shared consciousness was highly problematic, as was the role of religion.

The Union coincided with new socio-economic and extended relations aided by improved communications that led to increased exchanges of ideas and knowledge that then helped alter men's consciousness and sense of collective belonging. The UK opened Ireland to all-British influences and consciousness, particularly the Enlightenment, heavily identified with Protestantism (Colley, 1996, pp. 19–59), which posed problems for Catholic inclusion in being British. Irish Catholics, "the people," already had a collective organization (the Church) and consciousness easily transformed into its own political being (nation), a unifying knowledge of their collective interests and leaders (middle classes) spurned by the new UK elite.

This was exemplified in O'Connell's great campaigns for Catholic emancipation (seats in Parliament, 1829) and repeal of the Union (1840s), where he explicitly utilized an existing Catholic consciousness, parochial structures, and priests in a truly national mobilization (Boyce, 1991, pp. 138–41). He referred to specifically Catholic grievances and raised their consciousness and interests against (Protestant) Britain: "Now O'Connell could use the expression 'Ireland for the Irish' . . . the Catholics of Ireland, 'that is emphatically the people of Ireland' . . . numbers not property, entitled a section of the nation to regard itself as 'the people'" (Boyce, 1991, p. 149). This Catholic consciousness, largely confined to rural peasant life, when numbers now counted, had logical implications for Protestants and their interests and relations, Ascendancy or Dissenter, especially as the franchise was extended.

However, in Ulster, Protestants formed a majority where they constituted the "people" with their own consciousness and exchange relations, reinforced as they underwent Ireland's only industrial revolution, which completely transformed their regional economy (Kennedy and Ollerenshaw, 1985, chapter 2). One result was the dominating priority of socio-economic relations with Britain and Empire, not Ireland, and shared consciousness of industrialization, scientific knowledge, religion, and Enlightenment.

Ulster's industrial relationships progressively extended into British spheres for markets and raw materials: "By 1849 the steam power needs of the linen industry accounted for 250,000 tons of coal imported into Belfast every year, which would quadruple by the end of the century" (Foster, 1989, p. 389). Ireland produced no coal.

Industrial division of labor and extended exchange relations producing organic social structures constituted the crux of social change for Durkheim, producing new knowledge (cognitive and moral), interests, ideas of welfare, belonging, and consciousness. Building on an existing religious consciousness a specifically Ulster Protestant collective identity and realities emerged: "It is useful here to emphasise the fact that most of the business men in the province were Protestant" (Ollerenshaw, in Kennedy and Ollerenshaw, 1985, p. 65).

This uniquely Protestant experience remained even after large numbers of Catholics migrated into her industrial towns, mostly working in Ulster's non-industrial sectors (McLaughlin, 1980, pp. 15–27). Thus a unique Ulster Protestant consciousness emerged with its own (Dissenting) legitimizing moral authority, increasingly tied into the Union, independent of Ascendancy landlords but opposed to the Catholic peasant experience, interests, and consciousness galvanized by O'Connell.

O'Connell also built upon a Catholicism that became increasingly ultramontane after 1815, especially after Cardinal Cullen returned to Ireland from Rome (1848) instilling a new organizational, moral discipline and orthodoxy as the century progressed (Lee, 1989a; Inglis, 1998). After the Famine (1845–47), ultramontanism imposed a new social and moral discipline that symbolically expressed and reciprocated the new economic discipline required of the new peasant-proprietor farmers who emerged after it (Lee, 1989a, p. 5). Later (post-1870s) it also conflated with an Irish nationalism that increasingly identified itself as non-British: "A 'nationalist' catholic identity was the largest political fact of Irish life in the mid-nineteenth century. . . Archbishop Cullen . . . stood for another and less well recognised 'nationalist' policy, namely, an Ireland with its own distinctive life and institutions" (Comerford, 1998, p. 31).

Ultramontanism was aided in this by a "new medievalism" in Vatican teaching, which idealized the medieval village community and condemned most things modern, industrial, and progressive (Chadwick, 1998; Burleigh, 2005; Remond, 1999). In 1864, the Papacy's *Syllabus of Errors* condemned 80 errors of the modern world; these errors included: allowing immigrants of a different religion the right of public worship; believing that Catholicism should not be the only state religion; to think freedom of the press and expression of opinion does not lead to a decline in public morality; and that the Pope can and ought to reconcile himself with progress, liberalism, and modern civilization (Chadwick, 1998, p. 176). All were rigidly enforced under Cullen's ultramontane orthodoxy, the bedrock of modern Irish Catholicism, and inculcated in Catholic minds via denominational education.

A Catholic consciousness emerged oblivious to Protestants, or even the necessity of considering them, exemplified in the McCann case (1910–11) where the 1908 Papal *"Ne Temere"* decree (effectively, that in mixed marriages children must be brought up as Catholics) was successfully applied in a Belfast divorce, the Protestant Mother losing her children purely on the grounds of religion: "Such 'encroachments of the Papal power in the United Kingdom' alarmed Ulster Protestants and confirmed them in their belief that under an Irish parliament a deliberate and sustained attempt would be made to drive Protestants out of the country" (Buckland, 1973, p. xxxiii).

Few Catholics grasped how sectarian and divisive they were, reflecting how Nationalists continually ignored Protestant realities: "Thus Parnell's gross underestimation of the Ulster opposition of 1885–86. Hence Redmond's timidity and obscurity of purpose when under pressure to concede something on 'Ulster'" (MacDonagh, 1983, p. 24).

From Cullen on, Catholics lived in an increasingly disciplined, all-encompassing, and isolated world (Inglis, 1998) with few reciprocal relations with Protestants and less knowledge of them. However, Catholic peasants still rented from Ascendancy landlords who still controlled most of Ireland's local government (Hoppen, 1999, pp. 97–99, 121–34) while maintaining their own exclusive relations: "the hunting-field, the marriage market, the grand jury and Dublin clubs" (Foster, 1989, p. 378).

This left them isolated from Catholic Ireland in an era of mass politics and where Catholics increasingly defined themselves against their landlords, especially once "land" relations dominated Irish politics (Lee, 1989, chapters 3 and 4). The Ascendancy, identifying with the Union, became "British" to the Catholics' "Irish." Later, after the Land Acts (1885, 1903, 1909: Foster, 1989; Lyons, 1973) deprived the Ascendancy of their land ownership, they ceased having even an economic function as landlords (Clark, 1979, pp. 348–49) and thus had no relevant knowledge with which to inform Irish conscious-ness, a traditionally elite function.

The Land Acts were responses to a Tenant League movement (1840s and 1850s) and the Land War (1879–82) (Lee, 1989, chapters 2 and 3; Lyons, 1973) against rural economic uncertainties and rents, which united tenant-farmer and Catholic Ireland against the Ascendancy landlords. Clark (1979, chapter 8) refers to the tenants as a "challenging collectivity," a structure of small-market towns and traders that extended to include a network of tenant-farmers, who they served in an intimate structure of local recipro-cal relations uniting farmers, laborers, and traders in a network of common rural-peasant interests. They met on church premises, where priests chaired meetings directed against their Ascendancy landlord and formed tight-knit, local collectives and political organizations that exerted enormous social con-trol within an already ultramontane Catholic discipline.

After the Land Acts severed Ascendancy relations, new autonomous, interdependent networks of farmers, small-town traders, and professionals emerged; collectives that were almost exclusively Catholic now dominated Southern Ireland:

> North and South, the tenant societies were strongly supported by shopkeep-ers. Indeed, almost all the societies were based in towns or large villages rather than in purely rural parishes. The interest of shopkeepers in the economic and financial wellbeing of the farmers is easily understood. So is the interest of clergymen. (Comerford, 1998, p. 22)

(Especially given the Papacy's new medievalism.)

Local collectives were increasingly linked via the growth of communica-tions, those vital links to exchange and the formation of relationships and consciousness: "A railway system begun in the 1830's (with, significantly, two separate growth points in Dublin and Belfast) had been developed through out the nineteenth century" (de Paor, 1986, p. 274). Catholic Ireland's chal-lenging collectivity linked previously isolated collectives into relationships based on Dublin, the traditional administrative center, while Ulster devel-oped its own exclusive relationships upon Belfast.

Ulster's industry exchanged with Britain, not Southern Ireland; signifi-cantly for Durkheim's emphasis on functional relationships in creating collec-tive consciousness, its relational, industrial imperatives were outward:

> North-east Ulster had more in common, and maintained much closer con-tact, with industrial regions of Britain than it did with other parts of Ireland. This characteristic was already apparent in the 1820's and became increasingly obvious towards 1914. In several important respects north-east Ulster and

especially Belfast benefited from a proximity to Britain, and from excellent cross-channel communications. (Ollerenshaw, in Kennedy and Ollerenshaw, 1985, p. 101)

Ulster's industrialization (cotton, linen, shipbuilding, and heavy engineering) implied external exchange relationships, importing raw materials and exporting finished products. And as industry increased in size it required capital in quantities only found outside of Ireland, where it also recruited much of the scientific skills and knowledge industry required, which Catholicism had long opposed.

It was an industrial Ulster that was almost exclusively Protestant:

> One estimate around 1820 put the ratio of Protestant to Roman Catholic capital in Belfast trade and industry at forty to one, and at the end of the nineteenth century it was pointed out that virtually everyone engaged in commerce in Ulster was a Protestant. It was not merely the process of industrialization but Protestant control of that process that gave the political economy of northeast Ulster its unique character. (Ollerenshaw, in Kennedy and Ollerenshaw, 1985, p. 65)

The industrial elite oriented Ulster Unionism, helped by the trade unions and Orange Order, whose industrial workers depended on the industrialists for jobs. The order from its inception played an important role in finding jobs for Protestants, which was part of its success, and provided a province-wide structure that linked most Protestants, geographically and across class, and was often sanctioned by local Ascendancy landlords. Thus it provided a single structure with an unofficial sanction: "Orangeism's success was based on the sanction of the state, and protection from judicial action by local notables, of popular Protestant attempts to restrict the labour market" (Gibbon, 1975, p. 41).

Ulster workers also joined British trade unions that linked them to British workers and shared interests, particularly in scientific, engineering, and technical occupations: "In contrast to linen, shipbuilding and engineering had a labour force with large groups of workers in categories with relatively high levels of trade union organization throughout the United Kingdom" (Patterson, in Kennedy and Ollerenshaw, 1985, p. 176).

Thus Protestant workers formed external, industrial relations that helped shape their consciousness within a cosmopolitan and scientific milieu as opposed to the rural, parochial, Catholic consciousness. And these better skilled workers also increasingly took the lead in Belfast's ongoing sectarian rioting, riots that significantly corresponded to world-trade fluctuations and job threats, reflecting an extended consciousness informed by abstract world relations (Gibbon, 1975, chapter iv).

Trade unionism and Orangeism blended around working-class interests and also linked the local and cosmopolitan industrial world. Orangeism provided a set of symbols, color, and pageantry with which to identify and express Protestant identity—rituals, symbols, and myths (important to Durkheim's sociology) to inform their consciousness and identity and a vitality in which they could participate: "It appealed to religious primitivism, but it also provided colour, poetry and its own kind of magic for ordinary drab lives" (Lyons, 1982, p. 136). Orangeism provided mediating relationships for all Protestants and continuity to cope with rapid industrial changes; even if the respectable middle classes initially kept their distance, it informed a shared Protestant consciousness and gave it symbolic representation.

However, Ulster's rapid industrialization led to changing socio-economic relationships within the Protestant community as machine and factory work replaced craft labor, with consequent economic and social, particularly status, loss. Skilled workers, particularly the independent weavers and spinners of 1798, who Gibbon identified as the center of traditional "political, economic and theological debate," most acutely experienced this loss. New relations had to be forged and new livelihoods found involving a dramatic loss of status and income for those previously central to the collective consciousness. Gibbon (1975) regards this as having a cathartic affect upon Ulster Protestants, which was experienced and transmogrified via a religious revival and a new "ethnocentric" consciousness in the 1850s (Gibbon, 1975, chapter III; Brooke, 1994, chapter 9).

The "revival" was an internal Protestant experience, of socio-economic loss and renewal (moral and cognitive) transmogrified into a religious and intensely experienced one because it was "inner" to the collective. It conforms to Durkheim's idea of "collective effervescence" (Mellor, 1998, pp. 87–114) both in its form, mass hysteria in places, and its outcome, a new ethnocentric Ulster Protestantism that emphasized the exclusion of alien elements and values for collective salvation.

Thus Protestant (Orange) Ulster became increasingly evangelical, ethnocentric, and concerned about excluding impure elements. A religious zeal emerged that encouraged close group membership and collective consciousness. For Durkheim this might represent the religious function of re-sanctifying the collective with its new interests and relations and preventing its profanity by external, corrupting influences. Religious exclusiveness now provides a moral corollary to economic exclusiveness—job discrimination and ethnic exclusion.

In a competitive economy, with economic insecurity it is rational to exclude outsiders and religion can morally sanction this. It was those once the core of political and theological liberalism and Enlightenment values (United

Irish) who lost their jobs, status, and security to industrial production and had to compete in a competitive labor market who led the revival thereby conflating economic salvation with religious knowledge and cognitive salvation with moral knowledge.

Gibbon (1975) and Darby (1986 both comment on the rise in Ulster's sectarian rioting and an imperative to exclude Catholics from Protestant territory: "From the 1857 inquiry, the process which witnesses described was clearly designed to rid alien elements from districts, factories and services" (Darby, 1986, p. 12). This was typical and correlates with Gibbon's "fluctuations in world trade" and indicates how a new (protective) consciousness developed in response to new economic relations and threats. This in turn equates with the new technical and cognitive knowledge (science) required in industrial society but threatened by that of a rural peasant society and traditional religion, while new knowledge (science) profanes the consciousness of old, rural knowledge, which it demystifies as it rationalizes. In this sense Durkheim's progress (Protestant knowledge) required protection if it was to realize individual salvation, especially from an increasingly ultramontane Catholicism opposed to science and industry.

However, knowledge was still of the collective so that when that knowledge is threatened the collective needs to recall itself to its social origins and for Ulster Protestants this was an essential aspect of their "ethnocentric" revivalist identity as they returned to their social roots to relearn and legitimate their interests:

> This legitimation, and the rhetoric of personal salvation and the imminent "solution" of worldly problems which accompanied it, made participation by the socially marginalised an attractive proposition. Fundamentalist "enthusiasm" provided a means by which personal and collective fears, frustrations and expectations could be handled. (Gibbon, 1975, p. 60)

That this consciousness was exclusive helps explain, along with Catholics' scholastic mind-set, the blindness of Catholic nationalism to Ulster: "This meant blind assumptions that Ireland was one and indivisible politically, and that religion was a false divider of Irishmen, used as such by British government's intent on maintaining control of the island" (MacDonagh, 1983, p. 23). Consequently, we see:

> Parnell's gross underestimation of the Ulster opposition of 1885–86. Hence Redmond's timidity and obscurity of purpose when under pressure to concede something on 'Ulster' during 1913, 1914 and 1916. Hence the failure in 1921 . . . to consider in time the issue of a boundary, and the modes of determining it. Hence the claim of the 1937 Constitution to be that of all Ireland. (MacDonagh, 1983, pp. 24–25)

For Durkheim, Catholics and Protestants formed alien consciousnesses, each an impurity to the other, especially since the cognitive bases for their knowledge were so opposed, Enlightenment versus Romantic, scientific versus scholastic.

Denominational education at all levels, including university (Hoppen, 1999; Lyons, 1973), further hardened attitudes and collective consciousness by transmitting only their own knowledge within themselves, thereby reinforcing two opposed systems of knowledge. Catholic education was based on scholastic (medieval) philosophy, the antithesis of modern scientific philosophy (Shapin, 1995; Russell, 1996; Grayling, 2007), which effectively made scholasticism redundant: "The vexing problems of scholastic philosophy were not so much solved as rendered irrelevant or meaningless, or shown to be confusions" (Berlin, 1996, p. 61). Industrial society requires a scientific education for the technical and moral knowledge functional to it, while a rural peasant society doesn't; indeed, for Durkheim, scholasticism corresponded to the moral needs of mechanical solidarity. Thus denominational education may also be regarded as symbolic of and functional to real differences.

Catholic consciousness, founded on its own exclusive inclusiveness (Remond, 1999; Inglis, 1998) rapidly became the reality of nationalist Ireland, which quickly conflated Catholic iconography and values with their nationalism:

> The symbol system of the new nationalism was parallel to that of Irish Catholicism and was a translation of the latter into political terms. Neo-Gaelic nationalism retained the values of self-sacrifice for the group, religious communalism, respect for women, fear of external evils and idealism which were taught by the Irish Catholicism of the period. (Garvin, 1981, p. 104)

Catholic Ireland, already mobilized by O'Connell, also experienced its own traumatic transformation in the Famine, 1845–47 (Foster, 1989; Lyons, 1973), reforming its collective consciousness. The Famine largely bypassed Ulster's industrial workers, who were not subsistence peasants dependent on the single potato crop. Thus the catastrophe, resulting trauma, and major reformation of Catholic peasant society was internal to it and generated its own transmogrification. This was molded via Cullen's ultramontane reforms and "devotional revolution," which rebuilt Catholic Ireland (Inglis, 1998) around the exigencies of a new post-Famine socio-economic order: a Catholic experience of relearning and reforming consciousness similar to Ulster's.

In post-Famine Catholic Ireland, domestic manufacturing declined, old estates were broken up, and new urban landlords purchased the land, often to re-let and then sublet to new tenant-farmers who began farming on a commercial basis, particularly shifting to cattle. The Famine had cleared the land of subsistence cottiers, leaving survivors with new opportunities to farm commercially, but often only on farms of 30 to 50 acres. They formed a new set of rural market relationships linked to a burgeoning small-town economy, which created a new stratum of traders, shopkeepers, merchants, and rural professionals to service farmers' needs. Most came from farming families, as did many priests and the new (state funded but Catholic controlled) school teachers, thus uniting them in a communal lifestyle and frame of mind.

Small towns linked local rural economies in a shared parochial experience, linked "nationally" by new communications (post and telegraph) and transport networks (roads and rail) centered on Dublin. And the development of such new links necessitated the standard use of English (the market language) and an increased literacy to follow the market. This in turn becomes the basis for a new social and political consciousness:

> It is not necessary to exaggerate the social isolation of rural people before the Famine to arrive at the conclusion that the farmers of post-Famine Ireland were more integrated into national and urban structures than could be claimed for the bulk of the rural population in the pre-famine period. With reference to other societies, a development of this kind has sometimes been called "social mobilization" and regarded as significant because it weakens the control of traditional or regional social units and increases the control of modern, national units defined in larger ethnic or territorial terms. (Clark, 1979, p. 151)

Establishing this new rural economy was arduous, requiring a new discipline, market orthodoxy, and values, which became part of their Catholic consciousness; a purging of their souls to create a new legitimacy and identity in a rapidly changing milieu:

> If the religious revival of the nineteenth century was partly a response to social cleavage, it was also a response to uncomfortably rapid change. In an age when unprecedented economic advance disrupted traditional ways of life, many found in religion a symbol of continuity, order and identity . . . By the middle of the nineteenth century, Larkin suggests, Irish Catholics were affected by an "identity crisis" arising out of the disappearance of the greater part of their traditional culture. For them the devotional revolution provided "a substitute symbolic language and offered them a new cultural heritage with which they could identify and through which they could identify with one another." (Connolly, 1985, p. 60)

"The Churches however, merely reflected the dominant economic values of post-Famine rural society" (Lee, 1989a, p. 5).

Ultramontane discipline mirrored and sanctified the new economic discipline of a peasant market economy, expressing collective needs, a new identity, investment in the land, a new knowledge of self, and collective interest. This was reinforced by a Catholic education, with teachers and priests (who ran the schools) recruited from the same socio-economic strata (Lyons, 1973, pp. 85–86). Thus an internal knowledge system emerged where all pertinent knowledge-producing relationships were contained within a Catholic structure and philosophy, whose reality and legitimacy was reconfirmed by everyday parochial life. The devotional revolution of Cullen was specifically designed to create an all-encompassing Catholic world that met all the needs of a peasant society.

Much of Catholic nationalism's rhetoric was later directed against alien and corrupting influences, particularly those associated with modernity and industrialization (Brown, 1981) sweeping into Ireland via modern communication networks that threatened to undermine an all-encompassing world. The new identity and collective life that modern communications helped forge within Ireland now also introduced non-Irish influences, such as international trade, science, liberal ideas and British media, potentially disrupting to the new rural socio-economic structures and Catholic consciousness: "It was the acute sense of Irish Catholic civilization under threat, with British materialism and irreligion flooding in by the myriad roads of modern communications, which drove the clergy hardest towards identifying with the traditions of absolute resistance" (MacDonagh, 1983, p. 103). Hence this was the appeal of an alternative knowledge (Catholic truth) for nationalism; Catholic and Gaelic, knowledge to erect barriers against an English-speaking (modern) world that had initially promised great opportunities for an all-encompassing Catholic peasant society, knowledge rejected by Ulster and modern Dublin 4 as dysfunctional to their needs.

Gaelic was traditionally associated with the Catholic community and linked to a past that gave it legitimacy, now it had a functional role mediating exclusive internal relations and knowledge and a barrier to English cosmopolitanism. Gaelic provided and symbolized separate knowledge and interests, a mystery for a new aspiring mandarin class to master and promote its own interests on, as opposed to modern science (which unravels mysteries), and so blended well with scholastic Catholicism.

Hence Gaelic became popular with a new urban middle class, which stimulated the Gaelic revival of the 1880s, particularly with teachers, to whom it gave a knowledge, status, and moral purpose, as possessors of and instructors in a unique knowledge, once ordinary farmers ceased using it, the "soul of the nation":

Schoolteachers themselves held a similarly uncomfortable middle position in society, in that they possessed education and quite considerable cultural influence in village society while often having little real security or political independence. National teachers (NT's) were conspicuous among Gaelic League and Sinn Fein ideologues of the post-1898 period, and were early involved in the project to revive the Irish language through the schools. (Garvin, in Boyce, 1988, p. 102)

Gaelic was the center-piece of a whole cultural package in arts, literature, sports, and the eulogy of peasant life that emphasized an Irish uniqueness and introversion (Lee, 1989, chapter 6; Lyons, 1982, chapter 3). The more parochial the interests and relations, the more relevant the local knowledge and means of expression to exchange in it (dysfunctional to universalizing and cosmopolitan science). Thus:

> The theme of Irish tradition was staunchly reiterated in reviews of plays, exhi-
> bitions and concerts. An attitude of xenophobic suspicion often greeted any
> manifestation of what appeared to reflect cosmopolitan standards. An almost
> Stalinist antagonism to modernism, to surrealism, to free verse, symbolism and
> the modern cinema was combined with prudery. (Brown, 1981, p. 147)

But it resonated with nationalist Ireland, although critically regarded as third rate and insignificant when compared with the contemporary Anglo-Irish revival (Lyons, 1982, chapter 3). However, it provided a cultural knowledge functional to the reality of a commercial peasant society whose aesthetic appreciation was minimal. Consequently, the Anglo-Irish revival, which often critiqued peasant society, such as Synge's *Playboy of the Western World*, was greeted with hostility and remained the interest of an isolated Anglo-Irish elite whose cosmopolitanism identified them as un-Irish. The Gaelic revival also blended with Catholicism:

> The Irish language, the Catholic religion and the ideology of political separa-
> tion intermeshed. Thus to the fear of "modernization" in its English form,
> and to the spiritual expansionism and missionary ardour which increasingly
> characterised the official church, was added—for the laity at large—a sense
> that Gaelic was coterminous with Catholic, and Catholic with Gaelic in Irish
> circumstances. (MacDonagh, 1983, p. 116)

A single consciousness and identity exclusive to Catholic Ireland was only functional there, making industrial Ulster alien and un-Irish, part of the cor-rupting, English-speaking, cosmopolitan, and scientific threat:

> The literary revival, and the whole awareness of Irish art, culture, language,
> were inspired by a concern that the Irish identity was in danger of erosion,
> perhaps even disappearance. The Young Irelanders and the Fenians had felt

this as well, for the crisis of identity in nineteenth century Ireland was a cyclical one, reflecting the growing Anglicization of the country, the disappearance of traditional ways of life, of the Gaelic tongue, and the industrialization of the north-east part of Ulster. (Boyce, 1991, p. 233)

This cultural imperative was functional to maintaining the socio-economic relationships and interests painfully built up after the Famine. These came under threat as part of a UK with global and modernizing international relations that were inevitably of an organic nature as opposed to Catholic Ireland's, inevitably, peasant mechanical nature, which they were invading. Consequently, there was a spontaneous legitimacy to defend Catholic Gaelic knowledge, given philosophical currency via Young Ireland's Romantic philosophy, which, significantly, was a product of the 1840s but only gained mass appeal after the 1870s.

## Modern Irish Nationalism

Only after the Land War (1879–82) did the cultural revival and separation gain support, significantly, just when the modern world and international relations made their first, negative impact on Catholic Ireland, mobilized en masse during the Land War: "Before the famine these landless or near landless elements comprised some two-thirds of the population, and outnumbered the tenant and independent farmers by four to one; by 1900 farmers outnumbered labourers . . . The farmer was the largest and most influential class in post-famine Ireland" (Boyce, 1991, p170).

This was partly due to larger and more market-oriented farming, signified in the shift to grazing and cattle and increased farm size: "By 1854, 60 per cent of Irish land was being farmed by 90,000 farmers holding above fifty acres. The larger farmers could achieve near-gentry status; many of them were, effectively, landlords if not landowners" (Foster, 1989, p. 379).

These were men who had survived the trauma of the Famine and bought cheap land from old encumbered estates ruined by it; working farmers seeking to build a business, investing their time, effort, and cash into improvements. They had a new vested interest in the land, formed new relations, and shared a new self-knowledge of interests and identity (Clark, 1979, pp. 249–62; Bull, 1996, pp. 79–82). A commercial peasant-proprietor set of relations emerged, requiring a new socio-economic discipline to save and invest in building up the farm, with its moral corollary in ultramontane Catholic discipline.

To build up and bequeath the farm became central to family survival:

The normal sequence was for the farmer to pass on his farm first to his wife and then to one of his sons. This meant not only had the favoured son to delay marriage until the death of both his parents . . . but that the other sons, and often enough the daughters as well, were condemned either to emigration or to chastity. (Lyons, 1982, p. 157)

And this made Ireland something of a freak:

Between 1845 and 1914 average male age at marriage rose from about 25 to 33, average female age from about 21 to 28. The decline in crude marriage rate from about 7 in the immediate pre-famine period to about 5 in 1880, and the increase in the proportion of females in the age group 45–54 never married, from 12% in 1851 to 26% in 1911, distinguished Ireland as a demographic freak. (Lee, 1989a, p. 3)

Social relations based on deferred gratification and self-denial become transmogrified into the prudery, abstinence, and moral teachings of Catholicism (Inglis, 1998), which helped morally legitimate the economic necessities and social relations of peasant-farmer society, central to modern Irish identity:

Asceticism in Ireland came to be opposed to a materialistic and opportunistic careerism in republican rhetoric. A persistent theme in late nineteenth century Irish Catholic and nationalist thought was the opposition between a materialistic, corrupt and 'unspiritual' England and a suffering, poor but spiritually superior, Ireland. (Garvin, in Boyce, 1988, p. 107)

And this kind of disciplined society required close communal cooperation with closely integrated relationships of mutual support and dependence, strong ties, and loyalty to help sustain the personal sacrifice required, not consumerism and the personal gratification of modern society.

Before 1879 this did not create calls for Irish independence, because the farming economy was "largely dependent upon the British market" (Foster, 1989, p. 379). Britain's burgeoning industrial cities provided expanding markets for all UK farmers due to agriculture's "natural protection"; that is, most foods, being perishable, were protected from foreign competition before steamships, railways, canning, and refrigeration made long-distance transportation of perishables viable. Before these were developed Irish farmers were close enough to Britain for their food exports not to perish before market, hence the initial shift to commercial farming identified with Britain as a source of prosperity: 1850–70 was a golden period for Irish agriculture (Comerford, 1998, p. 8; O'Grada, 1996). However, during the 1870s this changed:

The late 1870's was a time of crisis for agriculture throughout the British Isles . . . Economic recession in the manufacturing sector in Britain had led to changes in diet among the industrial population, adversely affecting the profitability of the beef and "breakfast" trade, especially the pork and dairy industries, which had developed so well in Ireland in the preceding decades. Underlying international factors, less evident at the time, were to turn this into a permanent trend. Increasing grain competition from North America, Australia and elsewhere was significantly depressing the price of the Irish product. And Irish butter was losing out in the British market to its Danish competitors. (Bull, 1996, pp. 72–73)

This was the background to the Land War, which reflected the concerns of a newly established tenant-farmer class, financing loans for expansion and years of hard struggle. The Land War was the cry of an endangered class (farmers and small-town traders) being threatened by international competition and markets. However, the initial demands (fixed rents, tenure, and sale of tenancy) were not for independence but security in the face of economic threat and could have been resolved within a protectionist UK, particularly given the Catholicism's hostility to nationalism throughout Europe (Remond, 1999).

However, as British industrial interests (better and cheaper food for industrial workers) and manufacturing benefited from international markets, so Irish farming increasingly lost ground to them, which made separation (initially Home Rule within the UK) and protectionism a reasonable response to agriculture fears:

Broadly speaking, while the market was generally buoyant between 1851 and the early 1870's it was more favourable to animals and animal products than it was to products of the plough . . .

Thereafter, with the intensification of foreign competition, bad times ensued for almost everyone and lasted for the next twenty years . . . from 1896 to the First World War agricultural prices began to rise again and every department showed an increase. This was, however, to a certain extent offset by the fact that for the first time for many years general prices had begun to move markedly ahead of food prices, thus confronting the farmer with a potentially dangerous threat. (Lyons, 1973, p. 48)

Modern science and technology undermined the farmers' "natural protection"; steamships, railways, refrigeration, and the telegraph created world agri-markets, cosmopolitan interests, and relations that even invaded Ireland's agricultural markets, domestic (craft) industries, and self-sufficiency:

The railway permitted the far greater diffusion of information through the tele-post and the rapid distribution of newspapers. It increased the range of small, personal wants by distributing imports and Dublin goods throughout the countryside, breaking down the stifling barriers of physical and mental self-sufficiency. Between 1861 and 1911 the number of commercial travelers, superseding local pedlars, rose from 500 to 4,500. (Lee, 1989a, p. 13)

Additionally, after 1900, farmers were threatened with increased taxes to help pay for new welfare and social legislation to deal with Britain's (including Ulster) urban and industrial problems: "After 1903 Irish farmers tended to be suspicious of the British state; but in significant degree, it was because they feared that they might have to subsidise the United Kingdom welfare state as taxation fell on their new-found profits and property" (Bew, in Boyce, 1988, p. 222).

A new consciousness of Catholic Ireland's interests emerged that found a symbolic expression and cultural shield in Gaelic revivalism. Industrialization, modernization, and cosmopolitan values were now bad for Irish farming, making ideas of a rural Catholic Gaelic idyll appealing and functional to Irish farmers and their dependents but threatened by being part of a UK whose "people" benefited from what threatened Irish farmers.

Not just the farmers but the whole rural economy, especially its newly educated middle classes, who felt threatened: "contrary to so many generalizations there was an Irish urban middle class, but it was largely comprised of people in service or distribution industries in provincial towns, whose occupations were rurally derived or 'professional'" (Foster, 1989, p. 379).

These constituted the local elites of small-town rural Ireland, such as teachers, solicitors, valuers, auctioneers, journalists, shopkeepers, publicans, and traders, dependent on farmers prospering. They were educated and central to local networks, where isolated farmers came and exchanged news, views, and information, collated it, and informed the wider public (collective consciousness). The priest, often of the same class, also played a similar role while also morally validating resulting views and actions.

And once the franchise was extended this class became the political voice of Catholic Ireland, expressing its consciousness and interests. Journalists played a particularly important role in uncovering, manufacturing, and disseminating vital knowledge; an occupation much favored by Romantic idealists who saw journalism as an acceptable living:

And so Ireland in the 1850's produced a small army of newspaper people fired with romantic nationalist ideals. It so happened also that during the 1850's the newspaper business in the United Kingdom in general entered an era of unprecedented opportunity and expansion. The economics of journalism were revolutionised by technical and, especially, fiscal factors. (Comerford, 1998, p. 36)

Local knowledge is vital to local professionals, which makes journalism a central activity, as knowledge-producing hubs in educated structures with an often heightened consciousness able to direct opinion. Meanwhile a prosperous rural economy was also in their vested interests to maintain their role and income (Garvin, in Boyce, 1988).

Small-town professionals thus united with farmers in a nascent political radicalism:

> Landlordism must stand down: a peasant proprietry must be established. This Fenian advance into rural Ireland must not be exaggerated; most of the farming classes remained aloof; but between 1866 and 1871 the occupation farmer appears among lists of Fenian suspects, along with the now familiar categories of builders, drapery workers, clerks, shopkeepers and labourers. (Boyce, 1991, p. 179)

As rural fears increased so did the political activity and message: "The strategy of tenant interest shifts from one of advocacy of tenant-right measures to the demand, at a general level, of 'the land of Ireland for the people of Ireland' and, at a particular level, for transfer of land ownership and the creation of a peasant proprietorship" (Boyce, 1988, pp. 32–33). It was then but a small step to translate this into a political ownership of the land (nationalism), which would ensure that political control matched economic relations, which could then be sanctified and legitimated via Catholicism.

The priest and small-town professional are both central to local structures and knowledge. The latter produces the cognitive knowledge that is then legitimated by the former's moral knowledge and both occupy positions that enable them to communicate and instill the new knowledge into popular consciousness. Officially the Catholic Church was wary of nationalism (in Europe it had lost them clerical control) but once it had struck a deal with Parnell (1882) that gave it denominational control over education and social matters (Boyce, 1991, pp. 218–19), they warmed to it in Ireland.

However, locally many priests had long been active in local politics. Priests were generally accepted as neutral arbitrators in local affairs and church services were a regular gathering place for rural communities, their grounds and halls used for formal and informal meetings and consequently another hub of rural relations. Churches always had been centers of consciousness:

> Before newspapers, mass based political parties or television it was a major means of communication between the government and people. It was an important centre for social organization at local level. It was a means by which moral and political values were inculcated and cultivated. It ensured in an age

> when contacts between even neighbouring localities were few that a common identity and world view were shared over wide territories. (Brooke, 1994, p. 24)

Churches were therefore ideal to spread the new consciousness, especially as urban populations grew and outlying rural areas were better linked to them, making regular church attendance more possible and collective action, locally and nationally, much easier:

> Between 1841 and 1861 the proportion of people living in settlements of 500 and upward increased from 17.8 per cent to 23.7 per cent; towns became centres of exchange and dispersal of goods as Ireland's transport revolution proceeded in default of an industrial revolution. Railways proliferated (nearly 3,500 miles of track by 1900); the "market" invaded the rural economy along with advertising, foreign goods, credit and, eventually, the bicycle. The rate of internal migration doubled between 1841 and 1881; the Post-Office quadrupled the number of letters carried and extended its network. (Foster, 1989, p. 385)

This enabled Catholic Ireland to share a common experience, cooperate, and coordinate in defense of it, using the same intrusive instruments of modernity that undermined it to defend it—a lesson that implied the importance of independence to control the media and means that threatened it.

Durkheim would have added to this that the closer social relations in the new "settlements" (previously peasants had lived on isolated patches of land on which they subsisted) would have more immediately acted upon and constrained individuals, the greater force—the idea—that correlates with the pervading ultramontanism of Catholicism. Religion also provides an alternative (mystical) knowledge to oppose science, protecting the collective as another barrier against English modernity.

This new rural urbanization and commercialization also required schools (clerically controlled throughout Ireland) to educate the new middle classes, which necessitated teachers who also found an interest in nationalism:

> Schoolteachers themselves held a similarly uncomfortable middle position in society, in that they possessed education and quite considerable cultural influence in village society while having little real security or independence. National teachers (NT's) were conspicuous among Gaelic league and Sinn Fein ideologues of the post 1898 period, and were early involved in the project to revive the Irish language through the schools. (Garvin, in Boyce, 1988, p. 102)

Teachers became leading "wordsmith" professionals, along with journalists and writers, in manufacturing and propagating the Gaelic revival. Garvin suggests this reflects the frustrations of "underemployed and politically subordinated literates" (Garvin, in Boyce, 1988, p. 104) carving out their own independent mystery for status fulfillment, unique purveyors of the idea. However, their success lay in articulating a special knowledge functional to real interests which then gave them a vested interest.

Most of these "wordsmiths" had strong rural connections or origins, were Catholic, and taught by Catholics from the same background, thus sharing in the consciousness of peasant-proprietor knowledge and helping negotiate important relations. Thus one expects to see teachers play an important role in Irish nationalism. However, their knowledge lacks relevance in modern Dublin 4 or Ulster.

After independence (1921) "Gaelicization" became the prime objective:

Gaelicizing the new state was a preoccupation. . . . From the early 1920's a series of important conferences and commissions on education stressed . . . that education should be structured 'in order to revive the ancient life of Ireland as a Gaelic state, Gaelic in language and Gaelic and Christian in its ideals.' (Foster, 1989a, p. 518)

This implied pre-industrial and, consequently, excluded industrial Ulster Protestants: "At this meeting, when the Belfast group explained one of their fears 'with regard to the question of the Gaelic language in the exams for public bodies they could suffer,' Asquith intervened, in an amazed tone: 'Are you really apprehensive as to that?'" (Bew, 1998, p. 63). Gaelic was useless, even an impediment to an industrial economy, which shows how divisive language and culture could be (and the ignorance of English politicians).

Education and cultural policy were the only real areas of radical change after 1921, thus reflecting nationalism's cultural "protectionist" nature: In 1922 Gaelic was made compulsory in National Schools at the expense of drawing, elementary science, hygiene, nature study, and most domestic studies. While Gaelic culture: "a vision of rustic dignity and rural virtue was popularized in speeches, poems, plays and paintings" (Brown, 1981, p. 3). It was further portrayed in the new state's Gaelic iconography and rural imagery, exemplified in the agricultural images on their currency (Northern Ireland's conspicuously sported industrial symbols).

Symbols are important for they represent knowledge and consciousness back to men, reflecting realities and interests that reminded them of important relationships and interests: "There were signs, nevertheless, that an Irish Censorship Bill might represent something more stringent than a government's rational attempt to suppress the more vicious forms of pornographic publication" (Brown, 1981, p. 69). This reflects the ascetic moral and cognitive knowledge functional to a peasant-proprietor economy, in lieu of any alternative, which explains the failure of the Anglo-Irish revival, since its cosmopolitan values critiqued peasant ideals and Catholic morality.

Meanwhile, Protestant Ulster's opposition to Home Rule produced its own icons and symbols that represented their consciousness, knowledge, and interests. The most spectacular symbol was the Great Convention (1892) to rally opposition to the second Home Rule Bill, and its center-piece, the Pavilion, displaying Ulster's:

> modernizing mission . . . It commemorated the qualities of rational imperative coordination in their most advanced form, and the components of the "Ulster tradition" from which it was purportedly realised (industry, endeavour, boldness, intelligence). It was a monument, moreover, to the existence in Ulster (without loss to each other) of "tradition" and "progress," the favourite twin theme of Ulster demagogues. A monument, finally, which made a silent comment on the lack of such qualities in the remainder of the Irish population. (Gibbon, 1975, p. 132)

An industrial culture, not a rural one, conscious of its own interests and relations: Durkheimian in its significance, where knowledge of drawing and elementary science was functional and Gaelic wasn't, making Gaelic useless knowledge and an anathema.

However, the Great Convention also consciously recalled a previous one in Dungannon, 1792, held by the Volunteers (militia) to call for radical reforms in Ireland, inspired by the American Revolution and Enlightenment ideals (Lucy, 1995, pp. vi–vii) rejected by Romantic nationalism. This was particularly pertinent because Ulster opposition to Home Rule was largely led by Liberals who feared for liberal values under an Irish Parliament.

Before Home Rule, most Dissenters were Liberals, not Conservatives, and one of its most prominent figures in 1892 was Thomas Sinclair:

> As a Presbyterian he viewed the established church as an undesirable legacy of the Protestant (i.e. Anglican) ascendancy and with distaste. He empathized on the land question with the tenant farmers of all denominations in general but with Presbyterian farmers in particular. His hostility to denominational education was a product of his mistrust of all forms of religious ascendancy. Predictably, he welcomed disestablishment in 1869 and Gladstone's two land acts of 1870 and 1881. These years, corresponding with Sinclair's involvement with the affairs of the Ulster Liberal Party's long hegemony in Ulster and were years of advance for Ulster Liberals as the province's parliamentary representation reveals. (Lucy, 1995, p. 89)

After 1870, Liberal MPs rose from 2 to 9 and Conservatives dropped from 27 to 18. But it was Liberals who were often foremost in their opposition to Home Rule, representing liberal politics and market economics (Thompson, 2001). For, while Conservatives were associated with landlords, Liberals represented tenant-farmers, commerce, industry, and the professionals who served their needs:

> Well represented in the business community, they felt they had good reason to believe that a home rule parliament's economic policy would inevitably jeopardize their hard won prosperity, dependent as it was on integration with the British market. Before 1886 they had seen Gladstone's reformist projects in Ireland, either in the spheres of religious privilege or land-lord tenant relations, as largely justified. They believed in short in the benign power of the liberal democratic Westminster Parliament of the leading country in the world to reconcile or at least arbitrate conflict between fanatical warring creeds and classes. (Bew, 1998, p. 4)

Liberals consequently saw Home Rule as threatening modernity and progress and so led in opposition to Home Rule.

Ulster's culture and language was English (a metaphor for modern, enlightened, cosmopolitan, and industrial) and part of the UK's, while being "Irish" implied a Catholic Gaelic world inimical to their interests and religion. This provided the catalyst for pan-Unionist solidarity, utilizing the Orange Order for organization and involving all classes and denominations: "Now in the mid-eighties, the gentry and the middle-classes returned to it once more and its lodges came to provide not only the nucleus for local Protestant patriotism, but also a meeting-ground where men of different social backgrounds could come together on a basis of equality and in pursuit of a common aim" (Lyons, 1973, p. 291).

Unionism represented a collective knowledge of the relations on which industry depended, hence also capitalist profits, professional fees, and workers' wages. Capitalist industry creates not just antagonistic class relations (rife in Ulster; Morgan, 1991; Probert, 1978; Kennedy and Ollerenshaw, 1985) but also symbiotic relations of class dependency and mutual interest.

Unionism also built on historical security fears and the often sectarian competition for jobs between denominations. Thus the failure of socialists and nationalists, such as James Connolly, to get Protestant working-class support (Morgan, 1991, chapter 7) even though they disliked their capitalist employers, indeed they had their own organizations in often hostile relations with capitalist Unionists:

> The Belfast Protestant Association had been founded in the early 1890's, and in 1902 one of its leaders, Tom Sloan, a shipyard worker and master of an Orange Lodge, heckled Colonel Saunderson, Belfast Grandmaster and leader of the

> Irish Unionist M.P.'s, at a "twelfth" demonstration, accusing him of prevent-
> ing the inspection of convent launderies . . . Sloan compounded his offence
> by contesting the by-election as an independent and defeating the Unionist
> candidate. (Buckland, 1973, pp. 28–29)

Class conflict is an integral set of relations peculiar to industrial society
and Belfast was the only city in Ireland to have such relations (Comerford,
1998, p. 8). Catholic Ireland had too little industry for industrial relations
and its anti-capitalism was based not on class antagonism but antipathy to
industrial society and its class relations.

That nationalism had little consciousness or interest in industrial society and its relations were graphically illustrated in de Valera's constitution
(1937): "Articles 40, 41 and 45 . . . implied or declared that a woman's place
was in the home; the image of rural utopianism was incompatible with an
industrialized female workforce, or, it might be added, with any industrialized workforce at all" (Foster, 1989, p. 546).

Yet the constitution claimed the whole of Ireland, while showing a mon-
umental insensitivity to and ignorance of Ulster, which may help explain
nationalists' confused attitudes to Ulster:

> Depending on political circumstances in the south, and on north-south rela-
> tions, northern unionists were claimed as Irish, or as alien colonists. Argu-
> ments that they were part of the nation were based on a denial of a separate
> unionist identity, and not on any form of compromise in traditional national-
> ism. While the rhetoric was primarily that of "one nation" there was an implicit
> exclusion of northern unionists from a nationalism which was wholly Gaelic
> and Catholic in ethos. (O'Halloran, 1987, p. xv)

Knowledge and understanding were lacking partly because of the absence
of informative relationships that could foster a shared "imagined community," probably also because nationalists lacked the critical scientific culture from which to analyze Ireland. The only way a scholastic mind could
cope was to assume an Irish-ness without critically examining it, while what
knowledge nationalists had of Ulster represented things they opposed, hence
Protestants were defined as un-Irish or British: "the whole tenor of Hyde's
argument was that Irish nationalism stood or fell by its cultural identity; an
identity, moreover, that did not include, and could not be shared by, what he
called the aliens of north-east Ulster, who had broken the continuity of the
Irish-ness of Ireland" (Boyce, 1991, p. 238).

Few Catholics were involved in its dominant socio-economic relations, at
least partly from self-exclusion and rival organizations (Hepburn, 1996) thus
Belfast's Chamber of Commerce:

Always representative of a cross section of businesses, membership increased from seventy-six in 1827 to 260 in 1893, at which date only eight members (3 per cent) were Catholics. R.S. Sayers once described the activities of chambers of commerce as 'that middle ground between business and politics.' (Ollerenshaw, in Kennedy and Ollerenshaw, 1985, pp. 65–66)

Meanwhile, for workers:

> Thus in Belfast, according to the 1901 census, whilst 24 per cent of the population were Catholic they made up only 8 per cent of ship, boat and barge builders, 6 per cent of shipwrights, 10 per cent of engine and machine workers, 11 per cent of fitters and turners, and 10 per cent of boilermakers. They constituted 15 per cent of carpenters, 27 per cent of bricklayers and 12 per cent of plumbers. In contrast they accounted for almost half of female linen spinners, a third of general labourers and 41 per cent of dockers. (Patterson, in Kennedy and Ollerenshaw, 1985, p. 178)

Catholics were a small minority in skilled, industrial trades involving important external relations, such as shipbuilding and engineering, with extensive external and abstract relations, and fewer were educated in scientific skills, culture, or appreciation. Irish Ireland could thus easily ignore Ulster as a rude intrusion.

Further, the sectarian strife in Ulster left many Catholics inured to predominantly Protestant losses. Even indirect losses accruing to Catholics from Protestant loss were less likely to impinge on their consciousness since Catholic skills lay in the service sectors (McLaughlin, 1980, pp. 15–27) not the manufacturing and productive sectors most directly affected.

Separate consciousness was deepened by segregated living areas (Tonge, 1998, pp. 90–91; Hepburn and Collins, in Roebuck, 1981) and by segregated education. For Ulster Catholics this meant an educational curriculum and teachers trained in an all-Ireland scholastic mind-set reflecting Southern, rural needs and realities, non-functional in industrial Ulster. This helps explain the ambiguous attitude of many Ulster Catholics to the Union (Moxon-Browne in Stringer and Robinson, 1991; O'Connor, 1993, chapter 9): They were caught between two cultures.

Catholic, Gaelic knowledge had little function in international economic relations or any industrial society and helped subordinate Catholics in Ulster. However, in their own Catholic state it would make them superior, reflecting the literature on industrial development and ethnic-separatist nationalism associated with underdevelopment (Breuilly, 1993; Hobsbawm, 1992; Gellner, 1983).

Education is also vital regarding the acquisition of social knowledge, of social structures, and how to negotiate them: access to the "right places," "contacts," the right attitudes, and social deference that helps integrate one into a shared consciousness. Murray (1985) in a study of Catholic and "state" schools in contemporary Northern Ireland observed how Catholic schools regarded official, state relations as outside interference: "The principal and staff in St Judes appeared to view educational legislative bodies as "outsiders"; necessities to be tolerated . . . He went on at great length about the interference by the department in the running of the school" (Murray, 1985, p. 81). Meanwhile everyday "interference" from priests and clerical bodies was accepted as natural and contacts of primary importance, which diverted attention away from Ulster's state and economic relations.

The opposite occurred in the "state" (Protestant) school where contact with the chairman of the local (state) Education and Library Board was seen positively: "His presence itself, however, demonstrates that he was considered to have an interest in and concern for the school. In fact, Mr Long served on several consultative committees with the chairman and knew him well" (Murray, 1985, p. 81).

Thus separate authority systems created different systems of legitimacy, status, and induction for their pupils, leaving Catholics at a disadvantage in terms of "contacts" in and knowledge of Ulster's structure of relations, inevitably affecting their consciousness. This was especially relevant in relation to jobs, where Catholic schools viewed contacts with and visits to local government offices, fire, police, and other state services negatively:

> It was interesting that the staff saw such outings in occupational terms only. They also considered such establishments as bastions of exclusive Protestant employment, which numerically is far from true. What is more disconcerting is that such negative perceptions within the school may well curtail the occupational aspirations and possibilities of the pupils. They may well not apply to these work sources because of the axiomatic knowledge, derived from teachers. (Murray, 1985, p. 83)

Thus Ulster's Catholic children are educated into a disadvantageous consciousness not relevant to Ulster's realities and ignorance of Protestants, which helps foster a sense of oppression since they are unable to fully utilize their knowledge and act out their consciousness in Ulster's dominant relations.

Catholic oppression is similar to Greenfeld's (1993) German Romantics experience, from whence Irish nationalism's cultural ideology was imported. Of course, in a single Irish state Ulster Protestants would be similarly disadvantaged, thus adding to their fears of Irish nationalism.

In his memoirs, Shea (1983) a Catholic and former senior civil servant in Northern Ireland's Department of Education, replicates Murray's findings:

Those in charge of Catholic education in Belfast, whilst always friendly and correct on official occasions, showed almost no desire to have me in their company on their own ground. Perhaps I was being spoiled by the attention I was getting elsewhere, but I cannot recall being invited to visit a Catholic school in Belfast. (Shea, 1983, p. 188)

While Catholics applying for posts in Northern Ireland virtually ranked as traitors:

It was my experience that some Catholics, and especially those in Belfast where, I had been told, the Bishop had advised them against seeking Government employment, looked with suspicion on Catholic civil servants. We had joined the enemy; we were lost souls. Within the civil service I saw the other side of the coin. To many of my colleagues Catholics were strange animals of which they had astonishingly little knowledge. (Shea, 1983, pp. 112–13)

Little knowledge was precisely the point, influencing identity formation, structural position, and consciousness.

Men become bonded (*religio*, Latin = bonds/relations) to society by shared knowledge and consciousness in both their individual and their social life: "Thus to love society is to love both something beyond us and something in ourselves. We could not wish to be free of society without wishing to finish our existence as men" (Durkheim, 1974, p. 55).

Durkheim accepted that societies can be changed but with great cost and effort. Men have become dependent on known social structures, relations, and knowledge, providing them with an important ontological security closely related to the idea of a superior force commanding deference and moral obligation. In this way, Durkheim defined religion as consciousness of society, which would make rule by another religion immoral and profane: "Ulster Unionists stressed the religious objection to home rule—the injustice of placing Irish Protestants under the jurisdiction of an Irish Catholic Parliament" (Buckland, 1973, p. 13).

Thus there is the need to protect one's God from sacrilege and profanity, to defend his truth against incursions:

The true-blue Sandy Row's Orangeman's "blueness" (i.e. "royalist" ethnicity) was true because he lived out its truth in faithfulness to his immediate comrades, and through them to the community as a whole. Further, since the threat posed by the enemy at the gates was a military one in some sense (invasion, annihilation, etc), the subjects of fidelity and reliability lived their roles as martial ones, embodied in the identities of stoutness—sturdiness, readiness, openness, boldness and redoubtability—indominatibility. (Gibbon, 1975, p. 80)

Equally, Irish Catholics wished to protect their truth against corrupting British (Protestant) profanities. These "crusades" against profanity are led by elites within the requisite structures because they have the best knowledge of it, are better educated, and have the greatest vested interest in it to create barriers to protect it. Thus small-town traders and professionals dominated Catholic nationalism, while industrialists dominated Ulster Unionism, reflecting the major interests at work.

Another Durkheimian index of interests and protective barriers is the law, equally important for nationalists for whom making laws, interpreting, and administering them is what independence is basically about, protecting relations and interests expressing their consciousness. As such, for Durkheim, law is more than a control mechanism, it is a symbolic representation, an "index" of social development, from repressive (mechanical, religious, and punitive) to restitutory (organic, non-religious, and contract) law (Durkheim, 1984; Lukes and Scull, 2013). Of Durkheimian significance therefore is how the new independent Irish state introduced a constitution and laws to reflect Catholic social teaching (Whyte, 1971) itself symbolic of economic, cultural, and moral interests:

> But the democratic, popular-sovereignty approach was combined with an assumption that the nature and identity of the Irish polity was catholic, reflected in five articles defining "rights." These were much influenced by Papal encyclicals and current Catholic social teaching. Divorce was prohibited; the idea of working mothers denounced; the Roman Catholic church granted a "special position. (Foster, 1989, p. 544)

This constitution was to protect and maintain internal relations important to a peasant-proprietor economy and social order (segmental and mechanical) and from external incursions, also reflected in bans on divorce (1925), contraception (1935), censorship laws (1929), the new constitution (1937), and attempts to Gaelicize life. For Durkheim these would be symbolic of mechanical, segmental, and repressive communal conformity typical of mechanical solidarity, especially in reaction against modernity, individualism, and growing (scientific) secularization:

> The symbol system of the new nationalism was parallel to that of Irish Catholicism and was a translation of the latter into political terms. Neo-Gaelic nationalism retained the values of self-sacrifice for the group, religious communalism, respect for women, fear of external evils and idealism. (Garvin, 1981, p. 104)

These now require a specific set of cognitive and moral knowledge to negotiate them, which implies particularly "professional," knowledge occupations, such as law, teaching, and wordsmith occupations, which are now restricted by the nature of that knowledge to nationals. And to legitimize this in opposition to a unification and enlightened state one logically had to adopt alternative Romantic ideals as the moral alternative, hence the Gaelic revival's success (totally irrelevant to Ulster).

A semi-new, or manufactured, unique knowledge was prescribed, creating imperatives for the "over-educated and under-employed" to create their own state and job opportunities, protecting and utilizing that knowledge, even opportunities for academics, to intellectualize and mystify into "national culture" what had previously been simple peasant folklore, myths and mysticism, a starting point for Durkheim:

> In fact, it would be no distortion to view Durkheim's entire sociological career as an intransigent and relentless battle fought on two major fronts: against the dark unfathomable forces of mysticism and despair on the one hand, and against the unsubstantial ethereal forces of the dilettantic cult of superficiality on the other. (Alpert, 1961, p. 18)

This supports Garvin's analysis of the social gravity of the I.R.A. (1919–24). They were economically vulnerable, yet also close to the center of rural relations, that is:

> the smalltown and rural "lower middle classes" of post-Parnell Ireland, but it also attracted very considerable support from groups both below and above that social level . . . Young men, particularly the younger sons of small and medium farmers, who had no alternative to emigration, appear to have been particularly active in the movement. (Garvin, 1981, p. 124)

Hart, in his study of the IRA (1919–23) makes a similar observation: "Drawn almost entirely from the working and lower middle classes but disproportionately literate, skilled and employed . . . the guerillas tended to be young men getting ahead in the world" (Hart, 1999, p. 12).

Getting ahead in a cosmopolitan and rationalizing UK with only a Catholic education made manufacturing a non-scientific peasant culture to legitimize small-town and peasant-proprietor relations, very attractive to them.

Concurrently, Ulster (Northern Ireland after 1921) gained its own home rule Parliament within the UK, becoming almost "time frozen" in its old class and sectarian relations. Semi-isolated from the rest of the UK it quickly manufactured its own internal structures, consciousness, and career opportunities. Both sides continued to defend their religious infrastructures, thus Lord Londonderry's plan for integrated education (1923) was dropped due to its hostile reception by all Churches, including a threatened Catholic boycott

(Lyons, 1973, pp. 722–23). And while a third of places in the new police force (RUC) were reserved for Catholics less than a quarter were taken up (Whyte, in Gallagher and O'Connell, 1983).

Meanwhile Catholic nationalist attempts to boycott the new Northern Ireland "state" (English, 2007, pp. 341–45; Fitzpatrick, 1998, pp. 177–86) helped ensure their exclusion, almost as much as Unionist determination to secure their Protestant state, and helped justify gerrymandering and discrimination in several districts (although Northern Ireland's administration remained scrupulously impartial). However, as Murray, Hepburn, and Shea (above) have indicated, the people of Northern Ireland were happier living in separate worlds, constructing carefully designed formulas for exchange and avoiding contentious issues (Harris, 1972).

The South was 90 percent Catholic, which ensured the moral superiority of Catholicism, but nationalist support indicated interesting variations. The eastern seaboard, part of an old maritime economy with Britain and the longest experience of "English" influence, exhibited more features of a modern society, including international trading relations, larger towns, more cosmopolitan, less communal, and a higher proportion of Protestants. Militant nationalism had a lower impact: "the Sinn Fein vote was based on communities rather than on generations or any distinction between old and new voters; it became more total the more Catholic, the more rural, the more western and the less northern an area was" (Garvin, 1981, p. 122).

The western areas, where Gaelic speaking "Gaeltachts" were established, constituted the essence of the nationalist Irish ideal and exhibited the peasant lifestyles Durkheim identified with mechanical solidarity, including a strong religious infusion. These also represent the regions where nationalism's rabid anti-modernism had most resonance, best expressed in Douglas Hyde's (a leading Gaelic Revivalist) 1892 lecture on "The Necessity for De-Anglicising Ireland":

> He equated virtually everything existing in his youth with "real" Irish, even though it may have been an earlier import from England, and denounced virtually every development during his adult years as "anglicisation" . . . He dreaded the threat of a modernized Gaelic Ireland as intensely as the prospect of a modernised anglicised Ireland. The whole infrastructure of modernisation appalled him, and he assumed that Irish could not survive in a modernised world.
>
> Hyde's confusion derived mainly from his equation of modernisation with anglicisation. (Lee, 1989a, pp. 138–39)

English (British) was symbolic of modernity and all associated with it that was destroying rural peasant society, in Ireland and throughout Europe, and this was precisely the appeal of the Romantics. Consequently, just as the German Romantics saw in France the agent of Enlightenment and loss, so Irish nationalists similarly viewed England and modernization. Thus nationalists used Romantic ideals in defense of a Catholic Irish economy, where mystical and non-material values blended with Catholic teaching, while Unionist unification identity reflected their interests.

Both had been through painful radical transformations that created enhanced ethnic identities and collective consciousness, expressed via national allegiance with opposed philosophical and moral imperatives, identical to Durkheim's mechanical and organic solidarities, symbolically represented in their religion and irreconcilable in their imperatives or as a single nation.

# CONCLUSION

# Knowledge, Truth, and the Problem of Useless Knowledge

From a Durkheimian perspective, the partition of Ireland was virtually inevitable and wholly comprehensible and the divisions and sectarian violence in Northern Ireland are wholly explicable. That Catholics and Protestants should form different national identities and aspire to different nation-states is highly rational from a sociological and nationalism perspective, where religion is merely the symbolic representation of two different societies/nations, with different social structures, "conscious collectives," and opposed systems of knowledge. These conform almost precisely to Durkheim's criteria for different societies/nations and also represent the core characteristics for his division between mechanical (Catholic nationalist) and organic (Protestant industrial), which are fundamentally incompatible because they produce truth and knowledge that contradict each other.

Most important, the division was not simply an "attitude of mind" open to psychological manipulation or technical fixes. They represented fundamental differences rooted in different "social milieu" that produced specific forms of social organization (segmental solidarity versus division of labor) that functionally produced different types of knowledge, the product of different structures of relations, which reflected the dominant modes of production. The most explicit representation of this lay in religion (Catholic and scholastic philosophy versus Protestantism and scientific philosophy) and the functional role, place, and value of science in each society, especially in relation to de Valera's explicit rejection of industry (peasant-proprietor versus industrial economy). And this was finally, practically, methodologically and symbolically represented in the "revisionist debate" and how one studies Ireland and the nationalist narrative.

Durkheim argued not so much for a preference for scientific over scholastic philosophy (although clearly preferring science) but that there was a functional imperative for each system of knowledge (culture) and that two such opposed systems of knowledge were logically incompatible within a single society (nation). This was further reflected in their attachment to either Enlightenment or Romantic ideas of national identity, emphasizing primacy of individual and scientific method or primacy of group and emotional attachment. Hence there was a rational basis for Catholic nationalist Ireland seceding from the UK, but an equally rational imperative for Protestant Unionist rejection of Irish nationalism for the UK. The socio-economic relations in each provided not only identity but knowledge of best interests and functional requirements.

However, this does not fully explain Ulster's fractured and conflict-laden history. Here the two identities (cultures or knowledge systems), although incompatible and diametrically opposed, cognitively and morally were forced to co-exist on the same territory under the same state authority. Additionally, they also offered different life opportunities and hence were bound to result in violence and/or a situation of domination/subordination, not equality.

Thus the stability and internal cohesion on which modern nations are premised (a single "people" who legitimize the state and give it authority) was totally lacking due to having two opposed moral and cognitive systems, producing two opposed ideas of legitimacy, authority, reality, and truth. On this basis, there can be no common understanding, shared or collective consciousness, popular will and agreed agendas, nor trust between different people, no imagined community or cohesion, no shared knowledge and truth. All one will identify is enemies, threats, and danger.

The Union was the logical place for Ulster as a whole but it left large sections of its population unable to share this interest because they were not integrated into its dominant system of relations, one of the most important being education. Education not only instructs pupils in the relevant moral and cognitive knowledge to enter into the major economic systems but also knowledge of vital social relations and how to utilize them. Segregated education left the Catholic minority isolated out, thus deepening their resentment and hostility to the new state. From a Durkheimian perspective Catholic nationalists were imbued with useless knowledge, redundant in most practical terms within their wider environment, although vital to maintaining their separate group identity (in an all-Ireland state, Protestant Unionists would have been confronted with similar issues).

In addition, segregated education and social relations left the Catholic community (North and South) fatally lacking in the kind of scientific knowledge required both to enter into a modern industrial economy (Ulster or the UK) or to run it. Gaelic has little use in an industrial economy, nor does scholastic philosophy. One needs scientific and technical subjects relevant to international trade and industry and a scientific frame of reference to successfully enter an industrial economy and administer and govern it, making a traditional Catholic education useless knowledge in Ulster. Of course, the opposite would arise in a Catholic, peasant-proprietor economy, where a scientific education counted as useless knowledge.

Admittedly the Catholic nationalist community chose to opt out of integrated education (the Protestant churches were also hostile) but Durkheim would have regarded permitting them to do so as a major error. Indeed, the entire thrust of his sociology had been how to create an integrated and cohesive France from a state that had been more ethnically and religiously divided than the UK. Integration was not an optional extra for stable, cohesive nations, allowing groups to acquire useless knowledge that was harmful to state cohesion and nation formation had to be resisted, especially in education, the primary agent of national socialization.

To effect such integration Durkheim identified two key principles: first, education should be geared to current and future dominant socio-economic realities (cognitive and moral) and not to reproducing romanticized or non-relevant religious knowledge. This maximized the potential rewards for entering the dominant relations, acquiring useful knowledge for the individual and enhancing their life opportunities, thus maximizing individual cooperation and integration. Second, to avoid ideas of win/lose the aim should be to deconstruct all old ethno-religious identities and redefine everyone in individual terms from which to develop a new single, inclusive group identity and structure of relations able to include all individuals on an equal basis. But this, of course, is a very scientific approach to conflict resolution.

For Durkheim, such integration based on new scientific knowledge had profound implications for all religions, but specifically Catholicism, because religion was primarily about social relations and order and its control over them. And this was particularly so for the Catholic Church whose core concern throughout the rise of nationalism was to retain its traditional control over social relations and agencies of them, such as education, marriage, socialization, community, or welfare, which had traditionally been the Church's role. This, from a Durkheimian perspective of social relations producing knowledge, also implied an attack on the Church's control over the mind, which now passed to science and the state, which also continued in its normal role of controlling political relations, physical force, and material assets.

New industrial and scientific relations (division of labor) therefore implied a fundamental attack on traditional religion, its role, place, and power in society because its knowledge was now made highly marginal to core social relations. Consequently, the Church's authority and power was inevitably undermined as its raison d'être as the agent of social order and control was removed and replaced by the modernizing, scientific state that alone now had the knowledge for functional social order, compatible with political order in an industrial society. Hence, the Church idealized the medieval village where it reigned supreme, also as the unquestioned intellectual agent of the state, where it had a functional relationship with its community.

But this traditional role no longer applied in the modern world, something Protestant Churches had already been partially forced to come to terms with in the Reformation, where the state asserted its primacy over Church. Also, given the association of Protestantism, science-and-industry Protestant Churches had equally been forced to come to terms with some of the key characteristics of modernity, especially personal judgment, individualism, and scientific method (the core elements of liberalism); indeed, some of the Dissenting sects were active proponents of modernity. In this sense, Protestantism already finds itself having crossed the Rubicon of Durkheim's mechanical-organic divide, its knowledge is more in tune with modernity, which also helps explain much of the antipathy of Catholic and Protestant.

This implied not only an incompatibility between religions but more specifically between Catholicism, or any traditional religion, and modernity because their knowledge, authority, and legitimacy would be superseded by science. Consequently, for Durkheim, the modernizing state must act decisively while also treating all religious and/or ethnic groups alike (to ensure equality) by pursuing a rational modernizing agenda to progressively take individuals forward. Of course, this would naturally advance the modernizing state further at religion's expense, especially as modernizing programs based on scientific philosophy exposed the inadequacies of scholastic philosophy to cope with modern problems.

The implication of this for Durkheim, and adopted in France, was to advance beyond all religion and separate ethnic identities—no religion, and for the state to clearly assert itself in a non-ethno-religious manner and scientifically derived identity. This meant a new civic society that recognized only individuals as citizens of France, not Bretons, Basques, Normans, Huguenots, Catholics, or Jews, all claiming special rights and privileges that merely served to foster ethnic and sectarian division and enmity. This was central to the development of a Republican sense of citizenship (knowledge of identity) in France and the realization of its ideals of Egalité, Fraternité, Liberté.

Meanwhile, in another major area of contentious relations (inter-denominational marriages), France led Europe in introducing civil marriage as the only legally recognized form of marriage (religious marriages became an entirely private affair with no legal standing, as was the religious upbring-ing of any children). At a stroke this negated the very divisions the *Ne Temere* decree had instigated and that exacerbated the bitter sectarian tensions in Ireland, as exhibited in Belfast's infamous McCann case.

This is where the European tradition of sociology, nationalism, and the role of the state come in, lacking in the UK and Ireland. Contemporary poli-cies of pluralism, parity of esteem, and multi-culturalism would have seemed very naive to Durkheim, even counter-productive, products of the lack of a clear national "idea" and reflecting Britain's anti-social tradition of empiri-cal individualism, contract theory, and laissez-faire utilitarianism. What is required is a national idea capable of including everyone equally, which implies a civic, secular constitution and social institutions and organizations that equally reflect that, de jure and de facto, in all social relations, permitting no opt outs.

Such a constitution and social institutions also need to be functional to dominant economic interests and needs to make them workable and accept-able, but additionally they require the development of a culture and social relations that reflect the dominant economic structure and is functional to it. Culture contains the moral cement that binds the structural building blocks, the lubrication that oils their operation and interactions, making them interactively smooth and efficient. In the modern world it must of necessity be scientific, which also implies liberal toleration. As such this may well pose bigger problems for the Catholic Church than the Protestants (it is difficult to believe that Durkheim did not specifically have the French Catholic Church in his sights). However, many Protestant Churches also have problems with science (Darwin and creationism being typical); con-sequently, science can genuinely rise above religion and provide a neutral culture that progresses on verifiable grounds that all can share, as opposed to balancing two essentially mystical sets of unscientific dogmas in the public sphere.

It is also useful to reflect here that most of the modernizing nation-states of Europe had to confront the churches about their role and place in politics and society to assert the state's primary role and function over them as direc-tors of social relations and order. This was vital to the success of modernizing states, especially Catholic ones such as France, Italy, and Spain (although less successful in the latter two under Mussolini and Franco) or where there was a strong religious division between Catholic and Protestant, as in Germany or the Netherlands. In all these states they had to face down especially the role and claims to primacy of the Catholic Church as an obstacle to national unity, integration, and progressive modernization, often involving extensive and bitter battles that lasted well into the twentieth century (Spain, its civil war, and Franco being the last great example, apart from Ireland).

This is not to attack the churches as such but, first, to assert the state as the one and only legitimate authority to order and run society, based on civic and liberal (scientific) values that treat everyone equally as individuals and where everyone's direct obligation is to the state as the same primary authority. Second, it is to ensure that knowledge of what is socially, economically, and politically functional (socialization) to society/nation, its cohesion, progressive development, and welfare, becomes the primary and shared knowledge of everyone, a shared scientific culture in a scientific world. It is to exclude "useless" knowledge in the public sphere, although what one wishes to believe and practice in the private sphere should be left alone; indeed, this was precisely the trajectory of most European States and America over the last two hundred years.

In Ulster this provides a way forward because there is already a strong link between Protestantism, science, and industry that provides Protestants with some security and continuity while at the same time offering Catholics a secular way in via a proven methodology with proven rewards. Even for Catholics, a civic society and the Union reflect a dominant reality from which they partly self-exclude themselves but whose material rewards are still attractive. In addition, as the revisionist debate illustrates, many Catholics have already found that science offers legitimate grounds for doubting much of the Catholic nationalist narrative.

Science can provide a basis on which to separate religion from politics and social relations to help build a shared political identity above religion for all individuals once the state takes the lead in creating a secular civic society, which as Durkheim observed can also play the role of a secular religion. This lead is fundamental since without it the social pressures to conform to existing communal norms, attitudes, and behavior will be too strong for most individuals to rise above, especially given the deeply entrenched opposed communities that currently exist.

What one is discussing is the creation of new knowledge via scientific method, a new identity to reflect basic realities founded not just on majority preference but also on what most people in Northern Ireland can identify with. The vast majority have a shared material and calculable interest in Northern Ireland's current position, most have historical roots in it that can be built on. But people also need a sense of security (ontological and more prosaic forms), hence an assured knowledge not just of their present state but also of their future is important. This lets people know where their future lies and hence they decide to invest in it, commit themselves fully, and engage positively. Currently, Northern Ireland stands in a provisional state and vacuum, where its future constitutional position can be altered by referendum.

Referenda on Northern Ireland's future not only raise doubts as to its future but also encourage dissident minorities and raise fears in insecure majorities, which mitigates against cooperation and integration and makes the development of any shared future and conscience collective almost impossible. It reinforces current sectarian knowledge while the current instability and enmities are maintained and even deepened. Equally, consociational government reinforces division by making different communal interests and opposed agendas the primary focus of both communities' politics, with the continual underlying threat and/or opportunity of potential change in the future to undermine cooperation at any permanent or meaningful level. The very relations built into consociational government reproduce knowledge of enmity and opposed interests, help develop a "spoils" approach to government rather than distribution of goods and services on a commonweal benefit basis, and undermine shared relations and collective consciousness.

For Durkheim the only long-term, cohesive society was one based on integrated relations, shared culture, and collective consciousness, founded on imperatives functional to the dominant needs of its milieu (primarily economic). This rarely just occurred; it required conscious construction by the state, conspicuously lacking in the UK but overtly recognized in Europe. The social world, especially the political, is always man-made and its success depends on grasping core truths and realities and responding to them adequately. This includes religion, hence the importance of Durkheim's understanding of God made in the image of man. The existence or not of God is another question, but the political implications of it (or at least the appearance of God in the image of man) are profound, especially in Northern Ireland: God must bear the same image for everyone.

# Bibliography

Abraham, J. H., *Origins and Growth of Sociology,* London: Penguin, 1973.

Akenson, Donald, *Small Differences, Irish Catholics and Irish Protestants 1815–1922,* Dublin: Gill and Macmillan, 1991.

Alder, Ken, *The Measure of All Things,* London: Abacus, 2002.

Alexander, Jeffrey, *Durkheimian Sociology: Cultural Studies,* Cambridge: CUP, 1988.

Alexander, Jeffrey (ed.), *Real Civil Societies,* London: Sage, 1998.

Alpert, H., *Durkheim and His Sociology,* New York: Free Press, 1961.

Alter, Peter, *Nationalism,* London: Edward Arnold, 1989.

Anderson, Benedict, *Imagined Communities,* London: Verso, 1991.

Anderson, Malcolm, and Bort, Eberhard (eds.), *The Irish Border, History, Politics and Culture,* Liverpool: Liverpool University Press, 1999.

Anderson, Perry, *English Questions,* London: Verso, 1992.

Anderson, Perry, *Origins of Postmodernity,* London: Verso, 1998.

Aron, Raymond, *German Sociology,* New York: Free Press, 1964.

Aron, Raymond, *Main Currents in Sociological Thought 2,* London: Penguin, 1967.

Augusteijn, Joost, *The Irish Revolution, 1913–1923,* Basingstoke: Palgrave, 2002.

Bardon, Jonathan, *The Plantation of Ulster,* Dublin: Gill and Macmillan, 2011.

BBC, http://www.bbc.co.uk/news/uk-northern-ireland-21345997

Beckett, J. C., *The Making of Modern Ireland, 1603–1923,* London: Faber, 1969.

*Belfast Agreement,* Belfast: HMSO, 1998.

Bell, John, Hansson, Ulf, and McCaffrey, Nick, *The Troubles Aren't History Yet,* Belfast: Northern Ireland Community Relations Council, 2010.

Bellah, Robert, *Emile Durkheim on Morality and Society,* Chicago: University of Chicago Press, 1973.

Berdahl, R. M., New Thoughts on German Nationalism, in *American Historical Review,* vol. 77, pp. 65–80, 1972.

Berger, Peter, and Luckman, Thomas, *The Social Construction of Reality,* London: Penguin, 1966.

Berlin, Isaiah, *The Crooked Timber of Humanity,* London: Fontana, 1991.

Berlin, Isaiah, *Political Ideas in the Romantic Age,* London: Pimlico, 2007.

Berlin, Isaiah, *The Roots of Romanticism,* London: Pimlico, 2000.

Berlin, Isaiah, *The Sense of Reality,* London: Pimlico, 1996.

Berlin, Isaiah, *Three Critics of the Enlightenment,* London: Pimlico, 2000.

Bew, Paul, *Ideology and the Irish Question,* Oxford: Clarendon, 1998.

Bew, Paul, *Ireland, the Politics of Enmity, 1789–2006,* Oxford: OUP, 2009.

Bew, Paul, Gibbon, Peter, and Patterson, Henry, *Northern Ireland 1921–1996, Political Forces and Social Class,* London: Serif, 1996.

Bew, Paul, Gibbon, Peter, and Patterson, Henry, *The State in Northern Ireland,* Manchester: Manchester University Press, 1979.

Bew, Paul, Hazelkorn, Ellen, and Patterson, Henry, *The Dynamics of Irish Politics,* London: Lawrence and Wishart, 1989.

Bew, Paul, Patterson, Henry, and Teague, Paul, *Between War and Peace, The Political Future of Northern Ireland,* London: Lawrence and Wishart, 1997.

Bew, Paul and Patterson, Henry, *The British State and the Ulster Crisis,* London: Verso, 1985.

Bhaba, Homi, *Nation and Narration,* London: Routledge, 1990.

BICO (British and Irish Communist Organisation), *On the Democratic Validity of the Northern Ireland State,* Belfast: BICO, 1971.

BICO, *The Economics of Partition,* Belfast: BICO, 1972.

Billington, Rosamund, Strawbridge, Sheelagh, Greensides, Leonore, and Fitzsimons, Annette, *Culture and Society,* London: Macmillan, 1991.

Blackbourn, David, *The Fontana History of Germany,* London: Fontana, 1997.

Blackwell, *Encyclopaedia of Political Institutions,* Oxford: Blackwell, 1987.

Bottomore, Tom, and Nisbet, Robert, *A History of Sociological Analysis,* London: Heinemann, 1979.

Bowler, Peter, and Whyte, Nicholas (eds.), *Science and Society in Ireland, 1800–1950,* Belfast: Institute of Irish Studies (QUB), 1997.

Boyce, George, *Nationalism in Ireland,* London: Routledge, 1991.

Boyce, George (ed.), *Nineteenth Century Ireland, the Search for Stability,* Dublin: Gill and Macmillan, 1990.

Boyce, George (ed.), *The Revolution in Ireland, 1879–1923,* Dublin: Gill and Macmillan, 1988.

Boyce, George, and O'Day, Alan (eds.), *Defenders of the Union,* London: Routledge, 2001.

Boyce, George, and O'Day, Alan (eds.), *The Making of Modern Irish History,* London: Routledge, 1996.

Brady, Ciaran (ed.), *Interpreting Irish History,* Dublin: Irish Academic Press, 1994.

Brett, David, *The Plain Style,* Belfast: Black Square, 1999.

Breuilly, John, *Nationalism and the State,* Manchester: Manchester University Press, 1993.

Breuilly, John (ed.), *The State of Germany,* London: Longman, 1992.

Brewster, Scott, Crossman, Virginia, Becket, Fiona, and Alderson, David (eds.), *Ireland in Proximity, History, Gender and Space,* London: Routledge, 1999.

Broadie, Alexander, *The Scottish Enlightenment,* Edinburgh: Birlinn, 2007.

Brooke, John, *Science and Religion,* Cambridge: CUP, 1991.

Brooke, Peter, *Ulster Presbyterianism,* Belfast: Athol, 1994.

Brown, David, and Harrison, Michael, *A Sociology of Industrialisation,* London: Macmillan, 1978.

Brown, Terence, *Ireland, A Social and Cultural History*, London: Fontana, 1981.

Bruce, Steve, *The Edge of the Union*, Oxford: OUP, 1994.

Bruce, Steve, *God Save Ulster*, Oxford: OUP, 1989.

Bruce, Steve, *The Red Hand*, Oxford: OUP, 1992.

Bruce, Steve, *Fundamentalism*, Cambridge: Polity, 2000

Bryson, Lucy, and McCartney, Clem, *Clashing Symbols*, Belfast: Institute for Irish Studies (QUB), 1994.

Buckland, Patrick, *A History of Northern Ireland*, Dublin: Gill and Macmillan, 1981.

Buckland, Patrick, *Irish Unionism, 1885–1923*, Belfast: HMSO, 1973.

Buckley, Anthony (ed.), *Symbols in Northern Ireland*, Belfast: Institute of Irish Studies, 1998.

Bull, Philip, *Land, Politics and Nationalism*, Dublin: Gill and Macmillan, 1996.

Burke, Peter, *History and Social Theory*, Cambridge: Polity, 1992.

Burke, Peter, *A Social History of Knowledge*, Cambridge: Polity, 2000.

Burleigh, Michael, *Earthly Powers*, London: Harper, 2005.

Carr, E. H., *What Is History*, London: Penguin, 1964.

Chadwick, Owen, *A History of the Popes, 1830–1914*, Oxford: OUP, 1998.

Clark, Samuel, *Social Origins of the Irish Land War*, Princeton: Princeton University Press, 1979.

Clark, T. N., *Prophets and Patrons*, Harvard: University of Harvard Press, 1973.

Clifford, Brendan, *The Economics of Partition*, Belfast: Athol, 1992.

Colley, Linda, *Britons, Forging the Nation 1707–1837*, London: Vintage, 1996.

Comerford, R. V., *The Fenians in Context, Irish Politics and Society, 1848–82*, Dublin: Wolfhound, 1998.

Connolly, Sean, *Religion and Society in Nineteenth Century Ireland*, Dundalk: Economic and Social History Society of Ireland, 1985.

Connolly, S. J., *Contested Island, Ireland 1460–1630*, Oxford: OUP, 2009.

Connolly, S. J., *Divided Kingdom, Ireland 1630–1800*, Oxford: OUP, 2008.

Corrish, Peter, *The Irish Catholic Experience*, Dublin: Gill and Macmillan, 1985.

Coulter, Colin, *Contemporary Northern Irish Society*, London: Pluto, 1999.

Cronin, Mike, "Golden Dreams, Harsh Realities: Economics and Informal Empire in the Irish Free State," in Cronin, Mike, and Regan, John (eds.), *Ireland, The Politics of Independence*, Basingstoke: Palgrave Macmillan, 2000.

Cronin, Mike, and Regan, John (eds.), *Ireland, The Politics of Independence, 1922–49*, Basingstoke: Palgrave Macmillan, 2000.

Crozier, Maurna (ed.), *Varieties of Irishness*, Belfast: Institute of Irish Studies (QUB), 1989.

Crozier, Maurna, and Froggatt, Richard (eds.), *Cultural Diversity in Contemporary Europe*, Belfast: Institute of Irish Studies (QUB), 1998.

Darby, John, *Intimidation and the Control of Conflict in Northern Ireland*, Syracuse: Syracuse University Press, 1986.

Deane, Seamus, *Strange Country*, Oxford: Clarendon, 1997.

Delaney, Enda, *Demography, State and Society*, Liverpool: Liverpool University Press, 2000.

De Paor, Liam, *The Peoples of Ireland*, London: Hutchinson, 1986.

Dingley, James, *Flags and Parades Protest, Belfast 2012–13,* ongoing research, Queen's University, Belfast, 2014.

Dingley, James, *The IRA, The Irish Republican Army*, Santa Barbara: Praeger, 2012.

Dingley, James, "Religion, Protestants and National Identity: A Response to the March 2009 Issue," *National Identities*, vol.15, no.2, 2013.

Dingley, James, "Sacred Communities: Religion and National Identities," *National Identities*, vol.13, no.4, 2011b.

Dingley, James, "Terrorism, Religion and Community," *Defence and Security Analysis*, vol.27, no.4, December, 2011a.

Dingley, James, *Nationalism, Social Theory and Durkheim*, Basingstoke: Palgrave Macmillan, 2008.

Dodd, Nigel, *Social Theory and Modernity*, Cambridge: Polity, 1999.

Duke, Sean, *How Irish Scientists Changed the World*, Dublin: Londubh, 2013.

Durkheim, Emile, *The Division of Labour in Society*, London: Macmillan, 1984.

Durkheim, Emile, *The Division of Labour in Society*, New York: Free Press, 1964.

Durkheim, Emile, *The Elementary Forms of Religious Life*, New York: Free Press, 1995.

Durkheim, Emile, *Ethics and the Sociology of Morals*, New York: Prometheus, 1993.

Durkheim, Emile, *Moral Education*, New York: Free Press, 1973.

Durkheim, Emile, *The Rules of Sociological Method*, London: Macmillan, 1982.

Durkheim, Emile, *Socialism*, New York: Collier, 1962.

Durkheim, Emile, *Sociology and Philosophy*, New York: Free Press, 1974.

Durkheim, Emile, *Suicide, a Study in Sociology*, London: Routledge, 1970.

Durkheim, Emile, *Professional Ethics and Civic Morals*, London: Routledge, 1992

Durkheim, Emile, and Mauss, Marcel, *Primitive Classification*, London: Cohen and West, 1970.

Eagleton, Terry, *Scholars and Rebels in Nineteenth Century Ireland*, Oxford: Blackwell, 1999.

Eisenstein, Elizabeth, *The Printing Revolution in Early Modern Europe*, Cambridge: CUP, 2005.

Elliott, Marianne, *The Catholics of Ulster*, London: Penguin, 2001.

Elliott, Marianne, *Robert Emmet, the Making of a Legend*, London: Profile, 2004.

English, Richard, *Irish Freedom, The History of Nationalism in Ireland*, London: Pan Macmillan, 2007.

Eriksen, Thomas Hylland, *Ethnicity and Nationalism, Anthropological Perspectives*, London: Pluto, 1993.

Erskine, John, and Lucy, Gordon (eds.), *Varieties of Scottishness*, Belfast: Institute of Irish Studies (QUB), 1997.

Farrell, Michael, *Northern Ireland: The Orange State*, 1st edition, London: Pluto, 1976; 2nd edition, 1980.

Febvre, Lucien, and Martin, Henri-Jean, *The Coming of the Book, the Impact of Printing, 1450–1800*, London: Verso, 2010.

Fennell, Desmond, *Heresy, The Battle of Ideas in Modern Ireland*, Belfast: Blackstaff, 1993.

Fitzpatrick, David, *The Two Irelands, 1912–1939,* Oxford: Opus, 1998.

Foley, Tadhg, and Ryder, Sean (eds.), *Ideology and Ireland in the Nineteenth Century,* Dublin: Four Courts, 1998.

Foster, Finlay, *The Presbyterian Church in Ireland,* Dublin: Columbia Press, 2000.

Foster, R. F., *Modern Ireland, 1600–1972,* London: Penguin, 1989a.

Foster, R. F. (ed.), *The Oxford History of Ireland,* Oxford: OUP, 1992.

Foster, R. F. (ed.), *Varieties of Irishness,* Belfast: Institute of Irish Studies (QUB), 1989b.

Fulbrook, Mary, *A Concise History of Germany,* Cambridge: CUP, 1990.

Gallagher, Tom, and O'Connell, James (eds.), *Contemporary Irish Studies,* Manchester: Manchester University Press, 1983.

Garvin, Tom, *The Evolution of Irish Nationalist Politics,* Dublin: Gill and Macmillan, 1981.

Garvin, Tom, *Nationalist Revolutionaries in Ireland, 1858–1928,* Oxford: Clarendon, 1987.

Gaukroger, Stephen, *The Emergence of a Scientific Culture,* Oxford: OUP, 2008.

Gellner, Ernest, *Encounters with Nationalism,* Oxford: Blackwell, 1994.

Gellner, Ernest, *Nationalism,* London: Phoenix, 1997.

Gellner, Ernest, *Nations and Nationalism,* Oxford: Blackwell, 1983.

Gellner, Ernest, *Reason and Culture,* Oxford: Blackwell, 1992.

Gibbon, Peter, *The Origins of Ulster Unionism: The Formation of Popular Protestant Politics and Ideology in Nineteenth Century Ireland,* Manchester: Manchester University Press, 1975.

Giddens, Anthony, *Capitalism and Modern Social Theory,* Cambridge: CUP, 1971.

Giddens, Anthony, *The Consequences of Modernity,* Cambridge: Polity, 1991a.

Giddens, Anthony, *Durkheim,* London: Fontana, 1978.

Giddens, Anthony, *Durkheim on Politics and the State,* Cambridge: Polity, 1996.

Giddens, Anthony, *Modernity and Self-Identity,* Cambridge: Polity, 1991b.

Giddens, Anthony, *The Nation-State and Violence,* Cambridge: Polity, 1987.

Giddens, Anthony, *Politics, Sociology and Social Theory,* Cambridge: Polity, 1995.

Glenny, Misha, *The Fall of Yugoslavia,* London: Penguin, 1992.

Goddard, Victoria, Llobera, Josep, and Shore, Chris (eds.), *The Anthropology of Europe, Identities and Boundaries in Conflict,* Oxford: Berg, 1994.

Graham, Brian (ed.), *In Search of Ireland,* London: Routledge, 1997.

Grayling, A. C., *Towards the Light,* London: Bloomsbury, 2007.

Greenfeld, Liah, *Nationalism and the Mind,* Oxford: Oneworld, 2006.

Greenfeld, Liah, *Nationalism, Five Roads to Modernity,* Cambridge: Harvard University Press, 1993.

Greenfeld, Liah, *The Spirit of Capitalism,* Cambridge, MA: Harvard University Press, 2003.

Hall, John, *The State of the Nation,* Cambridge: CUP, 1998.

Hamilton, P., "Emile Durkheim and the Philosophy of Nationalism," in Hamilton, P. (ed.), *Emile Durkheim, Critical Assessments,* London: Routledge, 1990.

Harris, Mary, *The Catholic Church and the Foundation of the Northern Irish State,* Cork: Cork University Press, 1993.

Harris, Rosemary, *Prejudice and Tolerance in Ulster: A Study of Neighbours and Strangers in a Border Community,* Manchester: MUP, 1972.

Hart, Peter, *The IRA and Its Enemies,* Oxford: OUP, 1999.

Hart, Peter, *The IRA at War, 1916–1923,* Oxford: OUP, 2005.

Hastings, Adrian, *The Construction of Nationhood, Ethnicity, Religion and Nationalism,* Cambridge: CUP, 1997.

Hennessey, Thomas, *A History of Northern Ireland, 1920–1996,* Dublin: Gill and Macmillan, 1997.

Hepburn, A. C., *A Past Apart,* Belfast: Ulster Historical Foundation, 1996.

Herbison, Ivan, *Presbyterianism, Politics and Poetry in Nineteenth Century Ulster,* Belfast: Institute of Irish Studies (QUB), 2000.

Herman, Arthur, *The Scottish Enlightenment,* London: Fourth Estate, 2003.

Heskin, Ken, *Northern Ireland, A Psychological Analysis,* Dublin: Gill and Macmillan, 1980.

Heslinga, M. W., *The Irish Border as a Cultural Divide,* Assen: van Gorcum, 1979.

Hickox, Stephen, *The Ideology of Intellectual Elites and Its Implications for the Sociology of Knowledge,* PhD thesis, University of London, 1976.

Hill, Myrtle, and Barber, Sarah (eds.), *Aspects of Irish Studies,* Belfast: Institute of Irish Studies (QUB), 1990.

Hobsbawm, Eric, *Nations and Nationalism Since 1780, Programme, Myth, Reality,* Cambridge: Canto, 1992.

Hobsbawm, Eric, and Ranger, Terence, *The Invention of Tradition,* Cambridge: Canto, 1992.

Holsti, Kalevi, *The State, War and the State of War,* Cambridge: CUP, 1996.

Hoppen, Theodore, *Ireland Since 1800,* London: Longman, 1999.

Howe, Stephen, *Ireland and Empire,* Oxford: OUP, 2000.

Hughes, Stuart, *Consciousness and Society,* New York: Vintage, 1961.

Hutcheson, Francis, *Philosophical Writings,* London: Everyman, 1994.

Inglis, Tom, *Moral Monopoly,* Dublin: University College Dublin Press, 1998.

Israel, Joachim, *Alienation: From Marx to Modern Sociology,* Hemel Hempstead: Harvester Press, 1979

James, Paul, *Nation Formation, Towards a Theory of Abstract Community,* London: Sage, 1996.

Jarman, Neil, *Material Conflicts,* Oxford: Berg, 1997.

Jenkins, Brian, *Nationalism in France—Class and Nation Since 1789,* London: Routledge, 1990.

Jenks, Chris, *Culture,* London: Routledge, 1993.

Jones, Susan Stedman, *Durkheim Reconsidered,* Cambridge: Polity, 2001.

Joy, Sinead, *The IRA in Kerry, 1916–1921,* Cork: Collins, 2005.

Kearney, Richard (ed.), *The Irish Mind,* Dublin: Wolfhound, 1985.

Kedourie, Elie, *Nationalism,* Oxford: Blackwell, 1993.

Kellas, James, *The Politics of Nationalism and Ethnicity,* London: Macmillan, 1991.

Kennedy, Liam, *Colonialsim, Religion and Nationalism in Ireland,* Belfast: Institute of Irish Studies (QUB), 1996.

Kennedy, Liam, and Ollerenshaw, Philip, (eds.), *An Economic History of Ulster, 1820–1939,* Manchester: Manchester University Press, 1985.

Kennedy, Liam, and Ollerenshaw, Philip, (eds.), *Ulster Since 1600,* Oxford: OUP, 2013.

Kenny, Anthony, *Medieval Philosophy,* Oxford: Clarendon, 2007.

Keogh, Dermot, and Haltzel, Michael (eds.), *Northern Ireland and the Politics of Reconciliation,* Cambridge: CUP, 1993.

Kingsley, Paul, *Londonderry Revisited,* Belfast: Belfast Publications, 1989.

Kinnvall, Catarina, "Globalization and Religious Nationalism: Self, Identity and the Search for Ontological Security," *Political Psychology,* vol.25, no.5, pp. 741–67, 2004.

Krolikowski, Alanna, "State Personhood in Ontological Security Theories of International Relations and Chinese Nationalism: A Sceptical View," *Chinese Journal of International Politics,* vol.2, pp. 109–33, 2008.

Kung, Hans, *The Catholic Church, A Short History,* London: Weidenfield and Nicolson, 2001.

Laffan, Michael, *The Partition of Ireland, 1911–1925,* Dublin: Dublin Historical Association, 1983.

Lee, J. J., *Ireland, 1912–1985, Politics and Society,* Cambridge: CUP, 1989a.

Lee, J. J., *The Modernisation of Irish Society, 1848–1918,* Dublin: Gill and Macmillan, 1989b.

Lehmann, Jennifer, *Deconstructing Durkheim,* London: Routledge, 1993.

Llobera, Josep, "Concept of Nation in French Social Theory," *Nations and Nationalism,* vol.4, no.1, Jan. 1998.

Llobera, Josep, *The God of Modernity, The Development of Nationalism in Western Europe,* Oxford: Berg, 1996.

Loftus, Belinda, *Orange and Green,* Dundrum: Picture Press, 1994.

Longley, Edna, "Belfast Diary," *London Review of Books,* vol.14, n.1, Jan. 9, 1992.

Loughlin, James, *Ulster Unionism and British National Identity Since 1885,* London: Pinter, 1995.

Lucy, Gordon, *The Great Convention,* Lurgan: Ulster Society, 1995.

Lukes, Steven, *Emile Durkheim, His Life and Work: A Historical Study,* London: Peregrine, 1975.

Lukes, Steven and Scull, Andrew, *Durkheim and the Law,* Basingstoke: Palgrave Macmillan, 2013.

Lux, Kenneth, *Adam Smith's Mistake,* Boston: Shambhala, 1990.

Lyon, Judson, "The Herder Syndrome: A Comparative Study of Cultural Nationalism," in *Ethnic and Racial Studies,* vol.17, no.2, 1994.

Lyons, F. S. L., *Culture and Anarchy in Ireland, 1890–1939,* Oxford: OUP, 1982.

Lyons, F. S. L., *Ireland Since the Famine,* London: Fontana, 1973.

MacCulloch, Diarmaid, *Reformation, Europe's House Divided, 1490–1700,* London: Penguin, 2004.

MacDonagh, Oliver, *States of Mind, A Study of Anglo-Irish Conflict 1780–1980,* London: Allen and Unwin, 1983.

Malcolm, Noel, *Kosovo, a Short History,* London: Papermac, 1998.

Mauss, H., *A Short History of Sociology,* London: Routledge, 1965.

Mayer, Arno, "The Lower Middle Class as Historical Problem," *Journal of Modern History,* vol.47, Sept. 1975.

McCann, Eamon, *War and an Irish Town,* 1st edition, London: Penguin, 1974, 2nd edition, London: Pluto, 1980.

McCormack, W., *Dublin 1916, the French Connection,* Dublin: Gill and Macmillan, 2012.

McCrone, David, *The Sociology of Nationalism,* London: Routledge, 1998.

McGarry, Fearghal, *The Rising, Ireland: Easter 1916,* Oxford: OUP, 2011.

McGarry, John, and O'Leary, Brendan, *Explaining Northern Ireland,* Oxford: Blackwell, 1995.

McGrath, Michael, *The Catholic Church and Catholic Schools in Northern Ireland,* Dublin: Irish Academic Press, 2000.

McLaughlin, Jim, "Industrial Capitalism, Ulster Unionism and Orangeism—An Historical Reappraisal," *Antipode,* vol.12, no.1, 1980.

Mellor, Philip, "Sacred Contagion and Social Vitality: Collective Effervescence," in *Durkheimian Studies,* vol.4, n.s., 1998.

Merton, Robert, *The Sociology of Science,* Chicago: University of Chicago Press, 1973.

Mestrovic, Stjepan, *Durkheim and Postmodern Culture,* New York: de Gruyter, 1992.

Miller, David, *Rethinking Northern Ireland,* London: Longman, 1998.

Milner, Andrew, *Cultural Theory, an Introduction,* London: UCL Press, 1994.

Mitchell, A., *The German Influence in France After 1870,* North Carolina: University of North Carolina Press, 1979.

Mitchell, Paul, and Wilford, Rick (eds.), *Politics in Northern Ireland,* Oxford: Westview, 1999.

Mommsen, Wolfgang, *Imperial Germany, 1867–1918,* London: Arnold, 1996.

Mommsen, Wolfgang, *Max Weber and German Politics, 1890–1920,* Chicago: University of Chicago Press, 1990.

Montgomery, Lord, *A Concise History of Warfare,* Ware: Wordsworth, 2000.

Morgan, Austen, *Labour and Partition,* London: Pluto, 1991.

Munck, Ronnie, *Ireland: Nation, State and Class Conflict,* Boulder: Westview, 1985.

Murray, Dominic, *Worlds Apart, Segregated Schools in Northern Ireland,* Belfast: Appletree, 1985.

Nisbet, Robert, *Emile Durkheim,* Greenwood: Connecticut, 1965.

Nisbet, Robert, "The French Revolution and the Rise of Sociology in France," *American Journal of Sociology,* September, 1943.

Nisbet, Robert, *The Sociological Tradition,* New Brunswick: Transaction, 1996.

Nisbet, Robert, *Tradition and Revolt,* New Brunswick: Transaction, 1999.

Nolan, Paul, *Northern Ireland Peace Monitoring Report, Number One,* Belfast, Northern Ireland Community Relations Council, 2012.

Nord, Philip, "Social Defence and Conservative Regeneration: the National Revival, 1900–14," in Tombs, R. (ed.), *Nations and Nationhood in France,* London: Harper-Collins, 1991.

Norman, Edward, *A History of Modern Ireland,* London: Penguin, 1971.

O'Boyle, L., "The Problem of an Excess of Educated Men in Western Europe, 1800–1850," *Journal of Modern History,* pp. 471–95, Dec. 1970.

O'Brien, Conor, *Ancestral Voices,* Dublin: Poolbeg, 1994.

O'Brien, Conor, *God Land,* Harvard: Harvard University Press, 1988.

O'Connor, Arthur, *The State of Ireland,* Dublin: Lilliput, 1998.

O'Connor, Fionnuala, *In Search of a State, Catholics in Northern Ireland,* Belfast: Blackstaff, 1993.

O'Dowd, Liam (ed.), *On Intellectuals and Intellectual Life in Ireland,* Belfast: Institute of Irish Studies (QUB), 1996.

O'Grada, Cormac, *Ireland, a New Economic History, 1780–1939,* Oxford: OUP, 1995.

O'Halloran, Clare, *Partition and the Limits of Irish Nationalism,* Dublin: Gill and Macmillan, 1987.

O'Leary, Don, *Roman Catholicism and Modern Science,* London: Continuum, 2006.

Ong, Walter, *Orality and Literacy,* London: Routledge, 2002.

Pagden, Anthony, *The Enlightenment, and Why It Still Matters,* Oxford: OUP, 2013.

Paine, Tom, *The Rights of Man,* London: Penguin, 1969.

Parsons, Gerald, *Perspectives on Civil Religion,* Aldershot: Ashgate, 2002.

Patterson, Henry, *Ireland Since 1939, Persistence of Conflict,* London: Penguin, 2006.

Patterson, Henry, *The Politics of Illusion,* London: Hutchinson, 1989.

Pickering, Bill, *Durkheim: Essays on Morals and Education,* London: Routledge, 1979.

Pickering, Bill, and Martins, H, (eds.), *Debating Durkheim,* London: Routledge, 1994.

Plamenatz, John, *Man and Society, vols. I, II and III,* London: Longman, 1982.

Porter, Roy, *Enlightenment,* London: Penguin, 2000.

Probert, Belinda, *Beyond Orange and Green: The Political Economy of the Northern Ireland Crisis,* London: Zed, 1978.

Purdue, Olwen, (ed.), *Belfast, The Emerging City 1850–1914,* Dublin: Irish Academic Press, 2013.

Ravetz, Jerry, *Scientific Knowledge and Its Social Problems,* London: Penguin, 1971.

Remond, Rene, *Religion and Society in Modern Europe,* Oxford: Blackwell, 1999.

Ringer, F. K., *Decline of the German Mandarins,* Harvard: Harvard University Press, 1969.

Riordan, Michelle, *The gaelic Miond and the Collapse of the Gaelic World,* Cork: Cork University Press, 1990

Roebuck, Peter (ed.), *Plantation to Partition,* Belfast: Blackstaff, 1981.

Roll, Eric, *A History of Economic Thought,* London: Faber, 1973.

Ruane, Joseph, and Todd, Jennifer, *The Dynamics of Conflict in Northern Ireland,* Cambridge: CUP, 1996.

Russell, Bertrand, *History of Western Philosophy,* London: Routledge, 1996.

Ruthven, Malise, *Fundamentalism, the Search for Meaning,* Oxford: OUP, 2005.

Ryder, Chris, and Kearny, Vincent, *Drumcree,* London: Methuen, 2001.

Schmauss, Warren, *Durkheim's Philosophy of Science and the Sociology of Knowledge,* Chicago: University of Chicago Press, 1994.

Scruton, Roger, *Kant,* Oxford: OUP, 1982.

Sennett, Richard, *The Fall of Public Man,* London: Faber, 1986.

Shapin, Steven, *The Scientific Revolution,* Chicago: University of Chicago Press, 1998.

Shapin, Steven, *A Social History of Truth,* Chicago: University of Chicago Press, 1995.

Shea, Patrick, *Voices and the Sound of Distant Drums,* Belfast: Blackstaff, 1983.

Singer, Peter, *Hegel,* Oxford: OUP, 1983.

Smith, Anthony, *Chosen Peoples, Scared Sources of National Identity,* Oxford: OUP, 2003.

Smith, Anthony, *The Ethnic Origins of Nations,* Oxford: Blackwell, 1986.

Smith, Anthony, *National Identity,* London: Penguin, 1991.

Smith, Anthony, *Nationalism and Modernism,* London: Routledge, 1998.

Smith, Anthony, *Nations and Nationalism in a Global Era,* Cambridge: Polity, 1995.

Sokal, Alan, *Beyond the Hoax,* Oxford: OUP, 2010.

Stace, W.T., *The Philosophy of Hegel,* New York: Dover, 1955.

Stern, Fritz, *The Politics of Cultural Despair: A Study in the Rise of Germanic Ideology,* Berkeley: University of California Press, 1974.

Stewart, A. T. Q., *A Deeper Silence,* Belfast: Blackstaff, 1998.

Stewart, A. T. Q., *The Narrow Ground,* London: Faber, 1989.

Stringer, Peter, and Robinson, Gillian (ed.), *Social Attitudes in Northern Ireland,* Belfast: Blackstaff, 1991.

Swingewood, Alan, *A Short History of Sociological Thought,* London: Macmillan, 1984.

Taylor, Rupert, *Consociational Theory,* London: Routledge, 2011.

Teague, Paul, (ed.), *Beyond the Rhetoric,* London: Lawrence and Wishart, 1987.

Thompson, Andrew, and Fevre, Ralph, "The National Question: Sociological Reflections on Nation and Nationalism," *Nations and Nationalism,* vol.7, no.3, July, 2001.

Thompson, Frank, *The End of Liberal Ulster,* Belfast: Ulster Historical Foundation, 2001.

Thompson, Kenneth, *Emile Durkheim,* London: Routledge, 1982.

Tint, H., *The Decline of French Patriotism, 1870–1940,* London: Weidenfeld and Nicolson, 1964.

Tombs, R., *Nationhood and Nationalism in France,* London: Harper-Collins, 1991.

Tombs, Robert, *France, 1814–1914,* London: Longman, 1996.

Tonge, Jonathan, *Northern Ireland, Conflict and Change,* London: Prentice Hall, 1998.

Turner, Bryan, *Religion and Social Theory,* London: Sage, 1991.

Turner, J. H., Beeghley, L., and Powers, C. H., *The Emergence of Sociological Theory,* Wadsworth: Belmont California, 1969.

Uglow, Jenny, *The Lunar Men,* New York: Farra, Strauss and Giroux, 2003.

Van der Veer, Peter, and Lehman, Hartmut, (eds.), *Nation and Religion, Perspectives on Europe and Asia,* Princeton: Princeton University Press.

Walker, Graham, *Intimate Strangers,* Edinburgh: John Donald, 1995.

Weber, Eugen, *Peasants into Frenchmen, The Modernization of Rural France, 1870–1914,* Stanford: Stanford University Press, 1976.

Weber, Max, *The Theory of Social and Economic Organization,* New York: Free Press, 1964.

West, David, *An Introduction to Continental Philosophy,* Cambridge: Polity, 1996.

Whyte, John, *The Church and State in Modern Ireland, 1923–1970,* Dublin: Gill and Macmillan, 1971.

Whyte, John, "Interpretations of the Northern Ireland Problem: An Appraisal," *Economic and Social Review,* vol.9, no.4, July, 1978.

Whyte, John, *Interpreting Northern Ireland,* Oxford: Clarendon, 1991.

Whyte, Nicholas, *Science, Colonialism and Ireland,* Cork: Cork University Press, 1999.

Witcher, Sabine, *Northern Ireland Since, 1945,* London: Longman, 1991.

Wolf, K. (ed.), *Essays on Sociology and Philosophy by Emile Durkheim,* London: Harper, 1964.

Zamoyski, Adam, *Holy Madness,* London: Weidenfield and Nicolson, 1999.

Zeitlin, Irving, *Ideology and the Development of Social Theory,* New Jersey: Prentice Hall, 1994.

# Index

Act of Union, 1800, 154; and Ulster,
    154–55; and Catholics, 155; and
    separate consciousness, 155; new
    economic relations, 155–56
ancien régime, 8, 68
Anglicans (Church of Ireland), 152
Anglo-Irish: as not Irish, 147
arts: and Romantics,71–72
Aquinas, Thomas, 9
Aristotle, 130
Ascendancy, 153, 155, 158–60

books: as revolutionary, 85
Britain/British: utilitarian individualism,
    87; ideas, 96; as Protestant, 156;
    industrial interests, 170

Catholicism/Roman Catholicism, 5–10;
    opposition to science, modernity
    and industry, 73, 81–82; Church
    in Ireland, 156–60; as sectarian,
    157–58; scholastic mindset and
    blindness to Protestants, 162;
    consciousness and exclusiveness,
    163–65; blends with Gaelic
    against English culture, 166; self-
    exclusion, 177–78; working for
    state as traitors, 179; education as
    opposed to UK needs, 181–82;
    useless knowledge in Ulster,
    186–87; concern to control social
    relations, 187–88; France and
    Durkheim, 188–89
ceremony and rituals, 21, 42

change: and development, 37; and
    unification nationalism, 85–87;
    and loss of identity, 166–67
civic: society as way forward, 190
class, social: middle class and
    nationalism, 90–91; within
    Unionism, 175–76; membership
    of IRA, 181
communications: growth of
    19th century, 159–60; and
    consciousness, 172–73
community/collective: and barriers, 48;
    imagined, 78–79; and literature,
    music and arts, 85; nation as
    new, 93–95
conflict/social, political: causes and
    resolution, 19–20
consciousness, 68–69; early national,
    81; in Ireland, 124–25; Protestant
    in Ulster and 1798, 125; formation
    of Ulster Protestant, 161–62; new
    Catholic Irish interests, 170–71;
    informed by religion, 172–73; and
    segregated living, 177–78; nation
    requires single, 187
consociationalism, 1; creates division, 191
cosmology, 101
cosmopolitanism, 132; rejection of, 147
Creoles, 84
Cullen, Cardinal, 157–60
culture, 76–77; high, 79; high and
    development, 85–86; shared
    culture and division of labor, Irish
    nationalist as non-science, 127;

culture (*Continued*)
   Anglo-Irish and Gaelic-Irish,
      128–29; cultural studies, 129;
      and ultimate truths, 130; Ulster's
      as plain style, 131; Ulster as
      uncultured, 132–33; as symbol
      of living nation, 140–41; and
      language, 141; specificity in Irish
      nationalism, 144; nationalist
      reflects rural life, 145–46;
      importance of, 190

data and census collections, 89–90
De-Anglicizing Ireland, 147, 182–83
democracy: and language, 91–94
De Valera, 95, 176; opposed to
      industry, 185
development, 6, 50; and origins of
      nationalism, 77–78, 81–82;
      of Ulster, 151–52
Dissenters, 152–53; as Liberals, 174–75
division: in Northern Ireland and
      Europe, 4
Dublin: Dublin 4, 101–4; and reality,
      108–9
Durkheim, Emile: role of intellectual,
      144–45; and social relations in
      Ireland, 172–73; as opposed to
      mystic and dilettantic, 181–82;
      state response to modernization,
      186–87
   cohesion/social cohesion, 19–20
   consciousness/collective
      consciousness, 17–19; collective
      authority, 25–26; in Ireland, 155
   division of labor, 7–8, 26
   education, importance of integrated,
      186–87
   facts, 41–42
   knowledge, cognitive and moral,
      18–19, 23–24; segmental in
      Ireland, 25–26; social origins
      of, 36–50; as functional, 49–50;
      mechanical contrasted with organic
      and role of religion and science,
      50–51

   lack of analysis on Ireland, 118
   law, 25–26
   mechanical solidarity, 17–26;
      violence and passion, 28–29; and
      knowledge, 51–54
   organic solidarity, 17–26; and
      knowledge, 55–60; and rise of
      science, Positivism and nation,
      123–24
   progress, 24, 25, 44–46, 161–62
   reality/social, 23, 41
   religion, 19, 22–23; as knowledge,
      33–34; as society, 34–35, 36–49,
      179; superseded by science, 188
   Romantics, rejection of, 133–34
   segmental solidarity, 23–25
   society as nation, 14–15, 16–17
   structure, 15

economy/economics, 7; rewards, 73, 76;
      development, 80–81; traditional
      pre-modern versus modern,
      85; and Romantics, 86; and
      Marxist interpretation of Ulster,
      115–17; scientific economics,
      134; economic change and Young
      Ireland, 141–42; development in
      Ulster, 157
education, 21–22, 47–50; excess of
      educated/over-educated, 74–75;
      and nation creation, 89–90;
      over-educated, 94–95; role
      of educated middle class in
      nationalism, scientific, 134–37;
      denominational and scholastic
      versus scientific, 163; teachers
      and Gaelic, 165–66; segregated,
      177–78; Catholic rejection of
      integrated in Ulster, 181; segregated
      disadvantages Catholics, 182
England: consciousness, 81; as cultural
      enemy, 147–48; influence and
      degree of nationalist hostility,
      182–83
English economics and utilitarianism,
      60, 73–74, 85–86

enlightenment: Protestant and progress in Ireland, 24–25, 27, 49–50; and nationalism, 66; as corrupting, 70; and revisionism, 114; and Ulster radicalism, 153–54

ethnic/ethnicity, 1, 29–30; versus unification and rational knowledge, 43–45; and development, 76–77; formation of 78–81; and economic development, 87–88; used as subordination/domination, 94–95

Europe: different intellectual and political tradition from the UK, 67, 89

facts: interpretation of, 90, 111

Famine, 157–58; and reformation of Catholic peasant society, 163–64; dependent on British markets pre-1879, 167

farms/farming: Catholic in Ireland, 93–94; post-Famine rise of small market orientated, 167–70; loss of natural protection, 168–69; fear of tax increases, 170; peasant-proprietorship, 171

Fichte, 68

Field Day, 112–13

France: in 19th century, 13–15, 20, 26; French Revolution, 64; consciousness, 81; and education, 91; creation of modern, 189

freedom: Romantic concept, 67–68

functionalism, 21–22; success of nationalism, 97, 120–21; role of cultural knowledge in Ireland, 165–67; role of religion, 186

Gaelic: importance of to Young Ireland, 142; revival, 143; Gaelic and Catholicism as non-English, 144–45; and Romantic story chimes with peasants, 145; traditional way of life, 146; growth in popularity and anti-cosmopolitanism and compared to Anglo-Irish, 147–49; Gaelicization and exclusion of Protestants, 172–73; as useless knowledge, 173; as anti-modern and rural, 173–74; Gaeltachts, 182

Germany, 60, 66–67, 75–76, 87–88; and *Kulturkampf*, 90; Romantic influence on Young Ireland, 139

God, 27, 68, 69–70; in man's image, 191

Godless colleges, 134

government: growth of, 90–91

Hegel, 69–72, 79, 82

Herder, 72, 75–76, 82, 143

history: use of in nation creation, 89–90; helps construct nation, 123–24

Home Rule: Ulster opposition to, 174

idea: Hegel's, 69; of Irish nation, 98–99; lack of in Britain, 99, 191

ideas: religious and scientific, 41, 45–46, 47; British ideas, 99

identity: state and shared, 82–83

imagined community, 79; science and progress, 23–24

imperialism: and Ireland, 108–9, 130; as literary attack, 138; Marxist critique of, 138

individual/individualism, 38, 43, 66

industry/industrial/industrialization and standardization, 75–78; and unification nationalism, 85–86; and separatist, 93–94; organization in Ulster, 176–77; require new relations, 187

integration: Durkheimian ideal for Ulster, 189–91

intellectuals, 38, 92; role of in nation-state, 144–45

international trade: adverse affects on Irish farming, 168–69

Ireland, 1–2, 30; and partition, 124–25; consequences of Ireland in, 133–34; Catholic suspicion of science, 134–35; as Gaelic and non-English, 145–46

*Irish Historical Studies,* 102
Irish nationalism/nationalists, 71,
    76, 87–88; and economics, 93;
    as Romantic and anti-science,
    146–47; as eulogy of Catholic,
    peasant and Gaelic, 147–48;
    need to de-Anglicize, 147; as
    parochial self-defense, 148; as
    ascetic against English materialism,
    168; as anti-industrial, 170;
    attitudes to Protestant-Unionists,
    173–74; boycott of new Northern
    Ireland, 182
Italy, 88

Jews/Jewish, 11, 26
journalists: as manufacturers of
    knowledge, 170–71

Kant, Immanuel, 16, 37, 60–61, 67–68
knowledge, 18, 23–25, 33–34; as
    functional necessity, 35–36;
    social origins of, 36–50; mass
    and deliberative/sensate versus
    conceptual, 43–50; sensate, 52;
    mechanical solidarity and 52–55;
    and organic solidarity and, 55–58;
    and resistance to change, 59;
    nationalism as, 98; academics as
    producers and legitimating power,
    111; peasant and culture, 140; of
    collective, 162; industrial versus
    peasant, 163; Gaelic-Catholic
    against English-ness, 165–66;
    and journalists, 170, 172; Gaelic
    as useless knowledge, 173–74;
    nationalists lack of regarding
    Protestant/Unionists, 176; and
    segregated education, 177–78;
    professional knowledge producers,
    181; functional imperative, 186;
    Catholic as useless in Ulster,
    186–87; modern and Protestant,
    188; states role to ensure
    functional, 190

land: and ownership, 22–23; Acts and
    War, 159; and cultural revival, 167;
    Land War, 169; ownership and
    control, 170–71
language, 46, 70–71, 72, 81–84; multi-
    language states, 84; and unification
    states, 85, 89, 91; rise of vernacular
    separatist, 93; and vernacular as
    soul of nation, 140–41
law, 50; Romantic ideal, 234; as
    Durkheimian index in Ireland,
    298–99
liberal/liberalism, 14, 26–28, 130;
    opposition to Home Rule, 174–75
liberty, 58–59

Mandarins, 66–67; and intellectuals,
    87–89, 94–95, 181
Marx/Marxists, 1, 76, 60–61, 115–18
McCann Case, 158, 189
modernization/modernity, 6, 27;
    destructive of old knowledge, 58;
    and ethnicity, 77–78; and high
    culture, 92–93; modernization and
    social change disrupting Ireland,
    148; and technology undermine
    rural economy, 168–70; states
    confront Catholic Church, 189–90
morals/morality, 13, 19–20, 25,
    29–31, 33–37, 40–41, 51, 68,
    70–71, 98, 130; nation as
    moral force, 98, 130
multi-culturalism, 1, 4, 27; and
    revisionism, 112–14, 189
mysticism/myths, 13, 24–25, 27, 91,
    104, 108; cause troubles in Ulster,
    109–10

narrative: nationalist, 106–7
nation: history of idea, 67–72; as
    religion, 72–75; origin of word,
    124; social construction of 75–78;
    ethnic characteristics, 78–81; as
    reality, 79–80; as new community,
    94; nation construction and

academics, 119–23; construction
as two-way process, 121; role of
transport and communications,
121; defining and Durkheim, 123;
problem of definition, 123–24
national economics, 66–67, 87–88; and
Sinn Fein, 96–97
nationalism, 1–2, 5–6; Durkheim's,
11–13, 34; defined 60–61;
and vested interests, 86–94; as
reawakening, 95–96; as petit
bourgeois, 96–97; and Durkheim's
sociology; 98, as cognitive and
moral knowledge, 98–99; and
science, 128; as anti-material
literary and folk culture, 128–29;
as anti-science, 139; Catholic, 163;
identity in Ireland, 185–86
Northern Ireland, 1; as terminus
of revisionism debate, 109;
development of new integration,
190–91

objectivity, 5, 66, 98; and revisionism,
105; importance of in nationalism,
110, 131
O'Connell, Daniel, 141; and Repeal
and Catholic consciousness,
156, 163
ontology/ontological security, 23,
34, 37–38, 71; insecurity and
industrial development, 94–95,
111, 179, 191
Orange Order: origins of, 154, 160;
color and pageantry, 161, organizes
all Protestants, 175–76
order/social order: and change, 36–37
over-educated and under-employed,
75–76, 91–93, 94–95, 97

parochial, 53
partition of Ireland: as between
Enlightenment and Romantic,
148–49; Durkheimian
perspective, 185

passion, 28, 39
Pearse, Patrick, 40
peasant/peasant-proprietor, 28, 95;
and Romanticism, 139–40
penal laws, 152
plantation of Ulster, 152–53
Plato, 9, 130
pluralism, 4, 104
politics, 3, 42, 72, 171
post-modernism, 4, 21, 27
Presbyterians, 73, 152–54
print: and Reformation, science and
books, 81; print capitalism, 82;
and books, 130
progress, 23, 25–26, 27–29
Protestants/Protestantism: truth and
science, 24, 56; concept of nation,
67–68; efforts to write them into
Irish history, 113–14; revival
and ethnocentricity and new
socio-economic relations, 160–62;
and modernity, 186–88

rationalism, 29; and scientific
knowledge, 43, 56–57
reality/real world, 109, 114–15
Reformation, 82; and science, 131
relations/social relations, 35, 36–37,
39; mechanical, 52–55; extended,
45, 51, 55–60; science destructive
of, 58; industrial change and
Protestant consciousness, 157, 161;
and segregated education, 177–78;
importance of integrated, 186–87;
creating non-religious, 189
religion, 2, 4, 26–27, 38, 44; as false
freedom and reality, 37; different
systems as antagonistic, 37–38; as
relations, 59–60; and language,
71–72; and nationalism, 68–75;
as organized knowledge and
consciousness in nationalism,
68–69; opposition to modernity,
71; as collective expression, 161; as
form of communication, 171–72;

religion (*Continued*)
  as relations, shared knowledge
    and consciousness, 179;
    system of knowledge, 185–86;
    incompatibility between, 188
revisionism/anti-revisionism, 5; defined,
    101–2; origins of revisionists,
    102–3; as liberals, empiricists and
    enlightened, 102–3; as Protestant
    and colonial throwbacks, 104–5;
    English/British origins, 104–6;
    as scientific analysis, 102–4;
    anti-revisionist as Catholics and
    anti-science, single narrative to
    Irish history, 105–6; revisionists
    as value-free, 105–6; political
    implications of revisionism/
    defenders of Unionism, 119–20;
    reflects Enlightenment versus
    Romanticism, 120; relevance of
    Durkheim to debate, 120–23;
    anti-revisionists as Romantics, 122;
    and culture, 138
riots: sectarian, 161–62
Romantics/Romanticism, 26–27; and
    mysticism, 40; and emotional
    knowledge, 42–43, 53, 67–71;
    and economics, 87; and Ireland,
    129; and nationalism, 139–45;
    legitimizing philosophy for
    nationalists, 148
rural life: pre-industrial and Durkheim's
    mechanical solidarity, 124

sacred and soul, 20, 22; and profane,
    40, 50–52, 69–75
sacrifice, 20–21, 28, 36–37, 40;
    to nation/God, 74, 163
scholastic philosophy/scholasticism,
    9–10, 108, 130, 149, 163, 176
science/scientific philosophy, 5, 9,
    23–27, 30, 41–42; and rise of
    individual and liberty, 53–59;
    dearth of graduates in, 75; and
    history, 110; method, 110; as

political bias and Protestant,
    127–30; as imperialist and lifeless,
    130–31; clash with Romantics,
    132–34; and civilizing mission,
    134; and denominational
    education, 134–35; as
    predominantly British/Protestant,
    136–38; as killing, 140; and
    Catholicism, 141–42; supersedes
    religion, 187; rising above old
    differences and shared identity,
    190–91
scientists as international, 38–39
Scottish Enlightenment: Ulster as part
    of, 136–37, 155
Scottish nationalism, 97
self-determination, 41, 70
self-realization: Romantic, 112
small town: rise of in rural economy,
    163–64; threatened by
    modernization, 169–73; middle
    class and professionals, 170–71;
    priest as core figure, 171; and
    structures of knowledge, 173–74;
    increased numbers living in, 172;
    towns linked by modern networks,
    172, 180; and IRA, 181
social construction: of nations, 75–78, 79
social facts and realism, 13–15, 20–21
social organization/order, 20–23,
    27–29; types of knowledge, 185
social structure, 7, 35–36, 123–25;
    mechanical, 52–55; organic,
    55–60; Marxist socio-economic,
    116–18
Socialism, 98
socialization, 49, 97
society as nation, 2–3
sociology/social theory, 1–8, 15, 88,
    89, 115; and Durkheim's and
    nationalism, 98, 110; helps
    construct nation, 124–25, 130, 189
soul, 20–21, 38, 40, 58–59, 67, 74–75,
    104, 139, 141–74, 164, 165, 179
sovereignty, 64–65

specialization, 30, 55–59

spontaneity, 53, 70–71

state, 29, 50; defined, 64–67; British concept of, 67, 89; Hegel on, 69–71; and religion, 74; development of, 81–86, 90; modern state role, 189–90

structure, 131

structural-functionalism: Marxist on Ireland 114–18; non-Marxist and Ireland, 123–25

struggle and suffering (*sturm und drang*), 70, 75–76, 122–23, 143–44

*Suicide*, 15

*Syllabus of Errors*, 158

symbols/symbolic representations, 6, 8, 19; ethnic, 79; Catholic as Irish, 163–64; Ulster Unionism's, 173–74; in Ireland, 180; religion as symbolic of nation, 185

teachers: nationalism and Gaelic, 172–73

toleration, 54–58

trade unions: Protestants join UK ones, 160–61; and class relations, 175–76

tradition/folklore, 52–53

transcendence, 34

transmogrification, 38

truth: religious versus science, 23–25; social nature of, 34–35, 40–41, 46–49; as subjective, 67, and science, 133; political implications in Ireland, 149; nation requires single, 187

Ulster, 30; only division of labor in Ireland, 97; Protestant culture, 132–33; and science, 135; Protestant fears, 152–53; nature of Protestants and their experience, 153–54, 157–62, 174–76; Catholic experience, 176–79; after 1921, 181–82; fractured identities, 182; Union as logical, 183; way forward, 190

Ulster Unionism/ists, 30; southern and science, 138–39; culture as unfashionable, 148–49; symbols and opposition to Home Rule, 174; as collective knowledge, 175; as non-Irish, 176; religious opposition to Home Rule, 179

ultramontan/ultramontanism, 8–9; and new medievalism, 158; and post-Famine Catholicism, 172

unification, 28; nationalism and development, 85–86, 87–92; decline of, 92–95

United Irish, 66; and Wolf Tone, 113–14; in Ulster, 153–54

United Kingdom/UK, 134, 154–55, 181

universalism: rejection of standards by anti-revisionists and nationalists, 147

utilitarianism, 14, 60, 99, 132

violence and passion, 39, 72, 140, 143

volunteers, 174

war, 11, 12, 14, 70, 81, 82, 135

Weber, Max: on the state, 65

'Word', the, 132

wordsmiths, 38, 173, 181

Young Ireland, 141–43, 147, 166–67

Yugoslavia: identities in, 77

CPSIA information can be obtained at www.ICGtesting.com
Printed in the USA
LVOW04*2105240315

431832LV00010B/201/P